ALIENHOOD

ALIENHOOD

Citizenship, Exile, and the Logic of Difference

Katarzyna Marciniak

UNIVERSITY OF MINNESOTA PRESS

MINNEAPOLIS · LONDON

Poetry excerpted from *Borderlands/La Frontera: The New Mestiza*, by Gloria Anzaldúa, copyright 1987, 1999; reprinted by permission of Aunt Lute Books.

Lines from "Setting the Handbrake," by Stanisław Barańczak; reprinted by permission of the poet.

Chapter 4 was originally published as "Cinematic Exile: Performing the Foreign Body on Screen in Roman Polanski's *The Tenant*," *Camera Obscura* 43, vol. 15, no. 1 (2000): 1–43; reprinted by permission. Chapter 5 was originally published as "Transnational Anatomies of Exile and Abjection in Milcho Manchevski's *Before the Rain* (1994)," *Cinema Journal* 43, no. 1 (2003): 63–84; copyright 2003 by the University of Texas Press, all rights reserved; reprinted with permission.

Copyright 2006 by the Regents of the University of Minnesota

All rights reserved. No part of this publication may be reproduced, stored in a retrieval system, or transmitted, in any form or by any means, electronic, mechanical, photocopying, recording, or otherwise, without the prior written permission of the publisher.

Published by the University of Minnesota Press
111 Third Avenue South, Suite 290
Minneapolis, MN 55401-2520
http://www.upress.umn.edu

Library of Congress Cataloging-in-Publication Data
Marciniak, Katarzyna
   Alienhood : citizenship, exile, and the logic of difference / Katarzyna Marciniak.
     p.   cm.
   Includes bibliographical references and index.
   ISBN 13: 978-0-8166-4576-3 (alk. paper) — ISBN 13: 978-0-8166-4577-0 (pbk. : alk. paper)
   ISBN 10: 0-8166-4576-0 (alk. paper) — ISBN 10: 0-8166-4577-9 (pbk. : alk. paper)
   1. Aliens in motion pictures.   2. Emigration and immigration in motion pictures.   I. Title.
PN1995.9.A48M37 2006
791.43'6691—dc22
                                                          2006005015

The University of Minnesota is an equal-opportunity educator and employer.

This book is dedicated to my parents, Grażyna and Jan

Exile is strangely compelling to think about
but terrible to experience.

—Edward Said, "Reflections on Exile"

Contents

Preface — xi

Acknowledgments — xix

Introduction: Transnational Aliens — 3

1. Becoming Transnational:
El Norte and the "Elsewhere" of Exile — 33

2. Accented Bodies and Coercive Assimilation:
The Trespasses of the García Girls — 57

3. The Dialectics of Exile:
Resident Alienhood and *Lost in Translation* — 77

4. Claustrophobic Exile:
The Tenant and Ostracizing Logics of Difference — 101

5. Anatomies of Abjection:
Ethnic Cleansing and Liminality in *Before the Rain* — 129

Afterword: The Last Immigrant — 149

Notes — 157

Bibliography — 177

Index — 187

"No Aliens" sticker purchased at a gas station in Arizona, 2005.

PREFACE

> One can be either a resident or illegal immigrant,
> but one is always an alien.
>
> —Chandra Talpade Mohanty, "Crafting Feminist Genealogies"

On Sundays I typically used to log on to work as a phone interpreter, translating for Immigration and Naturalization Service (INS) officers who interviewed illegal border crossers and needed help communicating with non-English captives. Saturday nights must have been the busiest crossing time. One morning a female INS officer in Arizona initiated our phone contact in this way: "I've got an alien here that I need to interview." At first this sounded absurd, as if the officer had assumed Tommy Lee Jones's role as the suave INS Special Agent K in the film *Men in Black*. I knew, of course, that the officer was not referring to some slimy, bug-eyed monster but to an actual person. Her voice was kind and warm, reflecting the rhetoric of alienhood that I had heard so many times: it sounded deceptively innocent, its sweetness concealing the xenophobic undertones that frequently color anti-immigrant discourses in this country.

Situations like this usually shattered my effort at maintaining the professional neutrality of an interpreter and left me emotionally bruised. First, I myself fall into the state of alienhood. I have had the process of alien regulation and legalization inscribed on my flesh because of medical inspections and procedures through which my body was tested before being pronounced acceptable. So, paradoxically and painfully, I, a legalized alien, was helping INS officers sort out and remove aliens from the protected national space. In a sense, my work as an interpreter for the INS continually reminds me of my own process of legalization, which revealed to me not only my specific alienhood but also, however precarious, my sense of cultural privilege because my body was read as that of a white, Eastern European woman who could speak the language and understand its nuances. Even though I often heard condescending comments about my accented speech that, within the predominantly white community of Americans I lived in at the time, inevitably betrayed me as an alien, I nevertheless had the conceptual and linguistic means to express my anger and frustration over the INS legalizing process. Crucially, I had access to legal representation and could discuss the impossibly convoluted intricacies of the process with my legal counsel. As part of my legalization process, I paid mandatory visits to the medical clinics authorized to deal with aliens and to conduct mandated medical tests, and I could, at least in part, negotiate the medical experience, unlike many others with whom I shared waiting rooms who did not speak English at all, or spoke too little to communicate with doctors and nurses about the medical procedures performed on their bodies.

This medical element of legalizing one's alienhood is clearly set up not only to intimidate foreign nationals but also, ultimately, to humiliate and brand them. Similarly, the staff of the designated clinics that I visited had certain expectations of me: as an alien, I should be grateful for having an opportunity to go through the legalizing process; I should go through this process gracefully without complaining, arguing, and demanding any explanations; anger on my part was inappropriate; as an alien, I should understand that my rights are limited and that the success of the process depends on both the good will of the professionals assisting me and my own ability to accept "feminized" humiliation quietly. In other words, the process as a whole tacitly demands that an alien be grateful and quiet. When I think back to my days of INS evaluation, I can find no other explanation for the fact that other transnationals around me at the time did not warn me about their fingerprinting or medical experiences in order to prepare a novice like me for what was to come. Perhaps even those who have successfully completed the alien-testing process are so stigmatized by the experience that they do not wish to speak critically about its mechanisms. They simply hope to forget the abasement. They do not want to "mark" themselves as still alien.

The outcome of this silence, I came to realize, is compounded by the fact that we hardly ever hear the voices and points of view of those who are the focus of the immigrant debate in the United States. Although current cultural discourse is permeated by anti-immigrant sentiments or, at best, by obvious unease at trying to address immigration in complex, nondichotomous ways, the public knows very little about what is actually entailed in legalizing one's stay in this country. Many of us "aliens," women especially, are quite familiar with the misguided advice from sympathetic, "legitimate" Americans to reproduce so that the future baby "rightful" citizen would enable us to become "legal." Because the views of immigrants are rarely heard, even by academics and intellectuals, the general knowledge about alienhood is quite limited; and the arduous, costly, time-consuming, and, most important, humiliating parts of the immigration and naturalization process in its institutional, disciplinary forms remain largely unexamined. The seemingly infinite number of repeated interviews, fingerprinting, political screening, loyalty pledges, medical examinations and testing (for TB, HIV, venereal diseases, etc.) works to make the immigrant a completely disciplined object. The intrusion into the body—in short, the process of becoming an officially sanctioned subject—reveals the state's desire for a certainty that the body of the alien is "clean," free from any potentially dangerous impurities, both literally and metaphorically. And while these silent operations of alienhood remain under wraps (because they are often perceived as shameful by those who are subjected to them), the culture has historically authorized the grand narrative of immigration as the time-honored story of the nation.

These personal experiences led me to investigate aliens and the construct I call *alienhood*. Defining alienhood as a highly racialized rhetorical and disciplinary apparatus that classifies immigrants, refugees, and border crossers in relation to the U.S. territory, I start from the premise that the notion of aliens has a bifold, palimpsestic signification in American culture—meaning both foreigner and extraterrestrial creature. This intriguing semantic doubleness and the wavering, or even blurring, of the two significations creates a tenuous emotional climate around already unstable identities of various immigrants and adds yet another symbolic layer to foreigners' particular pejorative discursive markings. As I explore the tensions between these competing concepts, I will argue for the need to bring into focus the pathologizing politics of alienhood.

Alienhood and legitimation function as a conceptual apparatus that holds the exilic self within its parameters and discursively stamps the foreigner's body. It simultaneously stamps the symbolic identity of the nation. The INS rhetoric of alienhood is rooted in legal definitions of what the U.S. Supreme Court has termed "alienage classifications" in its dizzying multiplicity: "illegal alien," "resident alien," "nonresident alien," "immigrant alien student," "nonimmigrant alien," "enemy alien," or "alien of extraordinary ability." This language curiously collapses the distinction between the filmic, scummy nonterrestrial beings and the aliens-foreigners who, just like their cinematic counterparts, are inevitably perceived as strangers engaged in a threatening invasion of the national space. The notion of the alien brands exiles as outsiders, the ones who do not and will not fully belong, and may only aspire to provisional belonging. Thus, it seems that the INS's agenda is to imprint these "others" with the language of alienhood so that they will not easily blend in or become one of "us."

To write about aliens and alienhood from within the U.S. context runs the risk of universalizing these notions, of not doing justice to the myriad histories of immigration, because each ethnic and racial group has its own complicated past. Simply put, I came to realize that sketching a genealogy of alienhood is an unattainable goal. Indeed, alienhood has marked immigrants (legal and illegal) in polysemous, uneven ways—through racial, ethnic, gender, and economic privilege. It makes sense then, at the onset, to say that this book is not geared toward offering specific histories of various immigrant groups—there are already numerous projects that do this in most interesting and astute ways. But because this culture uses the term "alien" as if it *were* a universal concept, at the risk of essentializing alienhood and working against it, I want to examine the multiple deployment of "aliens" within the current context of transnationalism.

To do this, I offer a series of readings of literary and cinematic texts of exile—those of Julia Alvarez, Eva Hoffman, Milcho Manchevski, Gregory Nava, and Roman Polanski. These readings serve as case studies, relating dialogue narratives from both second and third worlds to first worldness. This dialogue underscores this book's two intertwined goals: to explore alienhood in order to problematize the often salutary meanings of the transnational, and to bring forth the issue of the so-called second world into these debates.

Although not a new phenomenon, since the early 1990s the analysis of the concept of transnationalism has been gaining rapid urgency across disciplinary boundaries.[1] Within the contemporary context of globalization, the term is often used to refer to current changes in advanced capitalist societies that reconfigure traditional boundaries of national economies, identities, and cultures. However, despite its somewhat salutary tone of mobility—"transnational" literally means "going beyond national boundaries"—various globalizing processes do not produce homogeneously empowering transnational conditions or identities. In order to establish a nuanced understanding of the much debated clash between exhilarating renditions of movability, and border crossings and painful limitations that immigrants often acutely experience,[2] I believe we need to inspect diverse categories of "aliens" in their ideological, gendered, and racialized formations.

Thus, my intention is to reorient the study of transnational immigrant or exile subjects, asserting that, although the concept of transnational positionality seems to embrace—even at times celebrate—the idea of border crossings, it is important to acknowledge that for many exiles such crossings are extremely problematic, risky, or sometimes not possible at all. Because I contest the idea that the condition of transnational identity is simply a liberatory position that allows an exile a special epistemological insight, I share, for example, Homi Bhabha's point that "despite the currency of new technologies and itinerant, diasporic cultural signs, *transnationality can be an experience of destitution and trauma*."[3] Hence, my discussions in this book work *against* celebratory conceptions of the transnational subject because frequently aliens experience the transnational status as a condition marked by painful disorientation, ostracism, or even abjection rather than by feelings of emancipation.

The contribution I wish to make here rests on the following thesis: even with the emergence of what Inderpal Grewal and Caren Kaplan call "transnational feminist practices,"[4] the dominant feminist discourses, even those that claim the space of "polycentric multiculturalism,"[5] "anti-racist, multicultural feminism," or "radical or critical multiculturalism" (Mohanty 1998, 485, 486), operate discursively within the first/third world axis and have very little to say, if anything at all, about the murky territory of the post-socialist-communist second world.

It is as if the second world, as a conceptual category and an actual geopolitical region, did not exist, despite the fact that the second world has changed the most thoroughly and the most rapidly in association with neoliberal globalization.

Perhaps the lack of this discussion in transnational feminist studies might be motivated by the fact that, as Danuta Zadworna Fjellestad (1995) suggests, "the refugees from the Communist system have seldom bothered to document their plight," and those who did so remain "exiled from American literary histories, anthologies and public discussions on ethnic literature." Furthermore, many feminist thinkers whose voices are prominent in the multicultural, diasporic debates in the United States come from spaces traditionally labeled third world—from the Middle Eastern, South Asian, or African regions. As a result of such a politics of location, the main feminist discussions have focused on troubling the West/non-West dichotomy; on showing how "there is a Third World in every First World and vice-versa" (Trinh 1987, 3); on scrutinizing the Eurocentric logic that, as Ella Shohat and Robert Stam argue, has valorized the West as "the world's center of gravity, as ontological 'reality' to the rest of the world's shadow," while often patronizing if not demonizing the non-Western spaces and peoples (1994, 2). The problem with the second world in these discussions is that it is now both Western and yet non-Western, a fuzzy in-between.

In fact, after the fall of the Berlin Wall in 1989, some scholars commented on the nonexistence of the second world (Shohat and Stam 1994, 26; Bauman 1997, 51). Such formulations presuppose that the very fact of the destruction of the Wall wipes out the socialist-communist legacy in once Soviet-bloc countries. Moreover, they also suggest that countries that were once behind the Iron Curtain are now already Western. But are they? Despite the fact that many of those countries wish to see themselves as Western, especially on the wave of the liberatory rhetoric of the unification of Europe, it seems more appropriate to claim that, as the second world slowly enters the economic realm of transnational capital, it still lingers between what it once was (non-Western, ideologically and economically, under the colonizing power of the Soviet Union) and what it is not yet (Western). Furthermore, the claims that now "the 'Second World' is no more" (Bauman 1997) create an impression that Europe is a uniform cultural and political space. They ignore the fact that Central and Eastern European regions, for a long time placed in Western imagination "behind the Wall," have been consistently treated as the "other" Europe, the impoverished cousin to the "real" thing, a treatment that consolidated the identity of "true Europeans" who saw themselves as legitimately and purely Western.[6]

My intention in bringing the narratives from Latin America and from behind the Wall into the discussion of transnational aliens is not merely to recover the forgotten space of the second world that needs to be added to the list of other worlds. Nor do I wish to create an impression that the second world needs to compete for attention with the third world. Of course, the notions of first, second, and third worlds are reductive ideological constructs that support the primacy of the first world.[7] By drawing attention to the deletion of the second world, my goal is not to privilege this space but to reflect on its discursive disappearance, which needs to be seen in the context of the end of cold war politics and the diversion of the Western gaze away from the "contaminating" communist legacy that is supposedly no longer threatening.

Toward that end, my interest is in considering the discursive affects—the emotions generated by the discourse—of the category "alien." Clearly, "alien" is not a hateful slur but a legally sanctioned concept. Bearing this in mind, to consider such affects means to analyze what the word, the institutional label, does to a person, how it injures the one designated as alien, often in covert, invisible ways. Only by dissecting the discourses that create and sustain alienhood can we begin to understand the often nuanced impact of discursive violence operating on "foreign bodies" and its correlation with ethnic and racial violence.

Most persons marked as aliens have felt at some time the legal, economic, emotional, or institutional, overall restrictive impact of alienhood because an alien's rights are formally and symbolically limited through visas and green cards, or lack thereof—papers that delineate one's right to lawful residence, visitations, work, or border crossings. And "alien" is not a pleasant word: to be coded by it means to have one's authority, legitimacy, and desirability perpetually questioned, especially when it comes to matters of public or institutional importance.

Etymologically, the word derives from the Latin *alienus* (of another place, other) and is defined by *The Oxford English Dictionary* as "a person belonging to another family, race, or nation; a stranger, a foreigner"; "one separated, or excluded from the citizenship and privileges of a nation." *The American Heritage Dictionary of the English Language* (4th ed., 2000) gives the following synonyms for "alien": "foreign," "noncitizen," "strange," "an outsider," "not natural." In 1982 the U.S. Supreme Court held, for example, that "aliens are by definition those outside the community."[8] Earlier, in 1952, the U.S. Supreme Court explained that "an alien, who is assimilated in our society," is afforded a large measure of economic opportunity and "is treated as a citizen so far as his property and his liberty are concerned." However, to remain in the country and "to protract this ambiguous status within the country is not his right, but is a matter of permission and tolerance. The Government's power to terminate its hospitality has been asserted and sustained by this Court since the question first arose."[9]

Given the etymology of "alien" and its interpretations by the U.S. legal system, one can see the waverings that arise when "we" find aliens desirable, useful, and properly assimilated. This hesitancy is underpinned by the fact that foreignness in general connotes strangeness, inadequacy, even illegitimacy—all, as if pulled together by the issue of legal birth.[10] The various U.S. Supreme Court rulings reflect the unresolvable tension regarding aliens' status. If assimilated, they are supposed to have rights equal to that of natural citizens, but they never completely do: "Under our law, the alien in several respects stands on an equal footing with citizens, but in others has never been conceded legal parity with the citizen."[11]

I want to probe these definitions. What does it mean to be housed by a nation and yet labeled "outside the community"? What kinds of mechanisms "measure" the desired level of assimilation? How does the nation decide to extend its "permission and tolerance"? Which kinds of *immigrant bodies* are affected most by various ostracizing categories of alienness? Who falls into the category of illegal, undesirable, even repugnant trespassing bodies? How does the coding take place, or more specifically, what kinds of mechanisms are employed in such a process of categorization? And in what ways is the popular understanding of science-fiction aliens as extraterrestrial invaders-colonizers linked with the legal referral to immigrants as "aliens"?

Acknowledgments

Linda Kintz, my mentor, early on recognized the "alien" spirit in my work and supported this book in unwavering, rigorous ways. My intellectual debt to her is one that many would be envious to owe. In the early stages of writing, I benefited from the erudition and guidance of Paul Armstrong, Kathleen Karlyn, and Julia Lesage. My dear friends Mara Holt and Amy Novak saw this book through its many reconfigurations, and I thank you for sharing your provocative arguments with me. You helped me infuse the project with complex ideas, energy, and spark—as only you can. To Sharon Willis, my most sincere gratitude for believing in this book. I thank Alden Waitt for contributing her editorial wisdom. Thanks to friends and colleagues for support and suggestions: Ann Brown, Marsha Dutton, Loreen Giese, Roland Greene, Margaret Johnson, David Lazar, Matthew McClellan, Robert Miklitsch, Áine O'Healy and Juruś Walczak and Marguerite Waller.

At the University of Minnesota Press, my editor, Richard Morrison, has been a terrific supporter of this project. I appreciate the astute comments from two readers whose advice was invaluable in working out the nuances of the book. Heartfelt thanks also to Heather Burns and Nancy Sauro for superb editorial assistance.

The Center for the Study of Women in Society at the University of Oregon generously supported this project with a dissertation fellowship. Ohio University, particularly the College of Arts and Sciences, Honors Tutorial College, and Ohio University Research Committee, assisted with research and travel grants, faculty development awards, and course release time. My two graduate seminars on transnational feminist practices have been wonderfully insightful, and I thank my students for the enthusiasm we all shared.

For art reproduction permissions, thanks to the British Film Institute, Milcho Manchevski, Goran Sipek, and Anna Thomas. Most grateful thanks also to the individual artists who permitted me to use their images: Don Bartletti, Lalo Lopez, and Kamil Turowski.

Finally, special thanks to my two favorite guardian angels, Jennie and Jennifer, for metaphysical and physical highs under the Big Sky of Missoula, Montana, and at Flathead Lake. And to my K2, Kaia and Kamil, for all the pleasures one could wish for.

Alienhood

Agent K (Tommy Lee Jones) and Agent J (Will Smith) as INS agents in *Men in Black*.

Introduction

Transnational Aliens

> Protecting the Earth from the scum of the universe.
>
> —Promotional slogan for *Men in Black*

Men in Black: Alien Spectatorship and the Politics of Ambivalence

Barry Sonnenfeld's "alien comedy" *Men in Black* (1997) is a film that may not be readily thought of as an example of cinema that foregrounds exilic experiences, yet it provocatively conflates meanings of "aliens." At first glance, it appears that, unlike a film such as Roland Emmerich's *Independence Day* (1996), which presents aliens as dangerous creatures—destroyers obsessed with invading and contaminating the American national space, *Men in Black* offers a sympathetic and less binarized view of otherness and difference.[1] That is, rather than creating a clear-cut, one-dimensional representation of us versus them, the narrative suggests that aliens are already among us—they are registered and under the control of the INS. The catch is that the public is not supposed to know it; Agent K remarks: "At any given time, there are around fifteen thousand aliens on the planet. Most of them right here, in Manhattan." Thus, ironically, the identity of "alien" here is not that of a slimy creature but one who is a nonnatural citizen. A comment by one of the film reviewers in the *Boston Globe* is therefore quite telling: "Where most movies make much of one or two space aliens, the joke in 'Men in Black' is that our planet is crawling with them. All we ask is that they behave themselves."[2]

I am less interested in science fiction aliens than in the bleeding of science-fiction discourse into U.S. nationalism. The analysis of the establishing sequence in *Men in Black,* featuring the misbehaving aliens, situates the diegetic focus on an unsettling ambiguity between an alien as a scummy nonterrestrial being and an alien-foreigner. It marks the narrative space as a site of wavering that collapses the distinction between both groups, suggesting that both kinds of aliens are engaged in a threatening invasion of national space. The film opens with a metaphorical image of bodily violence: we see a flying bug whose body smashes against the windshield of the moving truck. The first words spoken in the sequence are uttered by the truck's driver, Nick: "Goddamn bugs." The next shot takes us into the interior of a truck crammed with people being smuggled across the U.S.–Mexican border. The subject positions of the Mexicans shift at the very moment of crossing the national boundary: they are no longer simply Mexicans; the crossing gives them the status of illegal aliens. One of the first shots defines the way foreigners look: poor, dirty, shabby, dark-skinned, unable to speak English. The contrast between the Mexicans in the truck and natural citizens of the United States is emphasized when the truck is stopped by the border patrol. The border wardens are in official uniforms that mark their bodies as legitimately American, while the fatigued Mexicans wear tattered, unclean rags.

As the officials order the Mexicans to stand in a lineup, a slick black car approaches, and we are introduced to the businesslike Special Agent K, a black-suited man in charge of INS Division 6, a special unit regulating "alien activities." Even before the end of the opening sequence, the film has stigmatized the Mexicans as nonhuman, as "creatures." The initial conversation between Nick and one of the border patrols reveals the way the border-crossing creatures are already positioned outside the space of the privileged human "I":

>BORDER PATROLMAN: Where are you coming from, Nick?
>
>NICK: Fishing in Cuernavaca.
>
>BORDER PATROLMAN: I'm sure you are. Let's take a look at your catch, ah?

When Nick opens the back of the truck, in the left part of the frame we see, very briefly, the fearfully shaking hand of one of the crossers. Upon seeing all the crowded foreign bodies, the patrolman says: "Oh me. I would have thrown them back." Already at this moment, Mexicans-turned-aliens are coded for the audience in multiply degrading ways: they are dirty bodies, a less-than-human "catch," unwanted throwaways, and above all, they are marked as undesirable aliens who wish to smuggle themselves across the border to contaminate the pure inside of this nation.

When Agent K takes over, we learn that he is, in fact, searching for a "real" alien, a creature from outer space. He is positioned as a site of masculinist knowledge and authority, and the privileged space of enunciation belongs to him as he addresses the illegal border-crossers in a seemingly sympathetic way: "Welcome to the United States"; "How are you, Gonzales?"; "Grandma, don't worry." He eventually dismisses the border patrols: "You fellows can hit the road. Keep on protecting us from the dangerous aliens," and he pulls only one border-crosser, Mikey, out of the lineup, taking him aside and slashing his body in half. But Mikey's body, we see, contains yet another body—that of a space alien: what emerges out of illegal-human-alien-Mikey is Mikey-fantastical-slimy-bug-eyed extraterrestrial creature. Importantly, the act of slashing is an act of opening up the space of abjection, the abyss of nonbeing that is already coded as belonging to the crossers whose transnational position is not a cosmopolitan identity allowed to traverse national borders freely but a location of painful quivering. That is, the decision to mark the Mexican crossers as legal or illegal belongs entirely to the lawful Americans who have the power to decide whether the crossers are desirable.

The concept of an alien that emerges out of the film's diegesis is thus this unsettled wavering that confirms that this country needs to be on its guard against the flood of unwanted creatures that will supposedly seize any opportunity to usurp the rightful place of natural citizens. The slogan that ran as a promotional hook before the film's release only confirms the necessity to guard our national borders: *Men in Black*: "Protecting the earth from the scum of the universe." "Scum" refers to the racialized idea of pollution, dirt, refuse—matter that needs to be cleaned up, discarded, and removed. The narrative plays on the ambivalence of the marked-by-scum bodies that need to be purged from the protected national space. Both groups of aliens—foreigners and the extraterrestrial creatures whose bodies turn to blue goo after they have been exploded by the spectacular weapons of the men in black—are coded by the logic of dirt. That is, we see how both types of aliens are bodily inadequate, impure, dangerous, even repugnant. The darkness of Mexicans—visually emphasized via rags, sweat, and actual dirt as unclean and uncivilized—is associated with the slimy bodies of creatures and carries a symbolic weight. While the oozing alien is a standard figure in alien films, it is its leaking body that is important for my analysis. This leakage draws attention to materiality, suggesting that the bodily boundaries are permeable and unstable. Such an oozing flesh poses a discomfort, even a threat, to the Western bourgeois discourse that has historically authorized the proper, sanctioned body—the clean body that polices its own leakage of odors and dirt. In the Western humanist tradition, the privileged "I" constructs itself through excluding what Lynda Hart, for example, calls the "indiscreet body," the body that produces waste, blood, and fluids, thus affirming the seamless, generic, nonporous body (1994, xii). This historical banishment of the impure self supports the idea that the normative "I" envisions itself as indeed bodiless and clean.[3]

Such a reading of "scum" and "dirt" suggests several important points: the very notion of alienhood rests on the assumption that foreigners are polluters whose contamination needs to be controlled, contained, or eliminated; ascribing materiality and its weight to foreigners (as if it inherently belonged solely to aliens) allows rightful Americans to claim legitimate citizenry as organically

A slashing sequence in *Men in Black:* Agent K and Mikey (John Alexander).

Agent K with Mikey's head.

linked to the clean—that is, white—body; cleanliness has been traditionally associated with whiteness, purity, and nobility, and thus the right to racial superiority; and finally, the logic of purity justifies the treatment of unclean bodies as objects of violence.

This is, of course, *not* the way the film invites the mainstream public to read its narrative. The film and its sequel, *Men in Black II,* have been marketed as one of Hollywood's examples of light movies for wide audiences, summer fluff, an overtly comic mixture of science fiction and adventure flick, relying on high-tech special effects, "entertaining" violence. But I am not simply concerned with critiquing the film's ideological underpinnings and suggesting that Sonnenfeld's film utilizes a stereotypical vision of foreigners-aliens as substandard others. Rather, I am interested in switching the assumed spectatorial point of view and considering the film from the perspective of an alien. Only when we try to read *Men in Black* from the position of a foreigner does the film mobilize an interesting tension and reveal previously invisible discursive platforms.

Not only are the men in black cold-blooded INS agents whose job is to control and silence information, but they also use a special device called a "neuralyzer," "the film's neatest weapon," as one reviewer puts it,[4] a gadget that disturbingly wipes out people's recent memories, especially those who have had contacts with aliens. The justification for such troubling actions comes from Agent K, who tells us, "The public must be protected from itself." Given the fact that the agents' main occupation is to hunt aliens, the cultural resonance of their actions evokes the actual INS roundups of those who fit into the illegal category of alienhood,

The Mex Files, a remake of *Men in Black.* Courtesy of Lalo Lopez. Copyright Lalo Lopez Alcaraz, www.pocho.com.

the ones who are perceived as somehow not natural. Even if a newcomer gains the status of a legitimate alien, the aura of illegality, already inscribed in the paradoxical category of alien/resident, is not easy to dispel and serves to remind the foreigner of his or her social rank along the axis of alien-citizen opposition. In fact, all the legal and cultural meanings of "alien" I have engaged thus far suggest that such a newcomer is permanently coded as a stranger who, Bauman argues, historically "gestates uncertainty" and a sense of unease. This discomfort is frequently translated into phobic impulses on the part of the citizen, the privileged "I," to build barriers around itself through the perpetual creation and sustenance of the rhetoric of alienhood. The problem with aliens is that as "neither-nors" they are "cognitively ambivalent" (Bauman 1997, 46, 47). That is, the unease and ambivalence of the status of the foreigner disrupt the clear-cut national identification of rightful citizenry.

The analysis of *Men in Black* also brings up the idea that aliens have been historically defined in relationship to a specific national territory. In other words, one does not inherently and organically occupy the position of alienhood; rather, one becomes an alien when one crosses the border of a nation that then readily identifies the crosser as the non-native: a foreign-born person who wishes to become a resident. In addressing the cultural ambivalence of aliens, Annette Kuhn's argument about point of view is useful for this discussion. She writes: "The aliens of science fiction are capable of assuming many forms; but whatever its guise, the alien is always, by definition, *different*. The idea of the alien already assumes a point of view: whoever names the alien as such in the very act radically separates herself from it, and it from her. The alien's name is Other."[5] Two points here are important to consider. First, as Kuhn argues, the taxonomy of alienhood rests on the process of radical segregation, separation, and exclusion that needs to be performed by the sanctioned self. This separation, enacted via the binary logic of I/non-I, or what Trinh T. Minh-ha calls the "apartheid type of difference," ensures the presumed stability and superiority of the self that proclaims itself to be the rightful citizen (2001, 930). Second, the enunciative moment of naming coheres the sense of legitimate selfhood and anchors the "I" in what Edward Said calls the "superior ontological status" that historically belongs to Western whiteness (1979, 226). To put it simply, it matters *who* is deciding what or who is labeled as "alien." And alienhood is always envisioned as the opposition to the self and conceptualized as undesirable difference.

Deployment of Aliens and the Rhetoric of Multiculturalism

Many conservative Web sites such as IllegalAliens.US or Vdare.com have recently launched vigorous Internet campaigns against "aliens." Vdare.com's "How to Report Illegal Aliens—Updated DHS Version!" urges "rightful" U.S. citizens to report any suspicious aliens—these could be "illegal aliens" but also "criminal alien residents"—in order to "perform a vital public service." The increasing anxiety over aliens in many ways is an anxiety over ethnic and racial diversity, which, many believe, destroys the notion of a common American culture and leads the nation, in Lawrence Auster's words, toward "a new and more terrible age of ethnic imperialism" (1990, 54). IllegalAliens.US, for example, posted a sample letter concerned citizens can write to politicians and newspaper editors:

> In your recent article the misleading term "undocumented worker" was used. The accurate term is "illegal alien." Using "undocumented" means foreigners have the unconditional right to violate America's borders and immigration laws. There are an estimated 8 to 11 million illegal aliens in the U.S. today. What America needs is far less political correctness and far more honest reporting as to how illegal immigration has contributed significantly to school overcrowding, traffic congestion, our health care crisis, environmental degradation, social tension, and other negative impacts upon our country. Please support America's rule of law by using "illegal alien" in the future.

Paradoxically though, such passionate antialien actions and declarations obliterate the fact that while many crusade against undocumented aliens, or documented dark-skinned immigrants, simultaneously such aliens are willingly employed by legitimate Americans as a cheap labor force to care for their children, clean their houses, or do their gardening (see Hondagneu-Sotelo 2001). On a larger scale, these antialien discursive and material actions point to a disparity between present anti-immigrant sentiments and an alleged cultivation of a multicultural vision of a nation.

Typically, vehement antiforeign declarations characterize unwanted immigrants as aliens discursively linked to disasters that fatally puncture the civilized fabric of a nation. For example, in *The Path to National Suicide: An Essay on Immigration and Multiculturalism,* Auster sees the U.S. leniency toward immigration from the so-called third world as dangerous because the "new" multicultural American society (and he clearly sees multiculturalism as an import brought by immigrants) will lead us to the end of validated American greatness. His argument is rooted in a conviction that "open immigration and multiculturalism constitute a mortal threat to American civilization," and that they imperil not simply social cohesiveness but also the very basis of national existence (1990, 53). Another text that supports and praises the American "ethnic core" of whiteness is Peter Brimelow's *Alien Nation: Common Sense about America's Immigrant Disaster* (1995), which again stresses the perils of a racial imbalance that threatens to minoritize white Americans, as immigration continues to alter the true identity of "America," which is now becoming an "alien nation." Similar sentiments, warning us that uncontrolled immigration from Asia, Africa, and Latin America makes the great American nation a third world America, have been expressed most recently by Patrick Buchanan in *The Death of the West: How Dying Populations and Immigrant Invasions Imperil Our Country and Civilization* (2002). Buchanan starts his book on a note of sadness at the fact that American culture is now profoundly polluted by unwanted aliens, a "cultural wasteland," a "moral sewer ... not worth living in and not worth fighting for" (6). As a result, millions of rightful Americans, he believes, "feel like strangers in their own land" (5).

In all of these publications, antialien rhetoric links immigrants to the metaphors of pollution and peril, asserting the need to invest in the logic of racial purity. Such words as "death," "invasion," "mortal menace," "end of American civilization," and "end of the West" convey the calamities that await the American people if the nation does not stop this "path to national suicide." Dismissing discussions of indigenous populations as well as the fact that, before the birthing of the nation, "it was whiteness that was the absent color" (Shohat 1998, 44), these authors assume that America, from the start, had a white ethnic kernel that is now in great jeopardy.

Within such discursive practices, the stereotypical assumption is, of course, that if a foreigner is lucky enough to be formally accepted as a member of the U.S. community, then alienness is an inevitable marker of difference he or she should be willing to accept as well. On the other hand, there is the belief that anti-immigration discourse does not have an impact on natural Americans, that those born in this country are safe. But there is an ironic twist to this logic: the parameters of alienhood do not simply discursively codify the non-U.S. born nationals as different and coming from elsewhere. Often, those who look like stereotypical aliens—citizens who are people of color, the poor, those who speak English with accents—are already vulnerable to the charges of alienhood. To investigate this point, I argue, means to demonstrate how alienhood is not solely an immigrant issue, impacting the larger ethics of national identity.

I want to follow two examples that might further illustrate this discussion: a 1997 case of police harassment in Arizona and a 2001 incident involving Representative David Wu, the only Chinese American ever elected to the U.S. Congress. Both foreground the diverse range of critical issues at stake: privileged ethnicity in relation to nationhood, the right to call oneself an American or to verify the authenticity of citizenhood, and finally, the unspoken assumptions about the sanctioned national self linked to the desire for an ethnically white social order.

In 1997, during a weeklong roundup in a Phoenix suburb to capture and deport illegal immigrants, significantly called Operation Restoration, people from the Hispanic community were mistreated by city police. As a result of the harassment, sixteen Hispanic residents (most of them, ironically, born in this country) filed a civil rights lawsuit, claiming that police officers stopped people in the street and demanded that they prove their citizenship solely because they were dark-skinned and spoke Spanish.[6]

In a more recent case, a statement released by the Associated Press, "Chinese-American Representative Denied Entry," asserts that on May 23, 2001, Representative Wu had gone to the U.S. Energy Department to deliver a speech to Asian Americans in celebration of Asian Pacific American Heritage Month.[7] Along with an aide who is also Asian American, Wu was briefly denied entry to the U.S. Energy Department headquarters by security guards who asked twice if he was an American (even though he presented his congressional identification). The AP statement quotes Jeanne Lopatto, an Energy Department spokeswoman, who claims that "everybody entering the building, including Abraham [Spencer Abraham, the Department of Energy secretary], must present ID, and all visitors are required to confirm whether they are U.S. citizens under a presidential directive to protect classified information." Strikingly, Wu contradicts this supposedly uniform policy: "What they said was that they asked everyone, *everyone*, whether they are a U.S. citizen or not, but that proved not to be true. My friend and colleague, the gentleman from Massachusetts (Mr. Capuano), went yesterday and he was not asked the way that I was at all" (Wu's speech in the House of Representatives, May 25, 2001).[8]

Such incidents should not be considered in isolation, especially now when an intense anti-immigrant tonality in the post–9/11 period has been joined to the discourse of terrorism and evildoers. This cultural tenor has already revealed that in times of national crisis the framework of alienhood applies not only to all kinds of legal and illegal aliens but also to many U.S.-born Americans, particularly the members of nonwhite minorities, and even more so, to the ones who share the racial and/or ethnic background of the identified terrorists from the Middle East. Instances of discriminatory acts—from verbal bashing and physical attacks to detention without formal charges—that some U.S. citizens, members of the Arab-American community, experienced in the past three years poignantly confirm this point. Cases like the one of Mohamed Atriss, an Egyptian-born U.S. citizen, arrested in New Jersey and charged with multiple counts of conspiracy, are not exceptional. Attris ran a travel service business and was suspected of supplying two of the 9/11 terrorists with forged identification documents. He pleaded not guilty, and even though the FBI had interrogated him and concluded that he knew nothing about the 9/11 hijackers, he remained in jail for months after this because of secret evidence presented against him by the prosecutors.[9]

Given the current political climate and the initiation of the Patriot Act, there can be little doubt that those coded as aliens are now under a special inspection by the Department of Homeland Security. The agency portrays national safety as vulnerable and in continual need of protection and encourages citizens to be vigilant and cautious. At the same time, the media informs the public that new regulations in the immigration law are being introduced with the hopes of tightening the national security system.[10] On the surface, these laws may appear necessary to protect U.S. safety, and many citizens may welcome them, but they simultaneously generate a climate of witch-hunting, paranoia, and fear because the implication is that acts of terror are impending and may be conducted by any of the legal and illegal aliens. Clearly, the umbrella of protection does not embrace immigrants in this country the same way it does its natural citizens. Mary Louise Pratt notes, quoting Nadine Strossen's testimony to the Senate Judiciary Committee, "under the Patriot Act of October 2001 noncitizens may be taken into custody, held indefinitely in undisclosed locations, denied legal counsel, tried at secret hearings, and imprisoned or deported for charges as nebulous as suspicion of supporting terrorism or affiliating with groups who do."[11]

These contentions beg for an exploration of the friction between the current public rhetoric of multiculturalism in the United States and the continued attractiveness of whiteness as the marker of legitimate Americanness. Additionally, what happened to the Hispanic community in Arizona and to Representative Wu, and what is happening to many nonwhite citizens after 9/11, reminds us that the historical infatuation with whiteness has been supported by numerous governmental policies that have regulated immigrant influx via race and ethnicity-based restrictions cultivating the logic of ethnic purity.

The study of immigration restrictions, exclusion acts, and laws reveals that the stigmatization processes of certain aliens are very complex; foreign-born nationals have been marked by alienness in disparate ways through the intersecting axes of gender, racial, ethnic, or economic privilege. They also show that alienhood has never been a universal concept. For example, historically, white Europeans who colonized the indigenous lands of the Americas have certainly not been labeled as undesirable aliens the same way that present-day dark-skinned immigrants invariably have been. In "Who May Give Birth to Citizens? Reproduction, Eugenics, and Immigration" (1997), Dorothy E. Roberts discusses how the dynamic of current American nativism manifests itself not only through aggressive patrolling of the U.S. borders but also through efforts attempting to restrict reproduction within national boundaries. She discusses "laws that prohibit certain immigrants from using reproductive health services and the elimination of automatic citizenship to U.S.-born children of undocumented aliens" (205). These efforts, she claims, are a continuation of the historical push toward preserving a white national identity:

> These restrictions on the birth of citizens raise a fundamental question about the national identity: Who is an American citizen? In theory America subscribes to the ideal of civic nationalism, which

> defines citizenship according to shared political institutions and values rather than racial descent. But in practice American national identity has revolved around questions of race. From the founding of the nation, the meaning of American citizenship has rested on the denial of citizenship to nonwhites living within its borders. (208–9)

Indeed, the word "alien" in relation to noncitizens was introduced by the First Congress in the 1790 Naturalization Act in "A Bill to Establish an Uniform Rule of Naturalization, and to Enable Aliens to Hold Lands under Certain Restrictions." Crucially, in this document, an alien was described as a "free white person," consequently limiting the parameters of naturalized citizenship to whiteness (see Haney-López 1996, ch. 1, 1–36). Thus, as Matthew Frye Jacobson claims, "Citizenship was a racially inscribed concept at the outset of the new nation: by an act of Congress, only 'free white' immigrants could be naturalized" (1998, 13).

Significantly, however, it was not simply whiteness but *masculine* whiteness that was a foundation for the discourses of citizenship. In relation to gender and the issue of naturalization, the 1790 Act, although not limiting eligibility by sex, implicitly refers to an alien as male, rendering women rhetorically absent in the definitions of "free white persons." When considering the history of citizenship and women, one has to distinguish between U.S.-born women and non-native, immigrant women because their relationship to legal citizenhood was distinct, though, many argue, intertwined. Virginia Sapiro, for example, states that although "natural-born" women had access to citizenship (understood as morally and legally tied to a husband and his domicile), this privilege was "relatively meaningless," as she puts it, because women had no independent political rights: no right to vote and no rights over their children; they were also not expected to participate in governance.[12]

Similar to U.S.-born women, immigrant women's citizenship via naturalization was predominantly conditional on their marital status and thus motivated by a patriarchal and heteronormative conception of women's citizenship. However, as Marian L. Smith claims, the relationship of alien women to citizenship has been historically quite convoluted: "In general, women have always had the right to become U.S. citizens, but not every court honored that right. Since the mid-nineteenth century a succession of laws worked to keep certain women out of naturalization records, either by granting them derivative citizenship or barring their naturalization altogether."[13] Smith writes that by the late nineteenth century, marital status was the primary factor determining a woman's ability to naturalize, except, of course, for those women who were racially ineligible for naturalization.

Thus, as many scholars have argued, the valorized national identity has been sustained through the tactics of exclusion, repression, even abjection, which worked to solidify and cohere the legitimate American selfhood. In a 1927 publication, *American Citizenship As Distinguished from Alien Status,* Frederick A. Cleveland, when speaking of "aliens excluded from naturalization," enumerates two major types of considerations: moral and racial. Under the moral rubric, he lists several categories of aliens who would not qualify for naturalization, including polygamists, anarchists, those guilty of crimes, those who opposed the Constitution, those who spoke no English, and so-called alien enemies. Regarding race, however, Cleveland explains that, except for the Caucasian and later the African race (after the abolition of slavery), Congress excluded all other races: "We go to the extremes in colors, including the whites and the blacks, but leaving out the yellows and the browns. This seems like an absurd distinction in our law. Yet no Asiatics may be naturalized. No Mongolians or Malays, Chinese, Japanese, Burmese or East Indians can becomes citizens of the United States unless they are born here or are permitted to become citizens by a special act of Congress" (75).

Referring to these racial exclusions and the history of Asian immigration to the United States, Lisa Lowe states that "the period from 1850s to World War II was marked by legal exclusions, political disenfranchisement, and internment for Asian-origin groups in the United States" (1996, 9). Her argument is that "in the last century and a half, the American *citizen* has been defined over against the Asian *immigrant,* legally, economically, and culturally" (4). Similarly, Robert S. Chang sees multiple prohibitions against Asians imposed by Congress as motivated by "nativistic racism" that rendered Asian immigrants the Yellow Peril, unable to assimilate with "us," and dangerous to U.S. peace and security: "It is in part through the figure of Asian immigrants and their descendants as perpetual internal foreigners that the national community has been able to identify itself. Without Asian Americans, they (the 'real' Americans) would not have known who they were."[14] In the same way, Shohat sees the issues of legitimacy and foreignness as tied to the Eurocentric logic that demonizes non-Western peoples:

> Although immigration from North Africa and the Middle East dates back to the end of the last century, Middle Easterners are seen as "forever foreign." . . . Chicano/as are treated by the media as ontologically, quintessentially alien ("from there"), although many did not cross the borders to the U.S., it was the border that moved around them. The first "illegal alien," Columbus, is celebrated as a discoverer, while indigenous Mexicans are seen as "infiltrating" a barbed border, which in fact divides their former homeland. (1998, 43)

The above examples show that the racial logic of citizenry, initiated in 1790, has not operated simply according to whiteness/nonwhiteness, where whiteness is a preferred racial marker. Instead, this logic has been unstable, fluctuating, contingent; it has, in fact, historically privileged only a *certain kind of whiteness* as a metacategory that governs the notion of a rightful American.[15]

Thus, whiteness needs to be understood as a selective category that, through filtering, has privileged only the "appropriate" white bodies as materially and symbolically valid. Ian F. Haney-López, for example, asserts that whiteness is a falsely universalizing term: "Being white is not a monolithic or homogenous experience, either in terms of race, other social identities, space or time" (1996, xiv). Writing about her Italian stepgrandmother who, by her naturalization certificate, was defined as "Dark White," Louise DeSalvo concludes: "There was not one white race; there were several, and some were not as good as others" (2003, 27). Indeed, racial whiteness, as Jacobson argues, has been a highly contested and slippery notion—fluid and subject to multiple interpretations and reinterpretations, depending on various historical moments. "Caucasians are made and not born," he states, and "to trace the process by which Celts or Slavs became Caucasians is to recognize race as ideological, political deployment rather than as a neutral, biologically determined element of nature" (1998, 4, 14).

Hence, when it comes to the perception of white immigrants as unwanted pollutants, those immigrants who are white Western Europeans and pass for legitimate representatives of the first world have been typically privileged by U.S. immigration policies and generally valorized as more desirable than Eastern and Southern Europeans. Aristide R. Zolberg writes, "The coming of World War I and the Russian Revolution stimulated unprecedented efforts to insulate the United States from European dangers." After World War I, in the 1921 First Quota Act and in the Immigration Act of 1924, Congress implemented severe restrictions on immigration from Eastern and Southern Europe through national origin quotas, which were finally abolished in the 1965 Immigration and Nationality Act Amendments. The quota system, which cut off immigration of Italians, Slavs, and Eastern European Jews, was intended to restore the white ethnic profile of the United States and "was legitimized by supposedly scientific demonstrations of the mental, moral, and physical inferiority of the latest arrivals."[16] By contrast, the law then allowed for the greatest number of immigrants to come from Great Britain.

These various policies that have perpetuated the exclusionary ideal of an American identity demonstrate that, using the institutional apparatus of alienhood, the nation has been "cleansing" itself by keeping out those who are deemed threatening and undesirable, and disciplining those considered admissible. The impact of these regulations has been, to use Roberts's words, "mainly metaphysical" (1997, 205). That is, these restrictions have created ever-changing cultural conceptions about who deserves to have access to the rightful notions of Americanness.

The 2001 exhibit at the Ellis Island Immigration Museum, "Peak Immigration Years, 1880-1924: Between Two Worlds," further illustrates these ideas. Specifically, one quote, by Theodore Roosevelt in 1915, powerfully conveys nativist views that sketch out the desired idea of pure and true Americanness:

> There is no room in this country for a hyphenated Americanism. A hyphenated American is not an American at all. This is just as true of the man who puts "native" before the hyphen as of the man who puts German or Irish or English or French before the hyphen. Americanism is a matter of the spirit and of the soul. Our allegiance must be purely to the United States. We must unsparingly condemn any man who holds any other allegiance. But if he is heartily and singly loyal to this Republic, then no matter where he was born, he is just as good an American as anyone else.[17]

This passage demonstrates the patriarchally privileged vision of a model immigrant: a *man* expected to strive to become a whole American and, in the process, to sever his ties with the Old World and pledge his sole allegiance to the new nation. This strong rhetoric of national uniformity, couched in a discourse of spirituality, demonstrates the overall generosity and benevolence of the United States that is supposedly willing to accept newcomers as long as they are not the so-called hyphenated hybrids but are "heartily and singly" loyal to one nation.

To talk about aliens within such a historical framework means also to evoke the idea of what Bauman, for example, calls "strangerhood." The questions here might be: How in fact does one become "singly" and "heartily" loyal to one nation? How does the remodeling take place? What material and discursive practices need to be employed for this transformation to succeed? In "The Making and Unmaking of Strangers," Bauman theorizes the nationalist discourse of strangerhood as typically resting on either "anthropoemic" or "anthropophagic" strategies, strategies employed during the time of nation-building to ensure the control over the purity of a modern nation-state. The anthropoemic strategy involves ejection of the unwanted alien element. It is a tactic of exclusion that rests on barring strangers from entering the nation or confining them within specific ghettos—vomiting strangers, so to speak. The anthropophagic strategy refers to the nullification of a stranger's ontological otherness by consuming, or internalizing, his or her difference: "annihilating the strangers by *devouring* them and then metabolically transforming them into a tissue indistinguishable from one's own" (Bauman 1997, 47). This coercive assimilation smooths out the stranger's unsettling otherness and is historically conducted in the name of cultural homogeneity. An example of this strategy might be the seemingly innocent tactic employed by Ellis Island officials when they asked arriving immigrants to alter their names so that they would be more pronounceable. In one of the current Ellis Island Immigration Museum brochures, Zolberg describes the anthropophagic tactics prevalent in the first part of the twentieth century:

> The determination to reduce immigration to the U.S. in the 1920s was coupled with a major effort to "Americanize" those who had already come. The outbreak of World War I provoked a campaign

> against the use of the German language, which was especially widespread throughout the Midwest, and against bilingualism generally, which was considered unpatriotic and harmful to child development. Symbolized by an insistence on accentless speech, conformity in dress, and the performance of patriotic rites such as the daily pledge of allegiance to the flag in schools and the singing of the national anthem at sports events, "Americanism" was advocated by the school system and churches, as well as by employers. For example, Henry Ford required the wives of his workers to attend classes where they were taught to cook bland food that he considered truly "American."

What Zolberg describes are deliberate cultural practices that worked toward a monologic vision of Americanism. Today nobody is necessarily instructing immigrants to join special cooking classes, but I argue that the pull toward homogenization of Americanness is equally strong, in spite of the aura of multiculturalism. Anthropophagic and anthropoemic strategies still operate on postmodern strangers, but in more subtle, often covert ways. Bauman, in fact, comments that "today's strangers are by-products, but also the means of production, in the incessant—because never conclusive—process of identity-building" (1997, 54).

One might argue that the nationalist sentiments expressed by Roosevelt and Ford in the 1920s belong to the past, that, despite anti-immigrant rhetoric, with the current emphasis on cultural pluralism and ethnic diversity, a hyphenated Americanism is in fact not only permitted but also cherished, celebrated, and encouraged. To probe these issues, I turn for a moment to academic settings, believing that for many of us—teachers, students, administrators—educational institutions are places where we encounter and grapple with these notions and experiences on a daily basis.

When I discuss multicultural politics in my courses, my students are typically quick to point out, for example, that the recent stress in the mainstream media on Kwanzaa, an African-American holiday, could serve as a compelling instance of how contemporary American society tends to be more appreciative of its multicultural and multiethnic makeup. At a first glance, our own university campus appears to be a fertile multicultural ground as each May the university sponsors an International Street Fair weekend, featuring "ethnic" foods, music, artistic performances from "around the globe," and a march of students waving flags from various countries. All these activities are meant to convey a multicultural vision of our academic community and testify to the idea that our university "cherishes difference." Additionally, faculty and staff, especially around the time of holidays, receive memos from University Communications and Marketing: "Are you interested in an international experience without having to leave your home? If the answer is 'yes,' consider hosting one or two international college students for a Saturday overnight homestay one Saturday/Sunday this January."[18] And faculty members, at the end of each academic year, routinely receive a notice from the University Center for International Studies, encouraging educators to "internationalize" our courses: "As you are thinking about the courses you will be teaching during the upcoming year, consider adding an international component. The Center for International Studies can help you add an international component 'with a human face' to your courses."[19]

A careful scrutiny of our academic surroundings betrays the fact that such an officially promoted understanding of multiculturalism "with a human face" is fraught with tension. Although, for example, the practice of hosting international students is quite common on various university campuses, the encouragement to "have an international experience without leaving one's home" may give one pause; it invites an easy consumption of otherness while stressing the comforts of home in which one can safely become exposed to other cultures literally without stepping outside the boundary of one's own territory. An underlying implication is that by being at home the host remains in control of the experience, able to tailor it in terms of its duration and effect. The memos convey the American hosts' one-sided sense of unobliging hospitality, and therefore unintentionally highlight the superficiality and briefness of such an encounter with international students, who are authentic sources of knowledge about other cultures: "I learned a lot about Korea. My homestay students were great"; "I would definitely host students again. I learned so much from them."

My critique of the academic examples I give about my own institution is not intended to single out the campus I work on as a space that struggles with diversity issues. Rather, the often painful awkwardness that a lot of academics and students feel when it comes to issues of multiculturalism, ethnicity, and the discourses of difference is indicative of a cultural struggle on a larger scale.[20] That is, it reveals the way the dominant American discourse of honoring cultural diversity rests on what might be called a homogenizing multiculturalism, or what Slavoj Žižek terms "Western liberal multiculturalism," that is, a "Eurocentrist racism with a distance." Žižek's term is useful here because it suggests a certain patronizing Eurocentric *detachment* of a legitimate subject who, under the new heading of "multiculturalism," is willing to recognize, even respect, otherness cast in terms of authenticity, as long as this subject is capable of maintaining its own "privileged universal position" (Žižek 1997, 44). Moreover, such a view of otherness always perceives it as *outside* of the privileged subject itself. In short, the sanctioned "I" benevolently appreciates otherness provided that the other is understood as exteriority, without the possibility of touching the subject itself.

The idea of "Eurocentrist racism with a distance" is implicit in the notice from the Center for International Studies. Certainly well-meaning at a first glance, it presupposes that multiculturalism is a simple matter of "adding an international component"—sort of like adding an exotic spice to a familiar cuisine. Nothing in this notice speaks about the need to reconceptualize privileged notions of pedagogy that, for example, frequently translate themselves into the constructions of syllabi that map a conceptual trajectory of a course in such a way that multiculturalism or feminism appears as the last topic to be discussed and analyzed, and consequently, due to the obvious time constraints, receives little attention. Moreover, its addition as a tag end to the regular body of knowledge leaves the already validated knowledge intact and foils a more complex understanding of how multiculturalist feminist conceptual frameworks can potentially open up "a different terrain of consciousness" that might question the leveling of differences (Trinh 2001, 930). Instead, the invitation to internationalize our courses, luring us with the headline "Internationalizing Your Curriculum Made Easy," sounds like a seductive commercial that once again stresses the ease with which faculty can multiculturalize their courses and hence be more current. The notice explains that instructors just need to invite international students to their classes, and these students will act as cultural consultants.

One example of such a successful pedagogical arrangement is that of an instructor who invited African, Indian, and Filipino women to her Women's Studies 100 class "to give her students an opportunity to compare and contrast 'growing up female' in Western versus non-Western countries." Such a use of students designated as non-Western appears problematic on several levels: it assumes a certain universality of what it means to grow up female as Filipino, Indian, or African; it utilizes mainly students of color as exotic specimens that can represent non-Western cultures in front of predominantly white audiences; crucially, it treats these students as international components whose presence allows the instructors to claim that their courses have a multicultural element "with a human face"; and finally, it reduces discourses of multiculturality to elements that can be inserted into the already validated practices of teaching. Moreover, both examples presuppose that multiculturalism inevitably comes from "the outside" in the form of international students whose various cultural knowledges might be useful for the expansion of the ethnic horizons of American students and other community members.

This is certainly an interesting twist on the very idea of alienhood. These tactics demonstrate the sense of the privileged Western (American) self, which does not have to question itself in the process of doing multicultural work. Paradoxically, these tactics use alienhood to promote an idea of diversity that inevitably tries to make difference both usable and palatable.

AGAINST SALUTARY VISIONS OF TRANSNATIONAL ALIENS

To be understood, the current contradictory deployments of aliens that I have been theorizing must be considered within the context of late-twentieth-century processes of diasporic dispersals and transnational migrations. Although exile is, of course, not a condition peculiar to postmodernity, the post-1945 era has been characterized by many as "the age of the refugee, the displaced person, mass immigration" (Said 1984, 50). As the editors of *Travellers' Tales: Narratives of Home and Displacement* contend, "the world witnesses what is probably the largest ever movement and migration of peoples dispossessed by war, drought, 'ethnic cleansing,' and economic instability" (Robertson et al. 1994, 1). In the post-1989 period, the often turbulent and brutal events on a global scale, such as the destruction of the Berlin Wall, the collapse of the Soviet Union, the demonstrations in Tiananmen Square, and the war in the Balkans, resulted in the movements of economic and political refugees, exiles, and immigrants, mainly from non-Western spaces coded as second or third world, to industrially advanced Western nation-states. As Roger Bromley puts it, "Changes in the world since 1989 have refocused attention on the displaced person, the migrant and the stranger; people dispossessed and separated from their identity and their history. . . . This experience has to be seen in the context of a new global economy characterised by complex, interacting and disjunctive transnational flows" (2000, 3).

Against such a historical context, present discussions of transnationalism frequently refer to the transmittal of transnational capital and various economic and cultural processes of contemporary globalization that often mask imperialist tendencies, what Gayatri Chakravorty Spivak has summed up as "the neo-colonialism of *multi*nationals" (1997, 89). Scholars of transnationalism, in cultural studies and social sciences alike, typically point to the fact that contemporary experiences of transnationality are situated within the discourses and practices of late capitalism and enabled by current technologies of travel and communications. They also evoke the idea of the transnational as further linked with the notions of transculturality, translationality, cultural hybridity, and border crossings, and propelled by transnational flows of goods, images, and peoples.[21] There is then no doubt that, as Aihwa Ong argues, "transnational mobility and maneuvers mean that there is a new mode of constructing identity, as well as new modes of subjectification that cut across political borders" (1999, 18).

Yet, the discussions of the new modes of identity formation under the transnational processes rarely make space for the theorization of aliens and the discursive and material effects of alienhood.[22] This lack of sustained attention to aliens is especially troublesome given that it is precisely the disciplinary apparatuses of alienhood that have a legal, material, emotional, and symbolic impact on the daily experiences of various migrants. Instead, transnational practices are often conceived in potentially emancipatory ways, suggesting that new hybrid identities, although liminal and often marginalized by the very nature of being "across" or "beyond" the nation, have access to resistant, oppositional spaces. That is, the identities that are discursively produced via transnational conditions, what scholars refer to as "border" identities or "living hybrid realities" (Bromley 2000, 5), begin to function falsely as empowered, even at times celebratory.

One can see such contentions, for example, in Eva Hoffman's statement in "The New Nomads":

> Exile used to be thought of as a difficult condition. It involves dislocation, disorientation, self-division. But today, at least within the framework of postmodern theory, we have come to value exactly those qualities of experience that exile demands—uncertainty, displacement, the fragmented identity. Within this conceptual framework, exile becomes, well, sexy, glamorous, interesting. Nomadism and diasporism have become fashionable terms in intellectual discourse. (1999, 44)

Hoffman stresses a reimagining of the concept of exile as supposedly no longer a taxing and arduous condition that manifests itself in often violent uprooting—the loss of one's home, identity, cultural ties, and national moorings. Such a new vision of the exilic, by extension, rhetorically reconfigures an understanding of various immigrant lives—from painful to celebratory. As Hoffman suggests, although exile used to be thought of in terms of physical and emotional dispossession, at the end of the twentieth century, theoretically, "we" now presumably value those qualities that exilic positionings evoke—"uncertainty, displacement, the fragmented identity." Such a revised rendition of exile as "sexy, glamorous, interesting" creates a sense that those with access to an exilic consciousness are endowed with certain epistemic advantages. To be fair though, Hoffman is careful to attend to the contradictory nuances that frame what she terms "the exilic position." Although she acknowledges the pain of displacement and claims that "real dislocation, the loss of all familiar external and internal parameters, is not glamorous," at the same time she points out how for many displaced writers "exile can be a great impetus to thought and creativity" because it offers "the advantages of defamiliarization" (52, 50).

Hoffman's point about the potential pleasures of exile is evident, for example, in André Aciman's tempting statement that "exiles see double, feel double, are double" (1999b, 13). But such doubleness does not always uniformly translate into positions of privilege. Undoubtedly, there is a certain seduction in favoring bifocal experiences of exile and in recognizing that, for example, many artists have benefited from bicultural, or multicultural, aesthetic visions. However, such "salutary models of exile," to use Ali Behdad's words (2000, 407), frequently tend to obliterate the discrepancy between *theoretical*, liberatory renditions of mobility; border crossings; ensuing hybridization and experiences of conflictual emotionality; and the torn sense of belonging, pain, and oppressive liminality that forms the experiential reality of many migrants. A more contingent understanding of exilic positionings, reconfigured through a historically specific apprehension of transnationalism, would have to be one of unresolvable tension that while liberatory for some, for many remains the source of complex restrictions, curtailed mobility, and disenfranchisement.

Such an argument may compel us to be weary of the fashionable renditions of hybridity that are especially resonant in the current discussions of the "third space"—one of the most prevalent metaphors of transnationalism. For example, to conceptualize the third space, Trinh offers the concept of a "between-world reality": "It is a space of its own. Such a space allows for the emergence of new subjectivities that resist letting themselves be settled in the movement across First and Second. Third is thus formed by the process of hybridization which, rather than simply adding a here to a there, gives rise to an elsewhere-within-here/-there that appears both too recognizable and impossible to contain" (1994, 18–19). Working from the argument that "the experience of exile is never simply binary," Trinh attempts to account for the identities of those who are often complexly positioned between nations and who "belong" to more than one country, one culture, one language. Such a formulation of the third space destabilizes a traditionally static notion of cultural/national identity and seemingly problematizes most knowable (and intimate) categories of home, belonging, and nation, which we typically consider singular entities. Homi Bhabha, like Trinh preoccupied with the narratives of cultural and political diaspora, writes, "The very concepts of homogenous national cultures, the consensual or contiguous transmission of historical traditions, or 'organic' ethnic communities . . . are in a profound process of redefinition." What emerges out of this process is a "transnational and translational sense of the hybridity," a third space, "where the negotiation of incommensurable differences creates a tension peculiar to borderline existence" (1994, 5, 218).

I suggest that the metaphor of the third space has operated in a contradictory manner. On the one hand, it has been very helpful in rethinking the territorial boundaries, categories, and methodologies that we typically apply when studying, for example, literary or cinematic texts, all of which have been profoundly altered by the experiences of displacement and diaspora. On the other hand, as an often overused cultural metaphor, the third space, particularly when it is not anchored by historical specificity, begins to function as a free-floating, volatile notion, rendering the transnational "an empty conceptual vessel" (Guarnizo and Smith 1998, 4) and inviting an understanding of transnational migrants as unanchored hybrids. Though it is important to resist the impulse to privilege exilic consciousness as endowed with certain epistemic benefits, it is equally crucial not to romanticize hybridity and embrace it uncritically as a liberatory location. Put in a different way, I believe it is necessary to recognize that while it is fashionable nowadays to *theorize* in-betweenness, it is quite different to live it. For those who happen to be doing both, the experience comes with a realization of what Shohat called "a painful epistemological advantage" (1998, 4). Consequently, a rigorous employment of the "third space" requires not only a nuanced conceptualization of this term but also a strategic awareness of its conflicted applications.

To be sure, the ongoing efforts to theorize transnational, diasporic identity have already altered the contexts of national literature and cinema, which can no longer simply be identified by the parameters of monoculturalism and singular belonging.²³ Accordingly, literature that arises out of the political, social, and cultural changes of transnationalism and addresses these concerns has been called "the literature of new nomadism or diasporism," "transnational literature" (Hoffman 1999, 56), "narratives for a new belonging" (Bromley 2000), "writing outside the nation" (Seyhan 2001), and "diasporic writing."²⁴ Within a filmic context, Hamid Naficy's work (2001) on "transnational exilic cinema" has been particularly influential in approaching the diasporic filmmaking of the late-twentieth-century transnationals and exiles. All these new terms respond to the diasporic challenge, which, in the current era characterized by displacement, dislocation, migrancy, and border crossings, confirms the need to move beyond the more traditional parameters of national aesthetic categories.

At the same time, in order to avoid celebratory deployments of the transnational—and, by extension, salutary visions of aliens within those discourses— I follow a contention present, for example, in the work of Stuart Hall, who once remarked that the postcolonial is "a sign of desire for some, and equally for others, a signifier of danger" (1996, 242). For me, Hall's formulation is an especially useful and rigorous way to think of the transnational, allowing us to recognize asymmetries of power and privilege that affect immigrants, refugees, and border crossers through uneven processes of economic domination, wealth distribution, racialization, gender oppression, and class conflict. A watchfulness about specificities of racial, gender, and ethnic formations is crucial if we wish to be mindful of the conceptual trappings of Eurocentric and heteromasculinist logics that often erase heterogeneities and obscure histories of deprivation and exploitation. Hall's point also prompts the need to work against the impulse to conflate transnational identities. For instance, in the contemporary world, to be an alien means a very different thing than to be a cosmopolitan. I submit that even in the current context openly promoting movement and travel, the distinction between alienhood and cosmopolitanism is still maintained with a renewed force.

Clearly, both terms, "alien" and "cosmopolitan," refer to a transnational positioning, but their codings and cultural undertones are historically very distinct. As I have already argued, to be marked as an alien suggests a space of inferiority and unwanted otherness, but to be marked as a cosmopolitan, a term that exudes an aura of sophistication and elegance, is more readily linked with a desirable economic and racial position. "Cosmopolitan," etymologically deriving from the Greek *kosmopolítē*—citizen of the world—connotes mobility, autonomy, latitude, and it is most often associated with a class of elite Western subjects. A "cosmopolite" is defined as "belonging to all the world, not limited to just one part of the political, social, commercial, or intellectual world; one who is free from local, provincial, or national prejudices." Within current practices, Ong calls this position "flexible citizenship," even more enabled and validated by the multinational corporations and logics of transnationality.²⁵

Who then has access to this flexible citizenship? What kinds of identities might enter the transnational positionality? For whom is this term reserved? Are border crossers from Mexico to the United States performing a transnational act while traversing the nations' boundaries? In what sense are Mexican women who work in *maquiladoras,* U.S.-owned high-tech factories south of the border, transnational? Or more precisely, how do certain economic transnational practices delineate their gendered positions?[26] How might we understand the situation of transnational mothers, a large number of Central American, Mexican, and Caribbean immigrant women who are engaged in domestic work in the United States (as live-in nannies, housecleaners, home-care help for the elderly) and separated from their own children who often stay behind in their home countries? Pierrette Hondagneu-Sotelo argues, "The changing nature of U.S. labor demand and restrictive immigration policies have encouraged these new transnational family forms." Moreover, these transnational uses of alien women remain rooted in a long historical legacy of people of color being incorporated into the United States through coercive labor systems that do not recognize family rights.[27] In what sense can we talk about massive displacements of the peoples of the Balkans, dispossessed and traumatized by war, as having to do with transnational, albeit obviously often involuntary, movements? In what kinds of transnational interventions are the Muslim women involved who, seeking justice for their personal agonies, traveled to the Hague for the court hearings organized by the International War Crimes Tribunal in the mid-1990s? Many of these women endured violent acts of torture and rape at the hands of military men in the Omarska Detention Camp during the Serbian occupation of Bosnia and Herzegovina, and some of those who survived, out of the "obligation towards the ones gone," made a decision to testify in the Hague court against their perpetrators.[28]

Such difficult questions may propel us to consider the notions of hybridity and the third space differently and with caution. To speak of the third scenario in the context, for example, of the experiences of women who were exposed to violence, death, torture, rape, starvation, and killings in the Omarska Camp and who, having survived the camp, were forced to leave their native place and cross over from Bosnia to Croatia, feels deeply troublesome, almost an act of discursive violence. Furthermore, this example brings up yet another important point—the issue of a politics of representation within feminist discourses. If we agree with Ong that "besides the poor, women, who are half of humanity, are frequently absent in studies of transnationalism" (1999, 11), then we also have to ask precisely what kinds of female voices have been represented by current transnational feminist theories.

Even though the contestation of border identities has been perhaps most forcefully debated within feminism, specifically within what Grewal and Kaplan call transnational feminist cultural studies, the important critical work begun in this venue still seems rhetorically binarized, endlessly privileging discussions within a first worldness (associated with Westernness)/third worldness dichotomy. In proposing a theory of transnational feminist practices, Grewal and Kaplan aim for a praxis of resistance and critique, contingent on historically specific contexts, that transfigures the traditional theoretical divides in ways that "link our understanding of postmodernity, global economic structures, problematics of nationalisms, issues of race and imperialism, critiques of global feminism, and emergent patriarchies" (1999, 358). Although the stress is on the "global," the transnational multicultural anthologies that present the most cutting-edge, radical feminist scholarship systematically underrepresent, if not plainly exclude, any voices from the so-called second world.[29] In other words, it appears that the global, in transnational feminist cultural studies, has its already predetermined and limited set of meanings. Grewal and Kaplan contend that "what theorists of the diaspora often tend to forget is that *location* is still an important category that influences the specific manifestations of transnational formations" (1994, 16; my emphasis) It is to the notion of location that I wish to turn in the conclusion of this section.

If we conceive of postmodernity as a historical condition marked by heterogeneous experiences of exile and dislocation, feminist inquiries into the representational politics of contemporary transnational cultures necessarily need to take into account the diverse locations of various aliens and discourses and practices that create and sustain what I have been calling alienhood. Thus, an indispensable critical intervention into transnational feminist cultural studies would be to work against the erasure of the second world location so as not to eliminate or limit various voices, specifically female ones, from behind the Wall, and now post-Wall communities. That is, I opt for a feminist theory of transnational alienhood—one that would continue deconstructing the first/third world binary and simultaneously work against the deletion of the second world specificity. Thus, as I see it, to be engaged in transnational feminist practices (whether as teachers, cultural critics, or activists or across these locations) entails both stretching the meanings of the transnational and deromanticizing its employments within truly global networks.

QUIVERING BODIES: TRAJECTORY OF THE TEXT

In the context of what I have sketched above, I turn to contemporary literary and cinematic narratives of exile that fall within the genre, or category, of transnational exilic texts. In current literary and cinematic discussions, the term "transnational" is frequently used side by side, or at times interchangeably, with the notion of diaspora. Even though both concepts evoke the idea of the nation and displaced writers or filmmakers, it is important not to collapse these terms because each carries its own specificity. To some degree, I follow the distinction of an Asian-American writer, Shirley Geok-lin Lim, who suggests that "diaspora . . .

was appropriate at a time in human history when if populations left a location of origin, it was difficult for them to return." To situate her own writing, she prefers the notion of transnationality because it evokes a sense of "continuing relationships with the location of origin," enabled by current technologies of travel and communication.[30] While "the location of origin" may seem problematic because it evokes a certain unquestionable stability of a native home, presumed to be always localizable, Geok-lin Lim's argument points to a historical evolution in terms of how certain hyphenated writers choose to situate their work.

This book is about transnational aliens, those whose historically and culturally specific positions unsettle the traditionally coherent and stable narratives of the nation. To write about strangers-aliens is to enter the Derridean idea of the *pharmakon,* a concept with a dual meaning signifying both *remedy* and *poison.* As I have discussed, aliens can function symbolically and materially as remedy when institutionally they are employed as useful, noncontentious multiculturals. On the other hand, they are poison—especially if they are nonwhite and hence considered illegitimate citizens. This is because, as many anti-immigrant activists argue, the "color" they bring to bear on the mainstream culture, always understood as having an authentic white core, endangers not simply the "nation's body, but its soul" (Auster 1990, 56). In other words, aliens are useful when we need them, but only after their differences have been appeased and they themselves have been disciplined into nonthreatening bodies. The metaphor of the *pharmakon* is helpful here because it allows me to suggest that alienhood locks the exilic "I" in the space of undecidability, forever quivering.

The project traces the relation between the historical abjection of the alien body and the conditions of exile and assimilation. The readings focus on the discussion of "quivering ontologies," the term I have developed to explore the intricacy—and the intimacy—of cultural mechanisms that put the exile on a precariously wavering border between being and not being a valid, culturally sanctioned subject. I argue that the experience of exile—being catapulted out of the familiar mode of being—locks the foreigner in a complex, historically specific, in-between location. This location can be seen as a site of protest against a nationalistic dynamic of assimilation that accepts, while also absorbing and flattening, the exile's unsettling difference. The often fragmentary flow of the narratives I study reflects the protagonists' fragmented selves that are typically positioned in the interstices of two different cultural locations, between here and there, past and present, and, Bharati Mukherjee writes, between "two modes of knowledge" (1988, 189).

In what follows, I am treating exile as a performative condition, one that evokes a sense of shifting, or quivering, identity location—an experience of liminality and undecidability that destabilizes the traditionally static notion of national identity. Like the concept of an "in-between exilic location," in each text I analyze I consider liminality within particular historical and cultural parameters.[31] This contextuality is crucial for an understanding of how exilic subjectivities function performatively, resisting stable, homogeneous, and essentialist visions of the true exilic that can be applied across various ethnic and racial formations.

Chapter 1, "Becoming Transnational: *El Norte* and the 'Elsewhere' of Exile," opens with an inquiry into the contemporary transnational cinema of exile in the United States. In particular, I look at formal and thematic depictions of violence employed against impure aliens in Gregory Nava's 1983 *El Norte*, a film I locate in a larger context of recent U.S. border-crossing texts. The aliens here are exiled siblings, Guatemalan Indians, who are forced to flee their country in the 1980s. I argue that *El Norte,* by foregrounding the visual topography of the border crossing via the sewer, creates claustrophobic spatiality to eradicate any comfort traditionally associated with the idea of nationhood. Certain transnational aliens are not even invited to assimilate because the social structures they enter in the United States devour them and simultaneously spit them out as undesirable throwaways. Hence, even though the protagonists survive the abjecting crossing experience and emerge out of the sewer, they are materially and metaphorically relegated to living underground.

Chapter 2, "Accented Bodies and Coercive Assimilation: The Trespasses of the García Girls," turns to recent American transnational exilic literary narratives and focuses specifically on Julia Alvarez's 1992 novel, *How the García Girls Lost Their Accents*. I analyze the distinct ways that, even after the García family crosses the border successfully, escaping the Dominican regime of Rafael Trujillo in the 1960s, the stigma attached to them as trespassers haunts their unstable cultural positions. The Garcías are metaphoric trespassing transnationals whose experiences of the promised land are that of liminality often marked by disorientation and ostracism. It is, specifically, the accented body—the body semiotically coded as alien—that marks the Dominican-American García "girls" as strangers-hybrids and attracts the often violent force of coercive assimilation that invites them to lose their accented speech quickly so that they can begin to function socially at the level of successfully Americanized subjects.

Chapter 3, "The Dialectics of Exile: Resident Alienhood and *Lost in Translation*," broadens the discussion of "accented bodies" by examining Eva Hoffman's 1989 book *Lost in Translation: A Life in a New Language*. Exploring the position of a second world female immigrant caught between her Polish-Jewish cultural identity and her new position in the United States in the 1960s and 1970s, I inspect the way an exile lives the act of translation, both linguistically and culturally, and investigate the linguistic politics of assimilation. The text foregrounds the performative idea of translation, that is, an ongoing, shifting process of articulation and rearticulation—the performance of the self—that, specifically within the context of alienhood, does not allow us to settle meaning in stable and predictable ways. In other words, Hoffman refuses to purge alienhood out of her narrator so that she can emerge at the end of the text as a clean, nontroubling immigrant.

In the final two chapters, I return to the exploration of transnational exilic cinema and move the discussion outside of the U.S. context. Although the two directors whose films I study, Roman Polanski and Milcho Manchevski, have strong ties to the United States (Manchevski currently lives in New York; Polanski used to live here and made his films in the Hollywood studio system), the diegetic focus of the two films I explore grounds the discussion of second world aliens within a specific cultural and historical European context.

In Chapter 4, "Claustrophobic Exile: *The Tenant* and Ostracizing Logics of Difference," I use Roman Polanski's 1976 film, *The Tenant,* to explore the stylistic means of privileging claustrophobia, which the cinema of exile frequently engages to comment on the social constructions of alienhood. Specifically, the cinematic application of a restricted mise-en-scène paradoxically encloses the figure of the second world protagonist-alien in the Parisian community and comments on the very position of exile. The horror of Polanski's stifling urban space provides a way to illustrate the intense suffocation created by the foreigner's social ostracism. I examine how *The Tenant* works as a filmic narrative of abjection by foregrounding two critical moments in the film: the screams that open and close the narrative sequence. By reading the repudiated location of abjection, I investigate how the film discloses the phobic model of community that coheres and "cleans" itself through expelling the bodies of unwanted others.

The closing chapter, "Anatomies of Abjection: Ethnic Cleansing and Liminality in *Before the Rain*," examines the horrors of ethnic cleansing in the Balkans through an analysis of Milcho Manchevski's 1994 film, *Before the Rain.* This section suggests that alienhood, organized in a logic of purity, sameness, and oneness, does not simply work to abject certain *individual bodies,* but rather that the logic that propels its mechanisms eventually instigates ethnic cleansings and massive destructions of entire communities. That is, I argue that these textual, filmic structures, far from circulating harmlessly in aesthetic space, both reflect and reproduce the temptations of devastating kinds of genocidal violence. I consider the film's scrutiny of the dynamic of religious and racial violence and its inspection of the sociocultural mechanisms that produce xenophobic paradigms of the nation. Specifically, the liminal position of an exile, who returns to his native place in Macedonia and finds himself caught within the paradoxical logic of impossibility, reveals, in all its violent detail, the fact that an exile is no longer legitimate at home.

The conceptual trajectory of this book is thus motivated by the dynamic of border crossings. I start with the discussion of *El Norte:* the vision of refugees crossing the border, the foregrounding of liminality, of being at the threshold between the native and the host nation, the moment of becoming transnational;

and end with *Before the Rain*, which features the return of the exile, the return that underscores the logic of exilic impossibility as the exile discovers that he no longer counts as one of the natives. Manchevski's *Before the Rain* foregrounds the challenge of being reincorporated into an exile's native place and suggests that because an exiled "I" no longer has stable national identity, this "I" becomes curiously foreign to its own kin and, in contradictory ways, does and does not belong to its people. Such a condition of otherness complicates, once again, the positioning of a transnational exilic subjectivity. What *Before the Rain* shows is different from the experience of oppression and ostracism in *The Tenant,* from a linguistic struggle of a hybrid identity in *Lost in Translation,* from the location of shuttling transnationals in *How the García Girls Lost Their Accents,* and from the abjection of the protagonists in *El Norte* who are never even allowed to occupy a liberatory transnational bearing. A returning exile is not necessarily persecuted in any specific way, but rather occupies a place of paradoxical native-alien/outsider, a phantom, a tenuous "I" that returns to reclaim its old self that no longer is.

The diverse texts I work on are bound by their attempt to decolonize traditional representations of immigrants-aliens, which means to bring into focus often tabooed articulations of dissenting voices that respond to the ostracizing powers of alienhood. In this sense, this study is an effort to move the discourse of alienhood into a dialectical context. Thus, even if we accept Angelika Bammer's point that "marginality and otherness increasingly figure as the predominant affirmative signifiers of (postmodern) identity" (1994, xii), it is crucial to remember that the ideological discourse of purity has fostered the model of acculturation based on either absorption into normative social structures or ejection from them. The narratives in this book interrupt this binary trap by formally and thematically investigating the location of quivering as a site of both *painstaking complexity and possibility*. The transnational exilic positionality cannot be seen, depending on the context, as either fully liberatory or disempowering. At the same time, these literary and cinematic texts do not allow the readers and spectators to sublimate or romanticize otherness created by experiences of exile. Even more important, they do not simply tell "quaint stories from the Old Country" (Hoffman 1989, 202), therefore denying, through a benevolent gesture, the right to recontain them as marginal voices in literary and cinematic canons.

The category of transnational exilic textualities is not merely a new, fashionable terminology, but rather an attempt to open up the often stifling, reductive, and patronizing markers of immigrant, minority, and ethnic filmic and literary subcategories that, although historically valid, tend to lump the diasporic work into what Naficy calls "discursive ghettos" (1996, 120). Furthermore, these particular labels often work to code specific cinematic and literary texts as of ethnic interest, as if ethnicity inherently belonged to the so-called minority discourses.³² Instead, through a variety of literary and cinematic techniques, these texts tie the readers and the spectators to the protagonists in the most intimate ways. In doing so, they curiously estrange us from ourselves, asking us to feel our own otherness.³³ In other words, they do not offer specific points of view with which the readers and the audience are supposed to identify momentarily, but they problematize the traditional coercive acceptance of otherness and, in complex ways, move beyond the mere slogans of "embracing difference" and "celebrating diversity."

"Border Opinions," 1991. Copyright Don Bartletti/Los Angeles Times.

1
Becoming Transnational:
El Norte and the "Elsewhere" of Exile

> To be in exile means to be out of place; also, needing to be rather elsewhere; also, not having that "elsewhere" where one would rather be. Thus, exile is a place of compulsory confinement, but also an unreal place, a place that is itself out of place in the order of things.
>
> —Zygmunt Bauman, "Assimilation into Exile"

The landscape of critical writings on exile is permeated, to a large degree, by the notion of the exilic *elsewhere*. Julia Kristeva, for example, proposes, "Always elsewhere, the foreigner belongs nowhere" (1991, 10). One might read this point as liberatory, that is, the positionality of the foreigner may appear at a first glance as unmoored and hence unrestricted. But to propose such a "romantic," celebratory reading of the foreign—deriving from the Latin *forās*, meaning "outside" and connoting alienhood—would be a mistake. The unreality of exile described by Zygmunt Bauman in the above quotation compellingly captures the neither/nor territory of unbelonging in relation to the formation of transnational exilic identities. Exile here implies mobility, but the straightforward trajectory of a movement from one place to another is figured through a sense of paradoxical tension, through the idea of placelessness. The "elsewhere" of exile becomes almost unreachable as a space where the displaced could transport his or her body and claim that elsewhere as a new realm of home. Hence, Bauman's conceptualization of exile as a "compulsory confinement" offers an unromantic vision of almost claustrophobic spatiality, a place "unreal," marked by the quivering that suggests that an exile does not have a stable relationship to the new national space. Similarly, Trinh T. Minh-ha, when reflecting on exile and displacement, also speaks about the exilic elsewhere: "The traveling self is here both the self that moves physically from one place to another . . . and the self that embarks on an *undetermined journeying practice,* having constantly to negotiate between home and abroad, native culture and adopted culture, or more creatively speaking, between a here, a there, *and* an elsewhere" (1994, 9; my emphasis).

Does the elsewhere mark the transnational position? What does it mean to claim that the elsewhere is identified by "an undetermined journeying practice"? Conventionally, journeying implies mobility and movement between places, but Trinh stresses that "travel" has an ambiguous status; it is unsettled, unresolved, undecided, lacking precise limits. This kind of exilic journeying pertains not simply to the physical movement but also to identity shifts, linguistic traversings, bodily transformations, symbolic reconfigurations of one's "I"—what is often fashionably termed "hybridization," "translationality," and "hyphenated subjectivities." Unless we anchor these terms within specific material contexts, they all risk falling into universalizing traps, erasing discursive and material struggles of many exiles and border inhabitants. It is important to work against sweeping generalizations to avoid using these notions as simply the new catchphrases marking the latest intellectual fashions.[1]

In an effort to contextualize the exilic elsewhere historically and culturally, I take up the questions I have posed to examine the conditions of becoming a transnational subject through the heterogeneous, gendered experiences of transcultural border crossings. I am interested in the moments that, during national border crossings, rupture one's identity, putting exiles at the threshold of what they once were and what they are not yet. As my inquiry complicates the notion that transnational subjecthood is *universally accessible* within the contemporary processes of globalization, I inspect those who may claim a transnational identity and argue that for many exiles coded as aliens, especially illegal aliens, transnational positionality is an unattainable space of privilege. I start with Leo R. Chavez's definition of how to think of transnational identities within the culture of the United States, which, he argues, is fueled by new nativist sentiments that underscore the fear that, due to the influx of specifically nonwhite immigrants, America is rapidly losing its "true" Americanness:

> The "new" immigrants are *trans*nationalists, or people who maintain social linkages back in the home country; they are not bound by national borders, and their multiple identities are situated in communities in different nations and in communities that cross nations. (Chavez 1997, 62)

Although, as Chavez notes, many immigrants are certainly able to maintain social and cultural linkages with their native countries, there are also those who, often brutally expelled from their home cultures, have no access to these kinds of transnational ties that enable bidirectional mobility across borders. Hence, for some who fall into the category of alienhood, especially for those who classify as nation*less* rather than as *trans*national, the "trans" is not necessarily an attainable location.

Within such a framework, the specific focus of my analysis is the representation of alien contamination in Gregory Nava's 1983 film *El Norte* (cowritten and produced by his wife, Anna Thomas), which I examine in conjunction with his later production *My Family, Mi Familia* (1995). In this chapter, I first briefly discuss *El Norte*'s and *My Family*'s thematic and formal attention to the heterogeneity of cultural crossings and bridgings to link *El Norte* to the historical underpinnings of entering the United States as an immigrant. I then read the shifting, or quivering, location of *El Norte*'s protagonists as violently uprooted refugees whose exile relegates them to the position of abjected aliens. Finally, I turn to the examination of the gendered specificity of their abjection through a close reading of the border-crossing sequences. While addressing transnational exilic cinematic textualities and their frequent emphasis on the multiplicity of national belongings, I wish to show that it is important not to homogenize the transnational location, as each needs to be analyzed in its specificity, with attention to the heterogeneity of gender, racial, and ethnic modalities.

CINEMATIC BORDER CROSSINGS: ENTERING THE UNITED STATES

Nava's debut feature, *El Norte,* is one of the most poignant examples of border traversings in recent transnational American exilic cinema, and it forms a compelling commentary, Kristeva writes, on the global sociocultural "ability to accept new modalities of otherness" (1991, 2). An artist who comes from a border family, Nava is intimately concerned with immigration experiences involving Latin Americans and Chicanos. In one interview, he notes: "Even though I am a third generation native Californian, some of my immediate relatives, who live just a few miles from the house I was raised in, are Mexican. So I've always been raised in that border world, with that tremendous clash between cultures" (West 1995). Thus, the inspiration for *El Norte* springs from Nava's own lived experience of the border: "As a kid, I crossed the border several times a week, often wondering who lived in all those cardboard shacks on the Mexican side." The film visualizes the specificity of the Tijuana–San Diego border: "The border is unique—the only place in the world where an industrialized first-world nation shares the border with a third-world country. In California, it's just a fence: on one side are the Tijuana slums, on the other side—San Diego. It's so graphic! This was the germ of the story."[2]

Both *El Norte* and *My Family* are intensely preoccupied with borders, border crossings, and bridging cultures. In *My Family*, a Latino saga of the Sánchez family that spans three generations of Mexican Americans in the 1920s and 1930s, the 1950s, and the 1980s, Nava foregrounds both cultural separation, segregation, and symbolic and material bridges between Mexico and California and between Los Angeles and East Lost Angeles. In both films, the theme of crossings emphasizes the idea that while legitimate Americans historically manipulate the border and aggressively police it, it is mainly the Latino and Chicano characters who perform crossings that are either voluntary or forced. When the Anglo characters enact the crossings, their travel is always marked by a sense of a luxurious choice of making contact with a different culture.

For example, in 1933, the mother of the family, Maria Sánchez, pregnant at the time and an American citizen, is illegally deported by *la migra* (INS) to Mexico with thousands of other Chicanos, who like her were forcefully picked up in violent roundups during the mass deportations of the 1930s. It is only after her son is born in Mexico that she risks her and her baby's lives in a dramatic water crossing, struggling to rejoin her husband in Los Angeles. Throughout all three historical periods in the film, we see how the members of the Sánchez family perform the daily bridge crossings, moving from East Los Angeles, where they reside, to Los Angeles, where they work in the Anglo world as maids, nannies, gardeners, and waiters. One of the most memorable crossings in *My Family* comes at the very end of the film when the narrative features movement in the opposite direction. We see how Memo, a successful son in the family who becomes a lawyer, brings his white fiancée and her parents from Bel-Air to meet his family. Even though Memo's fiancée and her family have lived in Los Angeles all their lives, they have never been to East Los Angeles. The polite meeting of the two families is laden with discomfort and tension: the fiancée's parents perceive the Sánchez family as Mexican, that is, alien, foreign, and not quite fully American; their well-meaning compliments sound awkward and patronizing; Memo himself wishes to please his future in-laws at the cost of erasing his ethnic specificity (for the in-laws, he is Bill, not Memo) and silencing his family's diverse Chicano voices.

Whereas in *My Family* these kinds of physical and metaphoric border crossings formally tie together all three parts of the film and ask the spectators to consider the multivalence of the Chicano points of view and their place within the dominant Anglo culture, *El Norte*'s horrific crossing of the Tijuana–San Diego border functions on a slightly different level: as a violent narrative scar, a diegetic rupture underscoring visual anxiety—unhealable and paralyzing due to its asphyxiating mise-en-scène. The argument I will foreground involves the visual topography of the crossing designed to create claustrophobic spatiality that defamiliarizes any comfort traditionally associated with the idea of nationhood. To experience this unsettling crossing as a spectator means to plunge visually into what Caren Kaplan (1987) calls "deterritorialization" of space, to witness what I call "the abyss of abjection."

While it is pertinent to situate *El Norte* within the context of the aesthetics and politics of the New Latin American Cinema as well as in the larger category of ethnically diverse transnational exilic filmmaking, I would like to offer a perhaps unexpected conceptual route—that of Ellis Island—to ground Nava's film within the U.S. history of anti-immigrant discursive and material violence. This discussion will reveal the contradictory, double pull on the emotionally charged issue of contemporary immigration: the United States cultivates a sentimentalized, "congratulatory self-image as a 'nation of immigrants'" while, simultaneously, the history of American nativism shows how xenophobic sentiments continue to reinforce the ostracizing apparatus of alienhood (Chavez 1997, 66). After all, if we consider Peter Brimelow's discussion of the current immigration "disaster," which, he claims, manifests itself through the idea that "the United States has lost control of its borders," then the situation becomes transparent. The threat of foreign "contamination" harms the makeup of the American "national family," which is being transformed into an "alien nation" (1995, 4–5).

To speak of representations of border crossings within the history of the United States means to evoke Ellis Island as the paramount processing station for millions of arriving immigrants and as a symbolic site testifying to the troubled immigrant legacy of the United States. Until Ellis Island was closed in 1954, with its most active years between 1880 and 1900 during which nine million immigrants entered the country from Europe, Asia, and the Caribbean, it served as the main center that welcomed, but also often brutally sorted out, the newcomers (see Reeves 2000). To visit the Ellis Island Immigration Museum is to plunge into an unsettling visual and aural experience. In addition to more than two thousand artifacts, including jewelry, personal papers, clothing, and religious items, that are part of the permanent exhibition, many rooms are equipped with audiotapes that allow one to listen to firsthand interviews—recollections of border-crossing immigrants coming to the United States. As one sits in darkened rooms, with headphones over ears, it is hard not to experience chills as the voices from the past speak of their journeys to the port, conditions on the ship, arrival and processing at the Ellis Island facilities.[3] On VHS tapes, these voices come alive through supplementary documentary footage, illustrating the frightful yet hopeful arrivals of immigrants, their interrogations, and medical testings.

Listening to the interviews and viewing various documentary materials, a visitor quickly learns that immigrant processing was not a homogeneous experience. The oral and visual testimonies speak about all kinds of humiliations, brutality, discriminatory selections, deportation, and often violent treatment of the newcomers. Deportations, which often divided families, occurred for various reasons, the main causes being diseases such as trachoma (a contagious inflammation of the eyes) and favus (a fungal infection of the scalp), as well as suspicions of mental deficiencies, criminal records, prostitution, or "wrong" political tendencies.[4] Furthermore, the Ellis Island inspection and selection process was rooted in a discriminatory class system: the process involved only the poor; first- or second-class ticket passengers were processed aboard ship and allowed to pass directly into New York City. Hans Berger, quoted in *Island of Hope, Island of Tears*, speaks about the arrival experience:

> When we arrived on the 26th of December, on a very, very cold winter day, and the passenger ship was fastened to the pier . . . the first-class passengers were asked to leave the ship. The second-class passengers followed. Then the announcement went around—all third-class passengers were please to remain on board overnight. They would be fed on the ship, be given a breakfast the following morning, at which time a lighter would come to take us over to Ellis Island. And so there was this slight feeling among many of us that, "Isn't it strange that here we are coming to a country where there is complete equality, but not quite so for the newly arrived immigrants?" (Brownstone, Franck, and Brownstone 1979, 144)

In the History Channel documentary *Ellis Island*, historian Alan Kraut remarks that in the nineteenth century there was a well-known saying among immigrants: America beckons, but Americans repel. The contradiction embedded in this statement sums up the tension that surrounded the process of entering the United States. The promised land invited and welcomed the immigrants, but the welcoming process involved a careful scrutiny and frightening, humiliating bodily inspections. Aristide Zolberg claims, "There was a kind of fixation on disease as being something that an immigrant brought in" *(Ellis Island)*. Health was understood as being more than a physical condition; the newcomers were also examined with the intention of sorting out the feeble-minded and those whose moral standards appeared dubious. For example, women who arrived without a male escort were suspected of prostitution and treated as an LPC (likely to become a public charge).

The entire institutionalized processing of immigrants and their filtering had to do with selecting only "clean" and "safe" aliens in order to protect the United States from all kinds of "defective" foreigners. Once again defectiveness did not mean merely physical or mental illnesses; at stake was the preservation of appropriate categories of whiteness. Mandy Patinkin, who narrates the documentary *Ellis Island*, explains that in 1894, two years after the opening of Ellis Island, a group of wealthy Bostonians, alarmed by the influx of newcomers from Eastern Europe, formed the Immigration Restriction League. The league pushed for new laws to exclude undesirable foreigners, and its conceptual foundation was, in Senator Henry Cabot Lodge's words, the fear that "the Slavic immigrants threatened to contaminate America." Patinkin explains that the increasing anxiety over certain newcomers led to the revival of the Ku Klux Klan and more restrictive visions of who was worthy of entering the United States: "Despite all the restrictions placed on aliens entering the country, foreigners were seen as radical, criminal, and diseased."

A careful study of the rhetoric of alienhood historically used to refer to incoming immigrants reveals the systematic workings of the logic of purity as a predominant conceptual framework that governed the selection of the "right" foreign bodies that could be deemed acceptable—that is, with a potential to be safely turned into proper Americans. This kind of logic, fueled by the discourse of contamination and cleanliness, inevitably coded the immigrants as dirty foreign "polluters" and suspicious aliens. Speaking of the ideological impact of the national origin quotas established in the 1920s, historian Virginia Yans comments: "It is very clear that the effort was to limit people who were not thought to be of the same level of culture and civilization as resident Americans. What they [those establishing the anti-immigrant laws] wanted to do was maintain the predominance of white Anglo-Saxons in this country.... There was a tremendous fear that people who came in from Southern Europe, from Eastern Europe, would *pollute the blood of American population* (*Ellis Island*; my emphasis).

This context is important for the analysis of contemporary American transnational films because it allows us to situate the late-twentieth-century exilic experiences within a long history of immigrant racial and ethnic exclusion, cruelties, and segregation. One could argue, as Hamid Naficy does, that the Ellis Island documentary footage, as well as many early silent films enacting immigrant conditions, are early border-crossing texts, creating historical and conceptual foundations for the visual and ideological landscape of many contemporary transnational exilic productions (2001, 238). A close reading of virtually every "educational" film I screened that documented the Ellis Island experience reveals a double pull when it comes to the treatment of immigrants. David McCullough, in the narration of another documentary, *Journey to America,* when speaking of immigrants states: "We needed them, and yet we found them threatening." What he means is that while the United States needed immigrants to do the so-called dirty work—to work in mines, mills, and slaughterhouses—the presence of many of the newcomers caused discomfort and fears because of their different languages, skin color, foods, and customs.

McCullough's point about both needing and fearing immigrants does not belong solely to the history of Ellis Island. In contemporary American culture, this idea is perhaps most applicable to the treatment and perception of Mexicans, Mexican Americans, and other Latinos. The United States eagerly utilizes many Mexican migrant workers as a cheap labor force for grueling seasonal jobs in fields and sweatshops but conveniently keeps them within the discursive and material space of illegal alienhood. Chavez notes, "Employers in the United States have used Mexican labor for most of this century, helping to establish patterns of migration from specific regions in Mexico" (1992, 58). And Pierette Hondagneu-Sotelo argues, "Latina immigrant labor, and specifically the work of housecleaners and nanny/housekeepers, constitutes a bedrock of our contemporary U.S. culture and economy, yet the work and the women who do it remain invisible and disregarded" (2001, ix). Within the dynamics of the global marketplace, deprivileged immigrants, women of color in particular, are widely used as "transnational aliens," which I will discuss in connection with Nava's female protagonist in *El Norte*: "In the United States today, these jobs remain effectively unregulated by formal rules and contracts. Consequently, even today they often resemble relations of servitude that prevailed in earlier, precapitalist feudal societies" (x).

These ideas are embedded in many border films associated with the Chicano/a cinema because the Mexican–U.S. border has a particularly conflicted and painful history. Linda Rosa Fregoso notes that the concept of border for Chicanas and Chicanos as well as for Mexicans living on the borderlands has a politically charged meaning: "the border figures as an intrusive or invasive border, the division established after the Mexican-American War of 1848, that is, an illegitimately imposed separation" (1993, 65). We see this idea explicated in the beginning of Nava's *My Family* when the father of the family, Jose Sánchez, leaves Mexico in 1926 and crosses the border to seek out a relative who is said to live in Los Angeles. This relative has a special significance in the film: he is the only one who remembers the time when his house in Los Angeles used to be in Mexico, before the border was forcibly moved: "They called the old man El Californio because he didn't come from anywhere else. He was born right here in Los Angeles when it was still Mexico." El Californio requests that he be buried in the cornfield behind the house and to have the following inscription on his grave: "Don Alejandro Vasquez, El Californio. Died 1934. When I was born here this was Mexico. And where I lie, this is still Mexico." Thus within the narrative, the house itself becomes a site of memory that carries the violent history of the Mexican–U.S. border.

Hence, to speak of the cinematic border crossings and the exilic elsewhere within the context I have sketched above means to scrutinize the rhetoric of purity and contamination that governed Ellis Island's operations in relation to contemporary immigrants and specifically in relation to the Mexican–U.S. border and its inhabitants and crossers. Ellis Island also allows us to differentiate between the two modes of historical border crossings: entering the United States via Ellis Island carries the aura of a legitimate, historically sanctioned entry that has been honored, even glorified, in the American cultural imaginary, but the crossings of the Mexican–U.S. border are invariably couched in the racialized discourse of illegitimacy and unlawful trespassings. While the current rhetoric surrounding Ellis Island as an immigrant station marks it as a legendary landmark whose history sustains nostalgic and sentimentalized tonality, the Mexican–U.S. border is an aggressively policed zone, which, Gloria Anzaldúa writes, is "a shock culture": "The U.S. Mexican border *es una herida abierta* where the Third World grates against the first and bleeds" (1987, 11). Anzaldúa acknowledges the history of violence that is embedded in the border culture she describes: "The prohibited and forbidden are its inhabitants.... Gringos in the U.S. Southwest consider the inhabitants of the borderlands transgressors, aliens—whether they possess documents or not, whether they're Chicanos, Indians, or Blacks. Do not enter, trespassers will be raped, maimed, strangled, gassed, shot" (3).

Consequently, the rhetoric of purity surrounding complex issues of immigration and border crossings persists with a renewed force despite the stress on the importance of recognizing multicultural diversity. I have already argued that these ideas of purity frequently translate themselves into anti-immigrant discursive and material violence that, in many forms, continues to permeate the climate of the United States. Sociologist Joe R. Feagin sums up this point: "Contemporary nativism, the desire of many Americans to restrict, exclude, or attack immigrants, has taken many forms, ranging from verbal epithets against 'foreigners' and restrictive legislation to vandalism of property and murder" (1997, 13). Such nativist efforts are portrayed in Don Bartletti's 1991 photograph leading this chapter, "Border Opinions," which captures the gathering of Light Up the Border, a group known for its efforts to stop immigration. The photograph visualizes the border as a zone in need of special protection against undesirable trespassers. The statement on the shirt of one of the activists in the photograph reads: "The U.S. needs 16 miles of high steel fence at San Diego border." The photograph allows us to link anti-immigrant attacks and material efforts to protect the Mexican–U.S. border with the rhetoric of national purity and the perceived threat of immigrant contamination of this land. The banner in the photograph, "Control immigration or lose America. It's your choice," captures the nativist desire for the racial purity of the land and creates a nationalistic (that is, pro-white) argument using patriotic emotionality—if the border is not properly protected, "we" risk losing the nation.

MOVING TOWARD ALIENHOOD

> 1,950 mile-long open wound
> dividing a *pueblo,* a culture,
> running down the length of my body,
> staking fence rods in my flesh,
> splits me   splits me
> *me raja*   *me raja*
>
> —Gloria Anzaldúa, *Borderlands/La Frontera*

The politics and aesthetics of border crossings so powerfully represented by Anzaldúa's *Borderlands/La Frontera* intimately inform *El Norte*. The film's diegetic movement underlies transnational exilic positionality as it takes the spectators through three cultural and linguistic spaces, moving *el norte:* the narrative shifts from Guatemala under a military regime, through Mexico, to the promised land of Los Angeles. Nava remarks that the film foregrounds not simply a physical movement but also a "journey through cultural layerings."[5] Each distinctive layering and border crossing highlights an ideological shift, making an impact on the protagonists' formal status. Their identities become triangulated as they move from being Guatemalan refugees to Mexican migrants, and finally to occupying the position of unwanted illegal aliens in the United States. These cultural multiplications are also punctuated by the distinctive linguistic differences as the story is told in Mayan, Spanish, and English. Each shift painfully reconfigures the protagonists' identities and ironically relegates them to the material and symbolic underground. My reading of *El Norte* traces the protagonists' distinctively different codings as abjects and stresses the film's paradoxical tension: as the Guatemalan refugees escape a certain annihilation in their native land and search for freedom and emancipation by going north, they are progressively relegated to the space of alienhood and claustrophobically confined by the abyss of abjection.

The "cultural layerings" Nava mentions when commenting on the journeying aspect of *El Norte* shape the structure of the film as well. The film stresses hybridization thematically, yet it also performs it formally because the narrative consciously mixes various styles and genres. As other readers of the film have remarked, *El Norte* utilizes melodramatic tonality, the magical realism of modern Latin American fiction, the Mayan-Quiché Indian ritualistic iconography and symbolism, and political drama.[6] Because the narrative moves through different national territories, the changes are also registered visually and aurally in the altering diegetic pace, mise-en-scène, distinctive lighting, editing, and layerings of sound. Although the opening in Guatemala favors long takes, giving us access to an unimpeded view of the land, the later choice of shots relies on closed compositions and a more abrupt, often chaotic montage. Visually, we move from a Guatemalan openness, intense greenery, vastness of coffee fields enveloped in mist and fog, to a progressively tightening mise-en-scène in Mexico and Los Angeles. One way to read these shifts is to see the visual trajectory of the film as underlying the symbolic motion from openness to enclosure and claustrophobia, which comments on the protagonists' cultural dislocation and dispossession.[7] But the imagery of intense fog and mist in the Guatemalan section of the film mobilizes an intriguing narrative tension. Because of the fog, it is possible to read the initial location of the protagonists not as a romanticized, idyllic, and above all *safe* one, but rather as already murky and illegible.

A stylistic hybrid, Nava's film is hard to classify because it resists the logic of purity that would typically favor a particular narrative modality. Its refusal to be contained within a single aesthetic category might be read as a way to honor the journeying point of view of the refugees and an overall "non-Western understanding of the order of things" (Fregoso 1993, 107). That is, like the protagonists, who are catapulted out of their knowable mode of being and experiencing profound defamiliarization, the spectators are exposed to disorientation and rapidly shifting scenery and cultural codes. While the protagonists experience violent uprooting, the spectatorial comfort is frustrated inasmuch as the audience never quite feels at home anywhere either. Moreover, the film's insistence on privileging the refugees' vision produces one more dislodging effect for Western viewers: white American characters are peripheral within the diegetic framework, and the space of the United States appears both enticingly strange and dangerous. This impels a paradoxical tension: while the protagonists are classified as illegal aliens in Los Angeles, they themselves perceive the promised land as alien. This doubling and splintering of alienhood is what interests me in Nava's film.

El Norte focuses on the multicultural experiences of Rosa and Enrique Xuncax, Guatemalan Mayan siblings forced to flee their native village, San Pedro, and to go north as the only viable alternative to being executed by the Guatemalan military during the country's civil war in the 1980s. The diegesis forms a triptych punctuated by the national border crossings and is organized in the form of complex *exits* and *entrances*. The three parts, "Arturo Xuncax," "El Coyote," and "El Norte," enact a montage of horrors that begins with the murder of Rosa and Enrique's father, Arturo, a peasant leader who is beheaded for anti-government activism, and the disappearance of their mother at the hands of the ruling military regime.[8] The climax is evocatively tragic: Rosa dies from typhus at a hospital in Los Angeles after being infected by rats during the crossing of the Mexican–U.S. border, and Enrique is left alone, having missed his chance for securing a green card through a potential Chicago employer. The last shot of the film, mediated through Enrique's remembered vision of the past, is somewhat hallucinatory: against the beauty of the Guatemalan sunset we again see Arturo's severed head, hanging on a tree. Metonymically, the last moment of the film stresses the space of contradiction as it offers us the clashing image of violence and beauty, the realm of the horrible against the emphatic bleeding redness of the sunset in Guatemala. This effect once again underscores the impulse to

Enrique Xuncax (David Villalpando) receives advice from Don Ramón before fleeing for the North in *El Norte*. Reproduced by permission of Independent Productions Inc.

deromanticize the Guatemalan landscape so that it does not become an idyllic vision of the lost home that Enrique can remember nostalgically.

This feeling of conflictual emotionality frames the entire narrative. The film starts with emphasis on the logic of impossibility when it comes to the positioning of the protagonists. They wish to stay in their ancestral village but cannot. Because they lack the comfort of choosing their transnational status, a risky ejection beyond the limits of their native land operates as the sole mode of survival. Don Ramón, one of the old men in the village, tells Enrique, "If you stay here, the only way you can hide from the army is by turning into a flea." The contradiction emphasized by the film's last terrifying image is also stressed in Rosa's final words, when she reflects on the exilic logic of impossibility: "Life here is very hard, Enrique. We're not free. In our own land, we have no home. They want to kill us. There's no home for us there. In Mexico, there's only poverty—we can't make a home there either. And here in the north, we are not accepted. When will we find a home?" In Rosa's words, then, the elsewhere of exile is not some mythic space but rather the violent homelessness, a denial of belonging, a lack of space where Rosa and Enrique can be recognized as viable subjects. While the narrative is infused with their intense desire for survival and cultural acceptance, it is clear to both of them by the end that they are unwanted anywhere. The exilic elsewhere for the protagonists is a racialized realm of abjection that relentlessly envelops them, an expulsion beyond the validated space of subjecthood.

To track the idea of elsewhere means to pay attention to the dynamic of *El*

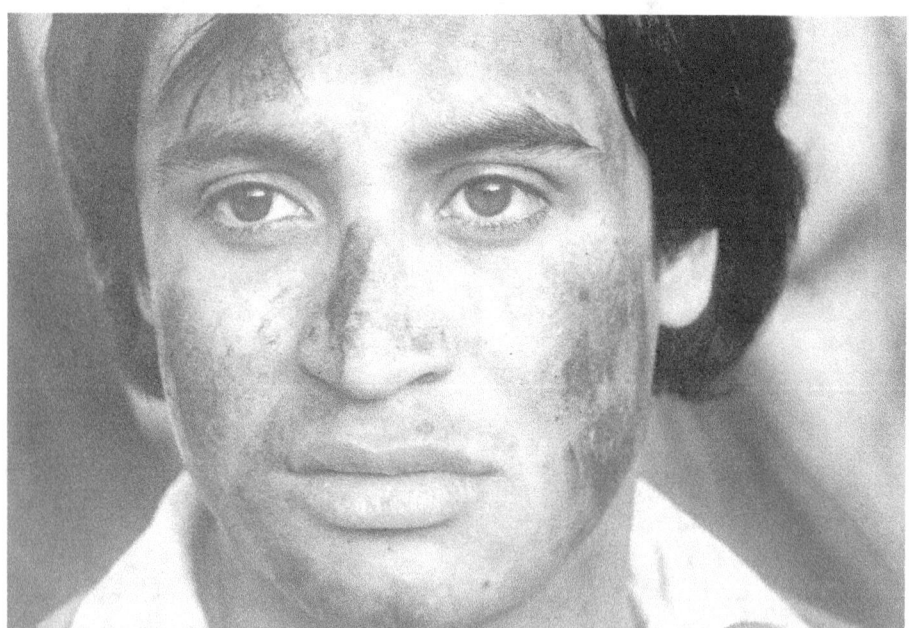

Enrique in *El Norte*. Reproduced by permission of Independent Productions Inc.

Norte's last image of Arturo's head. Like the conflictual emotionality, the hallucinatory effect of the film's closure has to do with a complexly structured temporality that permeates the entire diegesis. After Rosa's death, in the film's last sequence, we see Enrique returning to his "illegal" physical labor. As he shovels dirt with other illegals, the final sequence privileges several close-ups of a round cement mixer processing dirt. The grating sound of the mixer underscores Enrique's pain, his profound sadness about Rosa's death, and the harshness of his newly found experience of aloneness. Through a series of graphic matches taking us back to Guatemala, we see other round objects in the village: a water wheel, a tambourine, the sun. The outcome of these back-and-forth spatial and temporal switchings, punctuated by the dramatic drumbeat, undoes the present moment and produces an ominous displacement. The disorienting exchanges of scenery—between Enrique's work shoveling dirt in Los Angeles and the Guatemalan images of the coffee fields, the burial ground where their father's body rests, and a solemn Rosa carrying a white lily—perform a narrative rupture and stress Enrique's unbelonging.

As the film approaches its haunting finale, its last sequence one more time suggests that the temporality of the narrative is locked within a dialectical tension that foils the seemingly onward narrative movement. The mixing of the past and the present suggests a biconceptual reality that the protagonists inhabit and points out that both Rosa and Enrique are haunted by the Guatemalan imagery and never fully occupy the present moment. More than Enrique, whose double vision is privileged in the film's last sequence, Rosa is diegetically marked as the main carrier of the Guatemalan vision.[9] Throughout the film, Rosa sees images of the village; she sees her father and her vanished mother, both alive and surrounded by pleasant garden imagery. This kind of imagery has a quality of magical realism; it inserts the unreal, highly stylized images within the realist diegetic flow and stresses the refugees' time, the temporality of the displaced people who occupy emotionally and symbolically more than one space, bringing to mind Edward Said's discussion of an exile's "contrapuntal" awareness.

The way Said writes about contrapuntal exilic consciousness emphasizes how this kind of awareness gives access to "originality of vision" that underscores the "pleasures of exile":

> While it perhaps seems peculiar to speak of the pleasures of exile, there are some positive things to be said for a few of its conditions. Seeing "the entire world as a foreign land" makes possible originality of vision. Most people are principally aware of one culture, one setting, one home; exiles are aware of at least two, and this plurality of vision gives rise to an awareness of simultaneous dimensions, an awareness that—to borrow a phrase from music—is contrapuntal. (1984, 55)

Rosa Xuncax (Zaide Silvia Gutiérrez) in *El Norte*. Reproduced by permission of Independent Productions Inc.

Said's notion is useful here because it draws attention to Rosa and Enrique's bifocal experiences of time and space. However, although the film's last sequence accentuates Enrique's "originality of vision," this vision is certainly not one of pleasure: it is marked by a feeling of painful heaviness and a realization of oppressive liminality. Hence, the contrapuntal awareness does not work to enrich Enrique's exilic identity and expand his cultural horizons. Instead, the recurring motif of dirt that mediates Enrique's contrapuntal consciousness in the last sequence can be read as a symbolic marker of his abjection in both national spaces, in Guatemala and in the United States. Back home, he is a dispensable body; in Los Angeles, his abjection manifests itself through the notion that the social structures he and Rosa enter in the promised land relegate them to the position of burdensome and unwanted alien polluters. That is, their dark skin color becomes associated with dirt, suggesting symbolic and material uncleanliness.

THE ABYSS OF ABJECTION

After the arduous journey through Mexico, Rosa and Enrique find a sympathetic "coyote" who explains that going through the tunnels—"the old sewer tunnels that connect Tijuana with the other side"—would be the safest passage to the

North.[10] However, Enrique realizes that the tunnels are a place of unsettling contradiction. They are marked as a place of safety (they are safer than the passage through the mountains, the coyote claims), but they are discursively mapped in multiply frightening ways: "They haven't been used for years. So they are empty. The safest ones are the smallest." The safety of the sewers then is tied to their tightness and narrowness, which again, paradoxically, suggests that a successful crossing depends on painful self-entrapment. The coyote makes clear that to enter the sewer means to agree to experience the space of the horrible. He talks about going through "hell," about the necessity of crawling on "your hands and knees for miles," about paralyzing darkness, nauseating stench, and the feeling of unending enclosure. His words, "you can't hear, you can't see," accentuate aural and visual distress; they foreshadow the experience of relentless claustrophobia that awaits the border crossers and signals a consuming sense of torture.

Rosa and Enrique's experience of liminality in the sewer echoes the warning given to them by a friend in Guatemala: "And remember that the border between Mexico and the United States is like a war zone." As they are about to enter the sewer tunnel, they cover their faces and the coyote advises them again: "It will seem like you'll never get out. But I want you to keep going." Indeed, the severely restricted, darkened mise-en-scène, the pools of darkness relieved only by

Enrique and Rosa are led by a coyote into a tunnel across the U.S. border. Reproduced by permission of Independent Productions Inc.

the narrow streams of flashlights, the point-of-view shots that tie the spectatorial gaze to the extremely limited vision of the protagonists, the feeling of suffocation, the sensation of being permanently locked into the horror that is the tunnel—all these elements create a sense of penetrating discomfort that resonates on a visceral level. The tight and murky insides of the tunnel, the dreadful encounter with the musty corpse of a cat, and the prolonged shots of the protagonists crawling on repulsive surfaces mark this terrifying in-between space as the location of abjection and consumption.

The incident featuring the prolonged battle with the rats, a pivotal moment of the sequence, is especially assaulting visually and aurally. The coming of the rats is signaled by a piercing sound, enhancing a sense of being consumed by the interior. In the darkness of the tunnel, as Rosa and Enrique are attacked, it is difficult to distinguish their bodies from those of the rats. We see only fragments of crawling bodies and glimpses of frightened eyes. This sense of confused, panicked agitation is aurally emphasized as Rosa and Enrique's cries become almost indistinguishable from the shrieking of the rats. Because rats are typically perceived as dangerous pollutants, carrying contagious diseases and dirt, bearers of matter that need to be kept at bay to protect the safety of a particular space, the narrative association with the rats symbolically marks the protagonists' bodies as diseased, impure, and generally unsafe.

The tunnel sequence also underscores the aggressiveness of the U.S. border patrol's vigilant gaze and actions. As Rosa and Enrique enter the tunnel, we see the U.S. border patrol helicopter take off. The diegetic sound of the helicopter's whipping rotors quickly permeates the screen. Through parallel editing, we move several times between the gagging enclosure of the sewer and the open skies patrolled by the helicopter. The helicopter's noise and its searchlight pierce the darkness of the night, creating an uncanny effect: the sound reverberates through the tunnel, exacerbating the aural agitation, while the light visually exposes the outlet of the sewer on the U.S. side. The narrative tension escalates as the two spaces become linked by the blending of diegetic sounds that were initially quite distinct: the shrieks of rats, the cries of the protagonists, and the whipping sound of the rotors merge into one prolonged cacophony.

This unnerving maneuvering between a claustrophobic underground and the vastness of space in the sky comments on the paradoxical expression of the protagonists' exiled position. While the concept of transculturalism, especially for those globally mobile, invites the pursuit of border crossings as a liberatory movement, the protagonists' horrific experience of in-betweenness first and foremost operates as a material and symbolic stamp of abjection. We clearly see that for exiles in their position such crossings are infused with terror and panic and that contact with the desired promised land for some immigrants can actually turn out to be toxic. This suggestion becomes evident at the closing of *El Norte* when the American doctor discovers that Rosa's body, now sick with typhus, was contaminated by the rats in the tunnel. In retrospect, the rats may therefore also be read as a delayed metaphor for the perilous influence of the U.S. national space on the crossers' livelihood and heritage. The fact that it is the female immigrant body that becomes a carrier of disease certainly has important implications: symbolically, the film marks Rosa's flesh as a dangerous space that needs to be carefully contained in a way that a male body does not, underlining the unspoken threat of reproduction.

In "Phobic Spaces and Liminal Panics," Naficy comments on what he calls "transnational exilic cinema": "A sense of claustrophobia pervades the worldview, mise-en-scène, shot composition, and plot development of many transnational films. These are films of liminal panic, of retrenchment in the face of what is perceived to be a foreign, often hostile, host culture and media representation. This perceived threat is dealt with by invoking *confining but comforting* claustrophobic spaces" (1996, 131; my emphasis). Naficy certainly makes an interesting point claiming that claustrophobic spaces often figure as dominant iconography in transnational cinema. The sense of potential comfort, however, is seriously thwarted in such instances as *El Norte* because the film's claustrophobic spatiality is conspicuously coded as unbearable liminality—a site of panic, terror, asphyxiation, and abjection. Naficy suggests that "capitalism continually reterritorializes its liminars and transnationals through strategies of assimilation and co-optation, transforming them into ethnic subjects and productive citizens" (139), but it is important to remember that Rosa and Enrique are examples of transnational aliens whose prospects for assimilation have rigid limitations. In fact, soon after their desired assimilation has had an opportunity to begin, it is abruptly and tragically terminated by circumstances and the legal system. The social structures in Los Angeles devour Rosa and Enrique through illegal employment and spit them out as undesirable throwaways as soon as they are no longer useful.

The sewer tunnel thus functions as a pivotal point in the metaphorical trajectory for Rosa and Enrique's shifting cultural locations of alienhood as they move from the position of Guatemalan escapees in Mexico, through the status of illegal border crossers, to the peripheral status of foreign refugees. Even though Rosa and Enrique became exiles before they left their village (Enrique survived the military searches by hiding in the canyon and Rosa by hiding at her godmother's), the act of the Tijuana–San Diego border crossing relocates their exilic subject position yet again. This time, they are also nondocumented aliens, the potential usurpers of national space. This is, of course, highly ironic because while they anticipate emerging from the sewer will mean freedom for them, they exit the tunnel as unwanted migrants marked by an underclass status. They emerge as abjects. They have finally managed to reach their dream world of Los Angeles, yet, on many levels, they are forced to remain underground. It is as if they never emerge from the sewer.

For a moment, however, the third act of the film, "El Norte," postpones

Enrique is a waiter's assistant at a Beverly Hills restaurant. Reproduced by permission of Independent Productions Inc.

such a conclusive interpretation of the film as both Rosa and Enrique perform one more kind of crossing, an intercultural traversal into the Anglo world in Los Angeles, which they come to read on conflicting levels: as elegant, sophisticated, incomprehensible, and eventually dangerous.

For Enrique, the experience of elegance is linked to his illegal work in a posh Beverly Hills restaurant, Princess, first as a service boy and then as a waiter's assistant. Here, the narrative stresses his process of bodily translation. We see his rise from a nameless body taking care of dirty dishes, discreetly operating in the back of the restaurant, to "Ricky," who works on the floor, carrying silver pots of coffee and helping scoop caviar. (Ironically, Enrique's promotion has nothing to do with recognizing his skills but is an outcome of haphazard practices of hiring migrants and immigrants as dispensable, interchangeable, nameless bodies.) His groomed look, elegant uniform, and still awkward but polite version of English further underscore his remodeled identity. Enrique, in fact, reads his promotion as a possibility for his and Rosa's *mobility* and, for a moment, believes that they might be able to escape his father's brutal statement about Indians' doomed fate: "For the rich all peasants are just a pair of arms to do their work."

Similarly, Rosa, together with a new friend, Nacha, whom she meets at a sweatshop where she irons, gets a housecleaning job in a white, well-to-do neigh-

Enrique's remodeled identity: he proudly presents himself in his new waiter uniform before his sister. Reproduced by permission of Independent Productions Inc.

borhood. Their new employer attempts to position herself as sympathetic and kind: "Please, call me Helen," she insists several times. She then patiently explains how to operate the washer and dryer:

> Now, this is the washing machine and it's really very simple. First, you flip this to "on" and then you have eight seconds to put your program in, or else it will go to the default setting. Now, I usually leave the water on "extra high reset" because you can't move it from one level to another anyway without going to "restart" first. And I generally leave perm press here because that works for almost everything. Unless, of course, I am doing an extra heavy load of towels and then I use the towel setting. And that's really all there is to it. I don't bother with any of the other options. Oh, except for Chris's t-shirts and socks, and then I use an extra rinse, OK? Now, this is the hold function. If you press this, the machine goes off. But it's not off really, you see. Because if it was, you'd have to start over again and then you'd have to restart here. So you can see how simple it is.

The scene preludes the rising tension that comes from Helen's paradoxical speech: although she keeps stressing the ease with which one operates the machines, her language and tonality condescend to the women. Helen's treatment of Rosa and

Nacha appears polite and kind, and it is precisely the politeness of her discourse that effectively masks Helen's exercise of her unquestionable ontological superiority as a Western, white female. Rosa, of course, finds Helen's instruction impenetrable, and Nacha reminds her what it takes to be successful in contacts with affluent, white employers: "The important thing is, whatever they say, just smile and say 'yes.'"

The housecleaning sequence is reminiscent of an earlier moment in the narrative when, back in San Pedro, Guatemala, Rosa finds a *Good Housekeeping* magazine at her godmother's house. Captivated by the glossy pages, she looks at the polished images of modern Western interiors. She touches the pages, fascinated by the lure of the foreign visions. That moment prefigures Rosa's experiences at Helen's house, which can be read as Rosa's entrée into the clean and perfectly arranged world of *Good Housekeeping*—except, of course, that she enters this world not as its legitimate occupant but as an illegal maid locked in the relations of quiet servitude. Therefore, even though she has physically entered the American home she once fantasized about while looking at the images in *Good Housekeeping*, the narrative creates a feeling that she remains an inferior outsider, never expected to become a rightful participant of this new world's comforts, pleasures, and privileges.

Rosa's world is just as incomprehensible to Helen. When Rosa attempts to use the washer and fails, her solution is to wash the clothes by hand and lay them on

Rosa with Nacha (Lupe Ontiveros) at Helen's house. Reproduced by permission of Independent Productions Inc.

the grass to dry. She thus accomplishes the job of washing but the *way* in which she performed this task unsettles Helen: "By hand? Oh no, I mean it. I just couldn't let her do all that washing by hand. It's too much work. I can't stand the thought of her in here scrubbing." Of course, Helen's protest is meant to protect Rosa from excessively burdensome work, but ultimately, the narrative seems to indicate that Helen's response assumes an unquestioned superiority of the ways of her culture. Modern Western ways of washing become epistemologically privileged, and Rosa's Indian approach to the task is cast as shockingly primitive and obsolete.

Interestingly enough, in staging Rosa's and Enrique's crossing into the Anglo culture of Los Angeles, *El Norte* strives to avoid the stereotypical binarizing of blackness/whiteness and the oppressor/oppressed dynamic. The film resists casting the new reality for the protagonists in dichotomous ways that would feature them as illegal aliens who are entirely helpless victims of the discriminatory, racist logic of the white Anglo culture. We see how this logic works interculturally, penetrating all kinds of social interstices. In doing so, the narrative refuses to present the Latino ghetto as a romanticized space of purity inhabited only by good, though disenfranchised, groups. For example, the housing manager, Don Mote, a Chicano labor middleman, continually takes advantage of Rosa and Enrique and specifically manipulates Enrique when he introduces him to a white woman who wishes to employ him in one of her Chicago factories. Also, Princess, the restaurant where Enrique works, is not necessarily represented as a space where white, merciless employers victimize illegal workers. It is because of another Chicano, Carlos, who informs on him to *la migra,* that Enrique loses his promotion and job. It is ironic that the assault comes from a character ethnically related to Enrique rather than directly from the white culture. In another turn, racist insults directed at Carlos come from Jorge, a Mexican immigrant, who dismisses Carlos as a "pocho," a "dummy," someone who "cannot even speak Spanish." When Enrique does not understand the meaning of "pocho," Jorge explains: "He is a Chicano. He is an American citizen but he comes from a Mexican family. That's why he has to do the same shitwork we do."

All these unsettling moments accent the film's larger argument: the racialized structures of oppression that Rosa and Enrique experience and witness are not necessarily transparent and self-evident but often work in covert, subtle ways, coming from diverse directions. When speaking of the border culture of the United States and the rhetoric of fear that specifically surrounds Chicanos and Latinos, Guillermo Gómez-Peña makes a point that helps us to understand better the idea of such racialized structures of oppression: "The social and ethnic fabric of the U.S. is filled with interstitial *wounds,* invisible to those who didn't experience the events that generated them, or who are victimized by historical amnesia" (1989, 21; my emphasis). The social structures in the United States that Rosa and Enrique enter—that of illegal alienhood, specifically linked to the migration of peoples from other Americas—are precisely such historical structures of "wounds." *El Norte* shows how these wounds are invisible to Rosa's and Enrique's employers and to other characters who hold power over them; to some degree, they even remain invisible to the protagonists.

Overall, *El Norte* makes a compelling statement about acceptable immigrant identities that may be invited to enter structures of assimilation. More specifically, the narrative designates the parameters of admissible immigrant placement within the American symbolic configurations. In Rosa and Enrique's case, it is clear that they might be usable, even welcomed aliens as long as they embrace the prescribed conditions of servitude and discreetly obliterate their Indianness. In other words, to survive, the protagonists must erase the roots of their ethnicity. Indianness itself is represented as an ethnic modality at the very bottom of the racialized hierarchy; it becomes abjected—a handicapped feature that must be shunned, veiled, wiped out. The poignancy of the situation is represented through the idea that Rosa and Enrique need to perform this alteration themselves. For Enrique this means posing as a Mexican from Oaxaca at Princess, his body cloaked in his new waiter's uniform. For Rosa, this means refashioning her bodily image along the lines of normative representations of Latina women, despite Enrique's criticism: "You look like a clown." She replies, "No, I look like an American."[11]

Kristeva poetically writes about exilic reconfigurations: "Exile always involves a shattering of the former body" (1991, 30). On some level, this idea certainly may sound enticing as it implies the possibilities for identity reformulations or reinventions. In the case of *El Norte*, the "shattering of the former body," however eagerly taken up by the protagonists, only leads them to illegal servility. Clearly, Rosa is never expected to live anywhere close to Helen's neighborhood; similarly, Enrique is not anticipated to be capable of attaining a higher social status than waiter's assistant or, at best, a foreman at a factory. Nava's film invites its audience to probe the limiting expectations set up for abjected immigrants. It also provokes scrutiny of all kinds of privileged but often unquestioned social positions (like that of Helen, for example). Finally, it puts an interesting twist on the idea of exilic elsewhere by uncovering what we may call *the illegal elsewhere* of exile, a modality hardly addressed in the discussions of the exilic elsewhere.

To begin with, the common understanding of the term "legal aliens" is that in order to be legitimate one has to enter the United States legally. The film complicates such a simplistic rendition of legality. Clearly, being underground border-crossers, Rosa and Enrique become illegal the moment they emerge out of the sewer. Nevertheless, toward the conclusion of the narrative, they learn that they may be able to upgrade their formal status. When Don Mote attempts to convince Enrique that he should work for the white woman, one of his selling points is that the employer could arrange for Enrique's green card. "I can be legal?" ponders naturally surprised Enrique.

In *El Norte* the illegal space of elsewhere presents itself as a contradictory, hard-to-penetrate logic of white Anglo culture. The occupants of this space continually quiver in their under-the-table arrangements between the prospect of deportation and the lure of legalization. Supposedly unwanted in the United States, such illegal entrants as Rosa and Enrique easily find work in the sector designated for people like them; they operate underground, yet they openly learn English in a public school aided by government funds, where such classes are free and nobody questions attendees' legality. Nacha warns Rosa that comprehending this logic is beyond their reach: "If you try to figure out gringos, you'll just get a giant headache."

The film's insistence on exposing such paradoxical frictions seems to indicate that the legal and cultural construct of rightful U.S. citizenry is indeed a shrewd enterprise that takes full advantage of unlawful migrants. Materially, it takes them in, without any obligation, as a cheap labor force. Symbolically, it fabricates the space of alienhood as a reference point against which the legitimate "I" coheres its superiority.

"Passport to the Universe," American Museum of Natural History, 2000.

2
Accented Bodies and Coercive Assimilation: The Trespasses of the García Girls

> Thus the act of determining the "character" of a nation involves regulating who may and may not come in, who are "family" and who are strangers.
>
> —David Jacobson, "Introduction: An American Journey"

> A foreigner in principle is already a spy.
>
> —Trinh T. Minh-ha, in *Surname Viet Given Name Nam*

At the turn of the millennium, as a visitor to the American Museum of Natural History in New York City, I received a sleek pass, allowing me to enter the Rose Center for Earth and Space. This pass—an identity card of sorts, titled "Passport to the Universe," and also calling itself "Official Cosmic Passport"—is a fascinating cultural artifact, figured as a dark bluish rectangle to resemble an actual U.S. passport. The front cover features a hologram with an image of the cosmos and bears such words as "Earth," "Solar System," "Milky Way Galaxy," and "Observable Universe." The back of the card contains a blank line for the visitor's signature and, above it, the following text:

> The American Museum of Natural History hereby requests all whom it may concern to permit the citizen of the cosmos named below to pass without delay or hindrance. The bearer is empowered by knowledge and imagination to travel anywhere in the universe.

As someone who has been teaching within the area of transnational cultural studies, I have been captivated by the notions put forth by the "Passport to the Universe" and its celebratory mapping of what might be called a "transnational identity" in relation to the United States, a notion that is intimately connected to the cultural experiences and discourses of immigration. This particular model of an empowered citizenry interestingly speaks to the much-debated clash between current *discursive* liberatory renditions of mobility, travel, and border crossings and painful limitations that immigrants themselves often acutely experience. Undoubtedly, the visual-conceptual landscape of the "Cosmic Passport" offers provocative connotations, especially if we consider recent discussions within transnational studies that ask us to be wary of the favorable renditions of transnational positions.[1]

First, the "passport" plays on the idea that the contemporary era of transnational capitalism alters our national and cultural mobility in affirmative ways. The traditional idea of a U.S. citizen is stretched to include the notion of a citizen of the cosmos, inviting a reflection that such a citizen is free to roam the cosmic space. This freedom, of course, implies the unhindered ability to cross national borders, including venturing into outer space. Moreover, one could argue that this conceptual shift from American citizenry to cosmic citizenry reflects not only an ontological empowerment but an epistemological one as well, because the traveler is promised special access to "knowledge and imagination." Thus, the "Official Cosmic Passport," with its implication of the citizenry of the universe, opens up a space for an understanding of transnational crossings as a formation of a hypercosmopolitan identity ("the bearer is empowered . . . to travel anywhere") and as a presumably carnivalesque possibility for the museum's visitor to indulge in the fantasy of cosmic subjectivity. However, while the "Passport to the Universe" as a transnational text offers a flexible idea of the nation and the national self, it does so only by concealing the imperial desire of "America" to extend itself beyond all imaginable borders via the Eurocentric logic of domination. For a critical reader of such a transnational representation, the important issue is the interrogation of what kinds of national identities would be permitted to occupy the privileged position of a citizen of the cosmos. In other words, metaphorically speaking, who can use the "Official Cosmic Passport"?

To develop this discussion, I want to situate this question in the context of Nina Glick Schiller and Georges Fouron's explication of transnational migrations:

> Little research has been done on transnational relationships and their economic and political implications, because of a flawed historiography and ethnography of migration that, since the 1950s, has portrayed immigrants in the United States as displaced persons permanently uprooted from home and family. Current transnational research can correct these weaknesses only if we move beyond the stage of celebrat-

ing transnational connections and proclaiming the agency of transmigrants. (Schiller and Fouron 2001, 326)

Schiller and Fouron define "transmigrants" as those who "maintain multiple familial, social, economic, and political ties to both their country of origin and their country of settlement and live their lives across national borders" (322). In doing so, they call for a reconceptualization of immigrant identities not as permanently uprooted and alienated from their native cultures but in the context of transnational connections, more and more enabled by a global economy. In other words, they propose to revise the traditional meaning of immigration and exile via transnationalism. Linda Basch, Schiller, and Cristina Szanton Blanc define transnationalism as the "processes by which immigrants forge and sustain multi-stranded social relations that link together their societies of origin and settlement" (1994, 7). They caution, however, against a salutary understanding of those connections. These contentions interestingly expand on my previous question about the "Passport to the Universe": How do transnational bonds alter an understanding of immigrants in the United States? By implication, how do they modify the traditional grasp of American immigrant literature?[2] What does it mean to claim transnationality as one's mode of location? Who precisely might have access to a transnational subjecthood? What are the risks involved in theorizing such subjecthood in emancipatory ways?

Although a lot of groundbreaking work in the field of transnationalism has been carried out by anthropologists, sociologists, political scientists, and postcolonial theorists, relatively little attention has been devoted to the literary explorations of transnationalism in the context of current American literature. As Basch, Schiller, and Szanton Blanc observe: "individuals, communities, or states rarely identify themselves as transnationals. It is only in contemporary fiction that this state of 'in-betweenness,' has been fully voiced."[3] Indeed, contemporary American transnational literature, written by "bicultural" authors, many of whom are women of diverse ethnic and racial backgrounds, is an especially fertile ground for an exploration of the polysemous representations of transnationalism and its predicaments.[4] The recent "exilic" narratives I am referring to include the writings of such transcultural authors as Diana Abu-Jaber, Julia Alvarez, Edwidge Danticat, Chitra Banerjee Divakaruni, Ariel Dorfman, Cristina Garcia, Eva Hoffman, Jamaica Kincaid, Chang-Rae Lee, Bharati Mukherjee, Loida Martiza Pérez, and Esmeralda Santiago.[5] Overwhelmingly, their texts feature binational characters who transgress the boundaries of established nationhood by moving across national borders, languages, cultures, and competing ideologies.[6] In doing so, they explore and question the notion of privileged Americanness: they show how liminal identities, with their shifting subject positions, complicate the dichotomous hierarchy of citizen–legal subject/stranger–illegal other. What is particularly engaging about these narratives is the way they foreground the textual representation of exile as a critique of nationalism and accentuate the way that identities of "trespassing" strangers-foreigners unsettle monocultural narratives of the nation. Most of these texts, while insisting on the historical specificity and heterogeneity of their racial, ethnic, and gender modalities, enact transnationality thematically and stylistically. Emphasizing fragmentation, multiple and often conflicting points of view, and nonchronological narrative movements, the themes that emerge ask readers to think about what it means to be perceived as foreign or alien in the contemporary culture of the United States, or alternately, what it means to occupy the space of sanctioned citizenhood. In a variety of differing geopolitical contexts, these texts center on the experience of alienhood and give space to the often dispersed voices of those who do not quite fit within the validated limits of a nation.

With these concerns in mind, I inspect the voicing of transnational identities in Julia Alvarez's well-recognized, semiautobiographical first novel, *How the García Girls Lost Their Accents*.[7] Although I will approach the text through a textual close reading, my broader goal is to use Alvarez's novel as a starting point for a series of reflections on the need to scrutinize the idea that a transnational position implies a new, liberatory identity that allows an exile-immigrant a special epistemological insight and overall empowerment. The need to recognize the asymmetries of power of privilege that affect immigrants, refugees, and various border crossers in relation to U.S. territory prompts us to dissect the specific dangers in seeing the character of transnational connections as solely affirmative.

I focus on Alvarez's text as a representative example of American transnational literature for a number of interrelated reasons. First, the novel, self-conscious of the public rhetoric of multiculturalism in the United States, which often manifests itself in "happy pluralism" and "management of diversity" (Grewal and Kaplan 1999, 349), shows the dangers of the liberal multicultural model that often eagerly accepts, but also disciplines and consumes, difference through a subtle mixture of xenophobic and xenophilic undertones.[8] This notion is perhaps best represented through a nuanced textual portrayal of various accented identities that reveal that *accentless bodies* remain the markers of authentic Americanness.

Second, the Garcías' transnational status as political refugees from the Dominican Republic to the United States who maintain familial ties with the island mobilizes an interesting tension: even after the García family members have successfully crossed the border and begun to function as legal subjects in the United States, the stigma attached to them as trespassers haunts their unstable cultural positions. The narrative emphasizes their location as that of dubious strangers and foreign intruders whose national belonging is suspect: "The Garcias were only legal residents, not citizens."[9] As I will suggest, the trope of trespassing is interestingly woven into the text to carry a dual, bidirectional, function: it comments on the Garcías' position in the United States as metaphoric trespassing transnationals, and it also helps us read the cultural dynamics surrounding the transnational returning to her homeland. I will link the moments of trespassing to the underscoring logic of purity that, although manifested differently in the United States and the Dominican Republic, symbolically invests in "clean," that is, monocultural, identities.[10]

Third, keeping in mind Trinh T. Minh-ha's point that "the experience of exile is never simply binary," I will propose that *How the García Girls Lost Their Accents* represents what might be called an "exilic quivering" by foregrounding the experiences of transnational identities that, in a dissonant way, function in a precarious space of liminality as fragile yet threatening, privileged yet dispossessed. Placing Alvarez's novel within a context of other recent bicultural American narratives, I will focus on the portrayal of liminars whose multiple national belongings are frequently figured in various texts through a dialectics of pain *and* pleasure. Such representations of transnational subjectivities that occupy, to use Trinh's words again, "hyphenated reality" (1994, 13, 17) compellingly intervene in the celebratory discussions of transnationalism and in what Ali Behdad and Laura Elisa Pérez, for example, term a "multicultural euphoria" (1995, 70).

Finally, although *How the García Girls Lost Their Accents* has been traditionally read as an example of U.S. Latina literature (Vázquez 2003), I will turn to Alvarez's essay writing to discuss why the category of Latina/o literature, although certainly suitable and historically valid, seems insufficient in addressing the transnational location of the writer who belongs in the interstices of two cultures. As Alvarez remarks: "We travel on that border between two worlds and we can see both points of view."[11]

ACCENTED BODIES AND THE TROPE OF TRESPASSING

André Aciman compellingly describes accented identity: "An accent marks the lag between two cultures, two languages, the space where you let go of one identity, invent another, and end up being more than one person though never quite two" (1999a, 11). This sense of fractured doubleness that Aciman expresses—of cultures, languages, and identities—infiltrates the narrative of *How the García Girls Lost Their Accents,* especially since the text foregrounds the representations of the foreign bodies of exiles—the accented body, as I call it—whose exilic subjectivity comes into being through the process of border crossing. The experience of varied transnational crossings between the Dominican Republic and the United States permeates most of Alvarez's work: the poetry collections, *Homecoming* (1984) and *The Other Side/El Otro Lado* (1995); her novels, *In the Time of the Butterflies* (1994), *Yo!* (1997), *In the Name of Salomé* (2000); and her collection of essays, *Something to Declare* (1998). And Alvarez, positioned as a writer in the United States who grew up in the Dominican Republic and still cultivates strong family and activist ties to the island, has frequently commented on her doubleness and the fact that "being in and out of both worlds" allows her to "[map] a country that's not on the map" (1998b, 173). Asked about her national identity in one of the interviews, she stresses her hybrid position: "I am not a *Dominican* writer. I can't pretend to be a *Dominican*. By the same token, when people ask me if I'm an American writer, I have to say I don't think of myself as being in the same tradition as Melville or Hawthorne. I am a hyphenated person interested in the music that comes out of a language that hears both languages. My stories come out of being in worlds that sometimes clash and sometimes combine."[12]

The friction Alvarez speaks about is poignantly reflected in *How the García Girls Lost Their Accents,* whose intricate narrative structure at first glance moves us straightforwardly from the United States to the Dominican Republic, and unfolds from the present to the past, from 1989 to 1959. The novel is divided into three sections, each segment shifting backward in time, with the narrative focus on members of the upper-class García family who are forced into exile by the Dominican regime of Rafael Trujillo in 1960 because of the father's secret involvement in the underground political movement against the dictatorship. But even though it appears that the narrative takes us from the American immigrant present into the Dominican native past, the text clearly refuses any direct trajectory. Instead, while the larger diegetic framework moves us back in time, simultaneously we are asked to read the fragmented exilic textual space of the in-between. The narrative often impedes temporal consistency, moving back and forth between the two cultures, languages, and their ideological and ethical systems, not allowing us to anchor the characters according to the logic of monolithic cultural identity. In explaining her desire to experiment with the consistency of the narrative structure, Alvarez notes: "I wanted the reader to be thinking like an immigrant, forever going back" (1998a, 132). The effect is performative: the fragmented narrative the reader is asked to sieve through in *How the García Girls Lost Their Accents* reflects the sense of painful disorientation and confusion the characters experience as they cope with their exilic in-betweenness.[13]

Additional complexity of the novel is underscored by what David Mitchell calls multiperspectivity, that is, a lack of a singular enunciative position, or a lack of a coherent, narrating point of view (1999, 168). As Alvarez has acknowledged, all her novels give space to multiple points of view that, unlike the single perspective, do not privilege the protagonist and his or her singular story (Alvarez 1998a, 132). For example, her third novel, *Yo!,* often thought of as a sequel to *How the García Girls Lost Their Accents,* performs a compelling experiment with the diversity of narrating voices. One could say that *Yo!* is about Yolanda, a writer and poet, except that she does not utter a word in the text.[14] She remains the curious absence at the heart of the narrative, displaced as the authorial voice. Instead, the book is a weaving of interrelated stories that come from various characters whose voices speak about their lives being intertwined with Yo's: there is a story from the sisters, from Yo's mother, from her father, from her stepdaughter, her third husband, her best friend, and a Midwestern landlady. All get a space to express their point of view except Yo. Alvarez says that she appreciates "listening and being taken over by other voices": "We get the story of how this woman got to be a writer, but not from the writer's point of view" (1998a, 133). This intentional dispersal of an authorial voice is also movingly played out in Alvarez's most recent novel, *In the Name of Salomé*. A story of a Dominican poet, Salomé Ureña, and her daughter, Salomé Camila Henríquez Ureña, the novel has an elaborately structured narrative, allowing the voices of the two women to speak about their struggles with exile, poetry, family, identity—all wrapped up in the larger questions of cultural and national belonging.

In *How the García Girls Lost Their Accents*, too, we are invited to listen to different narrators. The multiperspectivity, or what might be called a dispersed focalization, allows various voices of the García sisters—Carla, Sandra, Yolanda, and Sofia—or "the four girls" as they are called, to speak their own vision of the exile, switching from a first- to a third-person narrative to a multiple "we." Yolanda, the poet in the family, also known as Yo (meaning "I" in Spanish), Joe, or Yoyo, has the strongest voice in the novel and occupies the space of a textual navigator who records the family's history.[15] The novel opens and closes with sections privileging Yolanda's experiences: the first part, "Antojos," is told in the third person; in the last part, "The Drum," Yolanda's point of view is emphasized by the first-person narration. By the end of "The Drum," in a self-conscious moment, she identifies herself as a diegetic creator and temporal manipulator by directly addressing the readers: "You understand I am collapsing all time now so that it fits in what's left in the hollow of my story?" (289).

The novel's title emphasizes the notion of an accented identity and its perceived loss, an experience that is often coded in the text as desirable because accentless identity, at least in an American popular imaginary, supposedly allows an immigrant to masquerade as a native. For example, "The Rudy Elmenhurst Story," a section that focuses on Yolanda's years in college and her failed romantic relationship with Rudy, explicates how the cultural mechanisms of coercive assimilation project the idea of an accentless speech as desirable. This explication is a result of Yolanda's critical dissection of her involvement with Rudy: "Why I didn't just sleep with someone as persistent as Rudy Elmenhurst is a mystery I'm exploring here by picking it apart the way we learned to do to each other's poems and stories in the English class" (88). This is the way Yo remembers her encounter with Rudy's parents: "His parents did most of the chatting, talking too slowly to me as if I wouldn't understand native speakers; they complimented me on my 'accentless' English and observed that my parents must be very proud of me" (100). The space of enunciation belongs to Rudy's parents who, assuming the authority of language, patronize Yolanda. Their comment plays on a common belief that an alien can pass as one of "us" once she removes foreign marks that code her as a suspicious stranger. Accented speech is obviously one such marking. It is thus the accented body—the body coded semiotically as an alien—that marks the García girls as strangers-hybrids and attracts the often violent force of coercive assimilation that manifests itself in subtle, invisible ways. The comment Yolanda hears invites her to lose her accented speech quickly so that she can begin to function socially at the level of a normative subject—successfully Americanized and gratefully assimilated.

In fact, many of the reviews of Alvarez's text echo these nativist sentiments. Donna Rifkind, for example, opens her review by saying that "to speak without an accent is the ultimate goal of the immigrant," clearly presupposing an immigrant universal desire of complete assimilation manifested by the perceived necessity of losing the accented speech. Similarly, Judith Freeman discusses the notion of a full American identity as one characterized by accentless articulation when she describes the García girls' cultural predicament: "The only choice left to them is to become fully American—lose their accents and plunge in."[16] I refer to these reviews not so much to point out how these critics failed to read the idea of an accent as transgressive, but rather to show how their formulations are indicative of a larger cultural logic that is conventionally applied to the immigrant identity. What motivates such statements is the reliance on the dichotomous thinking that privileges, even glorifies, the notion of speaking like a native over accented speech. Rifkind, indeed, sets up her review by displaying these binarisms up front, addressing the threshold "between accent and native speech, alienation and assimilation." Having an accent is hence equated with the perpetual mode of alienation, suggesting that an accented identity is always branded with strangerhood and doomed to cultural scrutiny and exclusion.

To lose an accent, however, does not necessarily mean to accelerate the desired acculturation. In Alvarez's novel we are confronted with subversive resistance to the metaphoric idea of losing an accent because to lose it means to obliterate the culturally and historically specific position marked by exile and to instantiate the idea of a full American whose uneasy, un-American differences have been successfully appeased or erased. Yolanda initially has no access to a conceptual apparatus that would allow her to dissect Rudy's parents' assumed position of privilege as natural Americans who cast her as a foreign object useful in their son's multicultural experiences:

> They encouraged him, his parents, to have experiences with girls but to be careful. He had told them he was seeing "a Spanish girl," and he reported they said that should be interesting for him to find out about people from other cultures. It bothered me that they should treat me like a geography lesson for their son. But I didn't have the vocabulary back then to explain even to myself what annoyed me about their remark. (98)

This is the moment that performs what might be called a conservative multiculturalism,[17] that is, the idea that ennobles the nativist vision of an American identity as the imperial center that, in a benevolent gesture, welcomes the encounter with difference, while still holding on to a politics of binary oppositions.[18] What I mean by a conservative multiculturalism is the traditional coercive acceptance of otherness under the slogans of "embracing difference" and "celebrating diversity."[19] The logic of binary oppositions that we encounter in this passage invests Rudy's parents with ontological superiority that allows them to entertain the idea that their son's education is enriched via multiethnic encounters. Yolanda becomes "a geography lesson" for Rudy, an attractive object of study to spice up his college life. In fact, Rudy loses his interest in Yolanda once he realizes that she does not conform to his vision of the hot-blooded Latina who can be useful as an erotic/exotic Spanish body (99).

The condescending comment about finding out "about people from other cultures" in many ways parallels the prevalent academic notion that students, especially education majors, should take world literature courses to be exposed to multicultural texts, which will help them learn about other cultures. Within this paradigm, the texts to be studied in such world literature courses are often positioned outside the realm of American literature, creating an impression that multiculturalism comes from the outside, or alternately, that it belongs to a subcategory of other cultures situated within the United States.[20] Thus, within this discourse, Rudy is already positioned as the full subject who does not need to question his privileged cultural location and who, certainly, does not need to lose an accent.

While Alvarez posits the idea of an accented subjectivity as the driving force of the narrative and prompts the readers to question the ideology behind the assumed necessity of an exile to lose an accent, *How the García Girls Lost Their Accents* does not necessarily celebrate the accented identity as liberatory. On the contrary, Yolanda and her sisters frequently reflect on the feeling of discomfort of being coded as different by an accent. In the section titled "Trespass," Carla, the oldest sister, a seventh grader in a Catholic school, becomes the object of violence of a gang of schoolboys:

> Out of sight of the nuns, the boys pelted Carla with stones, aiming them at her feet so there would be no bruises. "Go back to where you came from, you dirty spic!" One of them, standing behind her in line, pulled her blouse out of her skirt where it was tucked in and lifted it high. "No titties," he snickered. Another yanked down her socks, displaying her legs, which had begun growing soft, dark hairs. "Monkey legs!" he yelled to his pals. (153)

First, through the logic of dirt—that is, through the idea that cleanliness has been traditionally associated with whiteness, purity, and the right to racial superiority—Carla is being marked as an unerotic and undesirable dirty body. Her rapidly changing young female body becomes an object of ostracism, showing us how the racist discourse is in this context rooted in patriarchal violence. The epithet "monkey legs" painfully stigmatizes Carla as some savage, unclean creature. Second, the customary comment about going back to where one comes from rests on the unquestioned (and perhaps unconscious) right the boys feel as the legitimate possessors of the national space. It is this right that allows them to cast Carla as a usurper of a place that, as if organically, does not belong to her. And the feeling of not belonging is an emotion that Carla knows quite intimately. She hates, for example, being asked for directions in the street: "'I don't speak very much English,' she would say in a small voice by way of apology. She hated having to admit this since an admission proved, no doubt, the boy gang's point that she didn't belong here" (156). She is haunted by the boys' racist insults, remembering their "high voices squealing with delight when [she] mispronounced some word they coaxed her to repeat." And even after the tauntings stop, their voices and faces persecute Carla:

> But their faces did not fade as fast from Carla's life. They trespassed in her dreams and in her waking moments. Sometimes when she woke in the dark, they were perched at the foot of her bed, a grim chorus of urchin faces, boys without bodies, chanting without words, "Go back! Go back!" (164)

This oppressive imagery of "boys without bodies," which weighs on Carla's conscious and unconscious visions, reveals the devastating impact of discursive violence that pins her down as an unacceptable intruder who is repeatedly told to "go back."

In her fantasy of constructing possible defenses against this anti-immigrant abuse, she imagines herself being driven to school "in a flashy red car the boys would admire" (155). Although it is evident that Carla's desire is influenced by capitalist consumption (which she learns from the boys whom she observes being in awe over cars), at this point this is the only imaginary weapon she can call forth to counter the violation she feels.[21] But she realizes that even this fantasy cannot work: "Except there was no one *to* drive her. Her immigrant father with his thick mustache and accent and three-piece suit would only bring her more ridicule" (155). The accent is thus perceived as a burden, an unmistakable label of unwanted otherness that trespasses the protected boundary of privileged citizenhood. The exclusionary logic at work here that Carla senses is that even if she loses *her* accent, her parents' marked articulation will always serve as an unwelcome familial signifier that pins her down as a foreigner. Similarly, when Yolanda compares her parents with Rudy's parents, who "looked so young and casual—like classmates," she feels awkwardly self-conscious, sensing her parents' difference, not just audible in their accented speech but also written all over their bodies:

> My old world parents were still an embarrassment at parents' weekend, my father with his thick mustache and three-piece suit and fedora hat, my mother in one of her outfits she bought especially to visit us

> at school, everything overly matched, patent leather purse and pumps that would go back, once she was home, to plastic storage bags in her closet. (98)

Yolanda intuits that her parents' visible old worldness draws attention to her very self and singles her out as not quite adequate.

The idea of the García family as trespassers is interestingly figured in the opening of the section "Trespass," which underscores Carla's exclusion from the dominant culture:

> Down the block the neighborhood dead-ended in abandoned farmland that Mami read in the local paper the developers were negotiating to buy. Grasses and real trees and real bushes still grew beyond the barbed-wire fence posted with a big sign: PRIVATE, NO TRESPASSING. The sign had surprised Carla since "forgive us our trespasses" was the only other context in which she had heard the word. She pointed the sign out to Mami on one of their first walks to the bus stop. "Isn't that funny, Mami? A sign that you have to be good." Her mother did not understand at first until Carla explained about the Lord's Prayer. Mami laughed. Words sometimes meant two things in English too. This trespass meant that no one must go inside the property because it was not public like a park, but private. Carla nodded, disappointed. She would never get the hang of this new country. (151)

On a manifest level, Carla simply does not comprehend nuances of signification in English because the only context available to her is that of a Catholic upbringing in the Dominican Republic. Quite simply, she does not know yet that meaning is contextual. We see how at this point she does not have a position to speak from in the new culture, and she certainly has no access to a voice, understood, of course, not just as the ability to speak but also as an enunciative place of agency. The comment about Carla's inability to speak "very much" English, which I quoted earlier, also emphasizes that she expresses herself "in a small voice." This notion of a small voice underlines how Carla does not want to attract attention to herself as an accented identity and instead hopes to appear inaudible. But this passage is not only about how Carla does not know yet that "words sometimes meant two things in English." The no trespassing sign becomes a metaphorical warning that signals the prevailing aura of hostility frequently experienced by foreigners in the United States. This idea is aggressively expressed through the imagery of the barbed-wire fence as a protector of the purity of a nation.

The community that Carla scrutinizes in "Trespass" is characterized by patterns of sameness and cleanliness: "[T]hey had moved out of the city to a neighborhood on Long Island so that the girls could have a yard to play in, so Mami said. The little green squares around each look-alike house seemed more like carpeting that had to be kept clean than yards to play in" (151). The lookalike houses with neat carpetlike lawns embody the homogeneous vision of community that rests on orderly sameness, which Carla finds uninviting as a space of pleasure. She reads it as a place of exclusion—inhospitable and forbidding. She hungers for the greenery in the Dominican Republic: "Carla thought yearningly of the lush grasses and thick-limbed, vine-ladened trees around the compound back home" (151). In her childlike way, Carla romanticizes the vision of "back home" and invites the readers to perceive her world in a dichotomous, uncritical way: the luscious beauty of the island is clearly privileged over the mundane and asensual landscape of a Long Island neighborhood.

LIMINALITY: DIALECTICS OF PAIN AND PLEASURE

Although in "Trespass" Carla clings to the sentimentalized vision of home, *How the García Girls Lost Their Accents,* as a whole, refuses the predictable pleasant home/painful exile binary. Instead, the text creates a much more complex representation of exilic selfhood, which does not allow us simply to romanticize the Dominican Republic and to remain critical of hostility in the United States. This complexity is poignantly represented already in the first section of the novel, "Antojos," meaning "cravings," in which Yolanda realizes, to use Bharati Mukherjee's words, that she "flutters between worlds" (1988, 189). We begin to see how Yolanda's liminal position unmoors her sense of belonging to one nation and are invited to question the assumed natural connection between a person and her place of birth. Even though Yolanda is "the true geographical native" of the Dominican Republic (Mitchell 1999, 166), in an ironic and painful twist, "Antojos" shows that the space of home can be as unfamiliar and strange as the place of exile. Feelings of ambivalence, discomfort, and uncertainty permeate this section of the novel, as Yolanda tries to perform her homecoming.

Her wish to re-belong to the island is enacted by her desire to eat guavas, which she remembers from her childhood as an experience of pleasure, a desire that is underscored by the title of this section. Ironically, however, Yolanda is unable to figure out the meaning of *antojo*. This inability to capture signification parallels, of course, Carla's inability to understand the multiple meanings of "trespass," except that in Carla's case, we realize that she is still learning English, hence her lack of comprehension appears understandable. For Yolanda, however, her inability to understand *antojo* signals her estrangement from her native language and culture. In an interesting twist, Yolanda learns from her relatives that there is no one way to capture the meaning of *antojo*. Tía Carmen says, "it's not an easy word to explain." She translates it as "a craving for something you have to eat," while Altagracia, one of the family's maids, adds that "a person has an *antojo* when they are taken over by *un santo* who wants something" (8). Thus, the various shades of meaning that arise out of these translations mark *antojo* as an ambivalent desire, and this equivocal tension is associated with Yolanda as a character who has a craving that cannot easily be figured out.

"Antojos" opens with Yolanda's return to the island and it paradoxically establishes her position as a trespasser and foreigner. Instead of performing a pleasant encounter with the native culture, the beginning of the novel defamiliarizes the Dominican Republic for Yolanda. We learn that, after twenty-nine years of exile (and five years after the last visit), Yolanda secretly hopes to recover her old place among her extended family: "This time, however, Yolanda is not so sure she'll be going back. But that is a secret" (7). She is affectionately greeted by her aunts and cousins who prepare a cake to welcome her home. Yolanda is urged to make a wish:

> She leans forward and shuts her eyes. There is so much she wants, it is hard to single out one wish. There have been too many stops on the road of the last twenty-nine years since her family left this island behind. She and her sisters have led such turbulent lives—so many husbands, homes, jobs, wrong turns among them. But look at her cousins, women with households and authority in their voices. Let this turn out to be my home, Yolanda wishes. (11)

The yearning for home is problematized when Yolanda takes her family's car to search for guavas in the countryside. Even before she leaves, her aunts warn her about potential dangers: "This is not the States. A woman just doesn't travel alone in this country" (9). When her car gets a flat tire on a secluded road and she is met by two native farmers who offer their help, Yolanda is petrified, seeing the men as "strong and quite capable of catching her if she makes a run for it" (19). In her fear, she initially does not speak and is mistaken for an American tourist: "'Americana,' he says to the darker man, pointing to the car. 'No comprende.' The darker man narrows his eyes and studies Yolanda a moment. 'Americana?' he asks her, as if not quite sure what to make of her" (20).

We immediately understand the irony of Yolanda's position. Not only are the men "not quite sure what to make of her," but she does not know what to make of herself. Her inability to choose whether she is Dominican or American dramatizes her hyphenated, hybridized sense of selfhood and reveals her liminality. This liminality manifests itself bodily. She speaks and understands Spanish, but, being paralyzed by fear, she literally cannot articulate her cultural position: "[H]er tongue feels as if it has been stuffed in her mouth like a rag to keep her quiet" (20). Eventually, she admits to being *Americana* and begins explaining in English what happened to her car. The readers cannot miss the fact that Yolanda "others" the Dominican men (her "own people"), perceiving them as dark and dangerous, as if reenacting the xenophobic racism that her own family has experienced in the United States.[22]

The subsequent irony emanating from Yolanda's "choice" to present herself as *Americana* to the island's *campesinos* is underscored by an earlier moment in this section when, at her cousin's party, she is asked about her identity: "That poet she met at Lucinda's party the night before argued that no matter how much of it one lost, in the midst of some profound emotion, one would revert to one's mother tongue. He put Yolanda through a series of situations. What language, he asked, looking pointedly into her eyes, did she love in?" (13). The point about speaking one's mother tongue in the moment of emotion foreshadows, of course, Yolanda's encounter with the men on a secluded country road and sets up expectations that, in a situation like this one, she would naturally resort to Spanish. Additionally, these expectations are heightened by the fact that Yolanda, as a poet and crafter of words, obsessed with the workings of signification, is marked by the text as a character for whom language is not merely a tool of communication but mostly an aesthetic space of invention, reinvention, and enunciation of the self. Yolanda is not only hyperconscious of the process of meaning making, but she also treats language as a shelter: "In New York, she needed to settle somewhere, and since the natives were unfriendly, and the country inhospitable, she took root in the language" (141). All these expectations are foiled in the incident with the *campesinos*, pointing out that even the supposedly most intimate links like the one between one's native tongue and one's identity are not inherently stable. Thus, this performative moment of confused identity suggests that an exilic ontology is about quivering that is not always liberatory. That is, while Yolanda certainly has (unequal) access to two cultures, the episode on the country road shows us that her quivering is first and foremost viscerally painful. Later on, in "The Rudy Elmenhurst Story," Yolanda expresses this idea poignantly: "For the hundredth time, I cursed my immigrant origins" (94); "I saw what a cold, lonely life awaited me in this country" (99).

Contrapuntally, I am reminded of an intriguing 1998 *New York Times* article, "The New Immigrant Tide: Shuttle between Worlds." Focusing on binational immigrants who "lead a double life, with gusto," the article is permeated by the tone of cheerful exhilaration describing transnational crossings. The authors explicate the idea of modern immigrants who, supposedly able to straddle two worlds freely, live out "this here-there phenomenon" in ways not experienced by earlier immigrants and migrants: "Still, for the newest immigrants, technological advances and global political and economic changes have revolutionized the relationship with the homeland—just as the American embrace of multiculturalism allows it to flourish as never before." The article opens with the story of Fernando Mateo, a dual citizen of the Dominican Republic and the United States, who "simply commutes" between the two countries, conducting his business. The authors conclude, "There is nothing fractured about his existence." And Mateo himself confirms this point: "'I believe people like us have the best of two worlds. We have two countries, two homes. It doesn't make any sense for us to be either this or that. We're both. It's not a conflict."[23]

In applauding the experience of national doubleness and refusing the either/or model of monocultural identity, Mateo speaks about a hybrid selfhood as empowering and unproblematic. In a sense, we could say that this is a transnational person who metaphorically owns the "Cosmic Passport" and uses it with gusto. Although I think that most who live exilic lives understand the notion of multiple belonging, accepting the idea that a transnational existence is "not a conflict" seems prematurely celebratory. The *New York Times* article does not even mention those who, despite their wish to be transnational, often cannot go back home (political refugees, for example). Additionally, it is hard to miss the point that the idea of an "unfractured existence" that the authors foreground in their discussion of transnational identities takes us back to the humanistic notion of the "I" that historically is positioned as a whole, unfractured subject. Hence, even though Mateo's life is located between "yucca and plantains" and "bagels and lox,"[24] his in-betweenness is paradoxically refashioned as a postmodern wholeness. After all, Mateo is a shuttling transnational.

I refer to "The New Immigrant Tide" not because I want to discount the compelling experiences of people like Mateo, but because I am struck by the difference between how this article invites the general public to think about contemporary transnational crossings and the way *How the García Girls Lost Their Accents* and other exilic literature I mentioned earlier represent transcultural identities. Overwhelmingly, the transnational characters we encounter in these texts, through their unstable positioning in relation to the presumed stability of the Western self, exhibit how their identities are created in the dialectical space between pain and pleasure. And they show us how, to use Edward Said's words, "exile is fundamentally a discontinuous state of being," which complicates the logic of national identity (1984, 51). Furthermore, in Yolanda's case, her liminality reveals how she does and simultaneously does not belong to either the Dominican Republic or the United States. That is, in many ways, *How the García Girls Lost Their Accents* and other above-mentioned texts are about strangers, about those who—like the Derridean idea of the *pharmakon*, signifying both remedy and poison—remain in the space of undecidability, forever quivering.

Zygmunt Bauman's theorizing of the position of the stranger is helpful to explicate my point further:

> The strangers are not, however, the "as-yet-undecided"; they are, in principle, undecidables. They are that "third element" which should not be. The true hybrids, the monsters: not just unclassified, but unclassifiable. They therefore do not question this one opposition here and now: they question oppositions as such, the very principle of the opposition, the plausibility of dichotomy it suggests. They unmask the brittle artificiality of division—they destroy the world. [The stranger] is a constant threat to the world order. (1990, 148–49)

His discussion helps us to reflect on Yolanda's complex subject position that, as an unclassifiable third element, occupies the neither/nor exilic territory. However, Bauman does not suggest that strangers are merely occupying some neutral gray area that gives them the power to be perceived as a threat to the established social order. Nor does he suggest, I believe, that the ontological position of such strangers-hybrids as "undecidables" is necessarily a liberatory one. Rather, what underscores Bauman's discussion is what I came to call a quivering subjectivity that is both dangerous and in danger. For an exile's quivering self—neither firmly here nor there, but in the space of unclassifiable categories—constantly threatens to undo the normative idea of the self, one supposedly securely positioned in a given national territory. Simultaneously then, this exilic identity is in danger because, although it is a challenge to the historically privileged notion of the "I," it does not often count as a valid, sanctioned subject.

Interestingly, "The New Immigrant Tide" privileges the uplifting narrative of Mateo, but it also mentions Mersuda Guichard's family, whose story explores what it means to live the dangerous and in danger multicultural identity I am referring to. Although Guichard was born in Trinidad, her children "are a hybrid: part West Indian, part American—and all New Yorker." Despite the article's overall cheerful tone, the authors allow the strangerhood to speak its troubling modality in a rare moment: "The back and forth can be confusing, and some feel they fit in neither here nor there. 'Here they say, "You're from the islands,"' Starr [Guichard's daughter] said. 'In Trinidad, they call me a Yankee, and that's considered an insult.'"[25]

The sentiments that Guichard's daughter expresses are indicative of the way many American transnational exilic narratives foreground the neither/nor territory I am discussing. For example, the narrator of Hoffman's *Lost in Translation* (1989), Ewa, a Jewish-Polish exile residing in the United States, compellingly speaks of her location as being ridden with continual tension: "Of course, one of the shards sticking in my ribs suggests that maybe I'll never belong comfortably anyplace, that my sensibilities and opinions will always be stuck in some betwixt and between place." As Ewa uses the bodily imagery as a site of knowledge that foregrounds a sense of her hybrid self oscillating in the in-between space between different "I's"—past and present, Polish-Jewish and American—we see that, as she writes, "the gap cannot be fully closed" (216, 274). The "shards sticking in [her] ribs" become a metaphor for a sense of her flesh being torn and fragmented, and the place "betwixt and between" is not some idealized moment of suspension, but rather a lived experience that is both daunting and empowering. This experience of unresolvable doubleness also permeates Divakaruni's stories in *Arranged Marriage* (1995). For instance, in "Doors," Preeti, born in India but living in the United States since she was twelve, is paradoxically marked as "Indian and yet not Indian" by her husband, Deepak, who is "straight out of India" (189, 183). Ironically, Deepak thinks of Preeti's cultural location as exotic and mysterious; a sense of her mystery manifests itself in his inability to understand her desire for closed doors—for intimacy and privacy. Similarly struggling with the experience of bifocality, Jemorah, one of the protagonists of Diana Abu-Jaber's *Arabian Jazz* (1993), born in the United States of a Jordanian father and an American mother, wonders where she and her sister, Melvina, belong. Having experienced xenophobia, she probes the meaning of a legitimate Americanness: "It's not enough to be born here, or to live here, or speak the language. You've got to *seem* right." When for a moment she fantasizes about relocating to Jordan in search of "home," her cousin's words compel Jemorah to acknowledge her in-betweenness: "[T]his 'home' that you seek is not there.... People like you and Melvina, you won't have what your grandparents might have had. To be the first generation in this country, with another culture always looming over you, you are the ones who are born homeless, bedouins, not your immigrant parents.... You're torn in two. You get two looks at a world" (328, 330). And in Ariel Dorfman's autobiographical *Heading South, Looking North* (1998), the narrating "I" tells us about the resistance to "the madness of being double": "I instinctively chose to refuse the multiple, complex, in-between person I would someday become.... I refused to take a shortcut to the hybrid condition I have now embraced" (42).

I am not suggesting that the neither/nor territory I see revealed in these texts expresses a uniform diasporic experience that various characters share.[26] Although I draw attention to the multiplicity of national belongings, I do not intend to homogenize this location, as each needs to be analyzed in its specificity. What these voices collectively describe is an in-betweenness—a hyphenated Americanness—that threatens to rupture the nation's coherence, allowing for a critique of an exclusionary rhetoric surrounding the idea of rightful U.S. citizenry. This rupture is textually imagined in many of the narratives and certainly in *How the García Girls Lost Their Accents* as a space of nuanced resistance: to the binarized hierarchy of alien/native, as a protest against the elision of the foreigner's otherness, and as a defiance of the creation of a new "proper" subject that can successfully carry on in a new community once she moves through the trajectory of coercive assimilation. When I think about Yolanda's unbelonging, Said's words capture the conceptualization of this space: "Just beyond the perimeter of what nationalism constructs as the nation, at the frontier separating 'us' from what is alien, is the perilous territory of not-belonging" (1984, 51). It is ultimately the territory of not-belonging that discloses how the "hauntingly indeterminate" modality of transnational strangers works to "unmask the brittle artificiality of division" (Bauman 1990, 155) between the "I" rooted in nation and an exile who, by definition, is beyond nation.

Against Homogenizing Multiculturalism

Now that I have explicated the theoretical underpinnings of the exilic in-betweenness, the reader may wonder about the larger implications of these books for studying American literature or why the category of Latina/o literature seems perhaps too narrow. Moreover, pushing this point further, I would suggest that other various alternative categories of ethnic, multicultural, or immigrant literatures that might—at a first glance—successfully classify a novel like *How the García Girls Lost Their Accents* appear insufficient and problematic as well. In situating my response, I again turn to Alvarez's words:

> And though I complain sometimes about the confusion resulting from being of neither world, and about *the marginalizations created on both sides*—the Americans considering me a writer of ethnic interests, a Latina writer (meaning a writer for Latinos and of sociological interest to mainstream Americans), or the Dominicans reaming me out, saying she's not one of us, she's not Dominican enough—though I complain about the confusion and rootlessness of being this mixed breed, I also think it's what confirmed me as a writer, particularly because I am a woman. (1998b, 174; my emphasis)

The notion that a writer like Alvarez, who does not comfortably fit in a single compartment, experiences marginalization "on both sides" shows us the importance of the double critique she submits. Both of these critiques energize resistance to the necessity of being claimed by one nation as an author. Alvarez's unease with the category of "a writer of ethnic interests" demonstrates the narrowness of a conceptualization of ethnicity as an external, exotic subcategory that becomes of interest to literary studies as Latina/o literature—hence, not quite American. Not opposed to being classified as a Latina writer or to the category of Latino literature in general, Alvarez nevertheless expresses her ambivalence about traditional literary divisions. On the other hand, in speaking out against monocultural reductive categories—what David Palumbo-Liu terms "homogenizing multiculturalism" (1995, 15), she draws our attention to the marginalization from her native circles that cast her as not adequately Dominican—a stranger whose national loyalty is suspect.[27]

In closing, Alvarez's point takes me back to Bauman's discussion of the ambivalent ontology of strangers who "gestate uncertainty." He writes that in postmodern times "the age of anthropophagic and anthropoemic strategies is over" and that "the question is no longer how to get rid of the strangers and the strange, but how to live with them—daily and permanently" (1997, 46, 55). As I explained in the introduction, the anthropophagic strategy (*devouring* the strangers) he refers to is the process of nullifying the stranger's ontological otherness by consuming his or her difference. In short, this is the process of often subtle coercive assimilation that smooths out the stranger's unsettling otherness, historically conducted in the name of cultural homogeneity. The anthropoemic strategy (*vomiting* the strangers), on the other hand, is one of ejection, a process that rests on ostracism and, ultimately, on banishing the stranger from the cultural space in question. In stating that the problem for contemporary cultures is figuring out the ways in which to live *with* the postmodern stranger, Bauman, on some level, echoes Julia Kristeva's sentiments when she writes that "the question [of foreignness] is again before us today as we confront an economic and political integration on the scale of the planet: shall we be, intimately and subjectively, able to live with the others, to live *as others*, without ostracism but also without leveling?" (Kristeva 1991, 1–2).

Bauman's and Kristeva's theoretical positions, at first glance somewhat similar, are nonetheless predicated on a crucial difference. Bauman, perhaps unconsciously, seems to maintain the "us" versus "them" division because he locates otherness and difference "somewhere else," in the space of "strangerhood." For Kristeva, however—at least the way I read it—something else is clearly at stake. Disrupting the binary logic of "I"-sanctioned native/"other"-unwanted intruder–stranger, she asks for a recognition of the foreigner's foreignness within the "I" itself. This is a much more difficult paradigm of thinking since it does not allow for the sublimation and purification of the "I," a paradigm that, in fact, allows us to question the shadow of discursive violence that envelops a privileged notion of the self. Hence, given the context of Alvarez's novel, I read Bauman's statement that "ours is a *heterophilic* age" as troubling. Foregrounding the notion of heterophilia, he means that contemporary societies, unlike during the period of modern nation-building, are generally more appreciative of difference: "postmodern times are marked by an almost universal agreement that difference is good, precious, and in need of protection and cultivation" (1997, 55). But, as we have seen in the case of Rudy Elmenhurst's parents, the idea that difference is good and precious is a form of discursive multiculturalism, that is, an abstract cultivation of diversity that ultimately serves to cohere the identity of the rightful American and stabilize the desirable homogeneous vision of a nation. Although *How the García Girls Lost Their Accents* critiques such a nonthreatening notion of difference, it does not reject the importance of multicultural consciousness. The consciousness that the novel posits is not necessarily heterophilic in Bauman's sense, but rather one that demands considering transnational locations through a lens of unresolvable tension that, while liberatory for some, for many remains the source of complex restrictions, curtailed mobility, and disenfranchisement. Certainly, the García girls occupy a position of quivering ontologies that marks their Dominican American identities not as cosmopolitan, enviable hyphenated selves with the transnational passport in hand, but as exilic subjectivities who often painfully experience various shades of heterophilia on their very bodies.

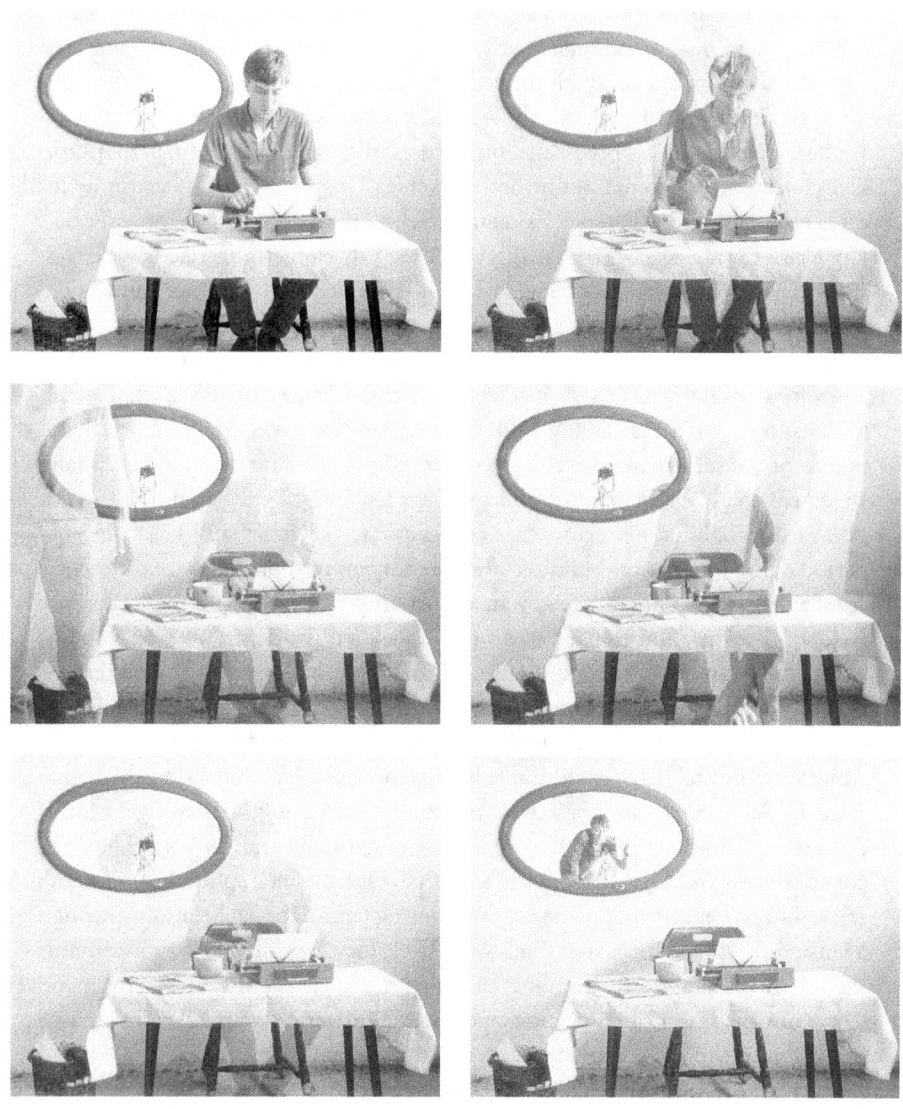

Metalanguage, 2004. Copyright Kamil Turowski. All rights reserved.

3

THE DIALECTICS OF EXILE: RESIDENT ALIENHOOD AND *LOST IN TRANSLATION*

> Perhaps I've read, written, eaten enough words so that English now flows in my bloodstream. But once this mutation takes place, once the language starts speaking itself to me from my cells, I stop being so stuck on it. Words are no longer spiky bits of hard matter, which refer only to themselves. They become more and more a transparent medium in which I live and which lives in me—a medium through which I can once again get to myself and to the world....
> ... But now the language has entered my body, has incorporated itself in the softest tissue of my being.
>
> —Eva Hoffman, *Lost in Translation*

"I have to translate myself," writes Ewa, the narrator of Eva Hoffman's 1989 autobiographical narrative, *Lost in Translation: A Life in a New Language.* In this statement Ewa locates the focus of the text on the process of translation, the process that—materially and symbolically—navigates an understanding of transnational exilic narratives. In this context, however, the concept of translating oneself questions the conventional understanding of translation as a mental act that, as the definition implies, usually refers to translating languages and their forms. The act of translation is not just about turning one language into another with the help of a dictionary. Rather, as the narrator suggests, the process of translation necessarily signifies merging between the "tissues of being," the living flesh and language itself.[1] This intricate connection between words and the flesh thus acknowledges the inseparability of body and language and implicates the translating "I" that needs to interpret itself in the process as well.

As the narrating voice in *Lost in Translation* invites us to reenvision the conventional dynamic of translation, she forces the reader to ponder the linkage between the flesh and the new language. How does an exile live the act of translation? And why does she insist on implicating her body in this process? In this text, the kinetic imagery of language entering the body and words flowing in the bloodstream underlines a dialectical dynamic of the narrative that destabilizes both the body and language and poses the idea that words have a material being.

Etymologically deriving from the Latin *trānslātus,* the concept of translation suggests "carrying across" or "bearing across." The narrator of *Lost in Translation,* grappling with her "life in a new language," makes us aware that to carry meaning across from one culture to another, from one language to another, she needs to carry her body across as well. And this act of carrying one's body across is both an obvious physical endeavor, since an exile is already borne across the world, and a more complicated journey through the process of translation, marked by an experience of slow bodily merging with the new linguistic system and its social configurations. Reading the text of this multifarious act of translation, however, one discovers that the process of language entering the body is not easily discernible because translation itself is not just about the transparency of words and their meanings; it is also about the struggle to make meaning and to decipher unknown cultural configurations: "But the terms don't travel across continents. You can't transport human meanings whole from one culture to another any more than you can transliterate a text" (175). In this passage Ewa makes us aware that the act of carrying meaning across is never quite complete, because what she experiences as her body is increasingly permeated—even re-created—by the new language both as translatable and untranslatable and as the simultaneous site of assimilation and resistance to the new cultural space.

As the English words start flowing in her bloodstream and language locates itself in the tissues of her being, Ewa, as a newcomer to the English-speaking world and an exile from Eastern Europe, acutely lives the process of translation. The idea of translation lived in her flesh poses the process of translation as both an abstract and material act, a performative act that underlies the materiality of meaning itself. Of course, her native language, Polish, already unquestionably is in her body and, to use the narrator's imagery, speaks itself from her cells (243). The acculturation that Ewa goes through does not, however, eradicate a previous self or create a new, English-speaking "I," but rather produces a new position that is situated "betwixt and between" (216). This new fluctuating in-between space becomes the always shifting site of her Polish-Jewish cultural identity and her new American subject position: "It is I who will have to learn how to live with a double vision" (132).

Drawing on these ideas, in this chapter I approach *Lost in Translation* as a transcultural narrative of exile that has been evocatively called "the first 'postmodern' autobiography written in English by an émigré from a European

Communist country."[2] Hoffman, an immigrant from Poland to Canada and the United States, an author of two nonfiction works, *Exit into History* (1993) and *Shtetl* (1997), and her first novel, *The Secret* (2002), has established herself as a compelling commentator on exile and displacement in the second half of the twentieth century. Of particular interest to my discussion of alienhood is her textualization of the *in-between space* as a site of resistance: resistance to a traditional notion of assimilation that works to accept, but also to absorb and flatten, the exile; resistance to smoothing out the foreigner's otherness; and a defiance against the creation of a new, proper subject that erases her past so that she can successfully function in a new community.

The Heaviness of Being: Inventing the Exiled "I"

Lost in Translation tells the story of a Jewish-Polish narrator who is exiled from Poland with her parents and sister at the age of thirteen in the late 1950s. The text chronicles Ewa's intellectual journey from Cracow to Vancouver, Canada, and eventually to a successful life as a professional writer, an émigré, in New York City. Even though the text ends on a note of immigrant success, Ewa's story questions conventional immigrant narratives of complete assimilation. From the very onset of a narrative that starts with a poignant image of closure and doom rather than the exhilaration of a beginning, Ewa's being is marked by heaviness: "It's April 1959, I'm standing at the railing of the *Batory*'s upper deck, and I feel that my life is ending" (3). The feeling of heaviness remains throughout the entire narrative, as Ewa struggles with the burdens of negotiating her subject position in a realm of new culture, language, and identity. This weight that Ewa emphasizes joins both the bodily conditions of exile and the process of lived translation. The pain and pleasure of the body-in-transition—which both translates and is being translated—that *Lost in Translation* foregrounds so eloquently draws our attention to the notion that translation is first and foremost a corporeal struggle, while it is simultaneously also symbolic.

The heaviness of being that Ewa experiences so sharply is contextualized within the literary history of narratives of exile. In the section on "Exile," the narrator refers directly to her literary predecessors, Milan Kundera, Czesław Miłosz, and Vladimir Nabokov, whom she calls "our world's experts of mourning" because they have lost "not an archeological but a living history" (116). Here, with specific references to the well-known literary figures, Ewa's narrative grows self-consciously intertextual. Her own story is told not in a cultural vacuum as a story of one individual struggle, but rather as a narrative that joins the tradition of exilic writing by authors-refugees from the communist system. While she clearly acknowledges this tradition, by inserting her own voice into the already established canon of male émigré authors she foregrounds the way in which gender shapes the cultural positioning of an exile. Especially interesting here is her direct reference to Kundera's famous phrase "unbearable lightness of being," which comes from his novel by the same title. This implied lightness of self, however unbearable, is not accessible to the narrator.

Her sense of being is marked by her Polish-Jewish past and the past of her parents, who are Holocaust survivors. Even though she imagines that her birth just after the war must have signified a new beginning for her parents, she is named in honor of her two grandmothers whose material traces had been erased during the war: "There aren't even any photographs which have survived the war: the cut from the past is complete" (8). Part of Ewa's heaviness of being is marked by the Holocaust imagery figured, for example, in her mother's tears on each anniversary of the terrible death of her sister, Ewa's aunt, who "was among those who had to dig their own graves" before being sent to the gas chamber. This excruciating, living pain is passed on to Ewa who, already as a child, inherits her parents' fear of the fragility of the self and the vulnerability of the present: "The ocean of death is so enormous, and life such a tenuous continent. Everyone I know has lost some relatives during the war, and almost none of my friends have grandparents" (7). Having been engulfed by the vision of "the ocean of death," Ewa is destined to carry the weight of her parents' past, even though she herself has access to it only through her mother's tears.

Paradoxically, even though there is so much stress on the heaviness of the past in Ewa's narrative, she has also introduced herself to the readers as an "I" whose "cut from the past is complete" (8). Consequently, the narrator emerges as a perplexing "I" with a conflicting connection to temporality. This clashing relationship between the narrating "I" and temporality is figured in the text's form itself. The formal arrangement of the text may seem linear at first as we move through subsequent sections called "Paradise," "Exile," and "The New World." But the reader quickly discovers that the structure of the text defies the linear onward progress of events and thoughts and emphasizes the self-reflexive and fragmentary mode of Ewa's story. In part 1 we are already given fragments that chronologically belong to part 3. All three parts thus paint a mosaic of experience that is not stable but fluctuates back and forth, confusing the temporal narrative mode. This fragmentary flow of the narrative reflects the narrator's fragmented self that is both here and there, in the United States and in Poland, simultaneously in the present and in the past. The writing self in the text floats in and out of the past, never fully either in the past or in the present. Instead, the narrating voice is stretched between the two temporal and spatial modes, accentuating Ewa's bifocal vision that makes her a "hybrid creature," located in the in-between space (221).

The notion of hybridity here, marked by the remaking of the narrator's identity, does not strive toward a resolution and the achievement of a new identity that would figure as some imaginary whole. The point of Ewa's story is that immigrant experience *is* as much about fragmentation, splintering, and dislocation as about assimilation:

> I share with my American generation an acute sense of dislocation and the equally acute *challenge of having to invent a place and an identity for myself* without the traditional supports. It could be said that the generation I belong to has been characterized by its prolonged refusal to assimilate—and it is in my very uprootedness that I'm its member. It could indeed be said that exile is the archetypal condition of contemporary lives. (197; emphasis mine)

The specific historical context in which Ewa and her friends find themselves is marked by the sense of exile that not only refers to those who are newcomers but also embraces her American contemporaries. When Ewa writes that the underlying experience of American lives is signified by exile and dislocation, she stresses the challenge of inventing both identity and a place in a country that can no longer be perceived as a stable and uniform social space. Therefore, Ewa's resistance to a dynamic of traditional assimilation is not a singular and individual gesture of defiance, because the entire generation that Ewa joins is characterized by its "prolonged refusal to assimilate."

The notion of assimilation, traditionally used in reference to exiles and foreigners, takes on a different tone here; it does not point solely to newcomers. Ewa notes that the whole American generation is characterized by its uprootedness, by not being moored firmly in the cultural stratum. Ewa's awareness of "an acute sense of dislocation" does not necessarily evoke a mourning for the supposedly once stable past, but rather pins down the cultural moment in which this presupposed stability is revealed as illusory. The assumed unquestioned superiority and security of the West, particularly the myth of the benevolent America as a democratic land of the free, is exploded as the marginalized voices begin to protest social injustice openly in the 1960s.

Despite sharing the same cultural moment, Ewa realizes an intense difference between her cultural aspirations and the desires of her American friends: "I want to live within language and to be held within the frame of culture; they want to break out of the constraints of both language and culture" (194). That is, Ewa desperately wants to figure out the workings of the language that she speaks and that speaks her; she wants to comprehend the signifieds underlying diverse signifiers around her in order to grasp various cultural meanings. However, her friends are in the process of questioning the very signifieds themselves. Thus, we see that Ewa cannot share with her friends the same sense of oppression or passion for social revolution because her "I" has not been organized by the same sociocultural forces that formed her friends' subjectivities in the first place. Her seemingly problematic desire for the solid frame of culture may become understandable if we remember that Ewa's position is that of an alien-outsider who does not really belong in the symbolic structures of this culture. In other words, being a marginalized "I," she cannot claim a terrain of American culture as her own. Consequently, she is not ready to start critiquing the cultural frame because she does not feel that she has one to begin with. Ewa's specific marginalization as a foreign "I" situates her in a different way from some of her friends who may also find themselves marginalized in American culture. In a culture marked by splintering and fragmentation, there is no one comfortable place where she may be able to locate her "I." She writes, "In a splintered society, what does one assimilate to? Perhaps the very splintering itself" (197).

We see that the specific moment of Ewa's immigrant experience sets her apart from those previous émigré authors who wrote their immigrant narratives at the turn of the century or before the Second World War:

> But insofar as I'm an outsider wishing to be taken in, I've come at the wrong moment, for in the midst of all this swirling and fragmenting movement, the very notion of outside and inside is as quaint as the Neoplatonic model of the universe. I do not experience the pain of earlier immigrants, who were kept out of exclusive clubs or decent neighborhoods. Within the limits of my abilities and ambitions, I can go anywhere at all, and be accepted there. The only joke is that there's no there there. (196)

Ewa sketches here a sense of the complexity of her own immigrant experience. On the one hand, she notes that her experience of being a foreign "I" may be less painful compared with earlier immigrant struggles because she does not face the same severe ostracism and exclusion from middle-class social privileges. After all, she is a talented undergraduate Rice University student whose scholarly commitment is recognized and awarded. However, the new difficulty, specific to her times, is the process of being positioned in a culture whose presupposed oneness and coherence is undercut in its "swirling and fragmenting." As she writes, the very division into inside and outside is under interrogation. What she means is the idea that the emerging social movements shatter the vision of the American culture as a self-sufficient nation-state whose supposedly solid basis lies in its unquestioned glory of being the promised land. When Ewa recognizes that "there's no there there" anymore, we see that she cannot be simply taken in and incorporated into the American social fabric. After the Kennedy assassination, in a time marked by general social unrest, the horror of the Vietnam War, and the rise of the counterculture, student protests, civil rights activism, and the women's movement, the assumed stability of the social ground is shaken. The cultural framework itself can no longer be perceived as a harmonious social machine that can take the newcomers in and show them how to be productive subjects in the land of prosperity. Instead, this time is marked by a sense of renegotiation of the cultural mechanism itself. There is no one "America" or one culture that can accommodate Ewa. Instead, Ewa senses the motion of fluidity and placelessness that removes the assumed stability of firm cultural references: "I find myself in the most fluid of generations" (195).

As Ewa articulates her sense of dislocation, the fragmented style of her narrative bears the marks of a crisis. The fractured diegesis pulls the reader in two different directions, showing us that despite her resistance to assimilation, she still needs to go through it. What she highlights in relation to the dynamic of assimilation is the task of inventing the *exiled "I"* without the help of a familiar cultural apparatus.[3]

Exile, derived from the Latin "banished person" and the Middle English "banishment," refers to a subject separated from her country or home, expelled from her native land either voluntarily or by authoritative forces. Since to be exiled suggests a removal from the roots that formed one's subjectivity, exile implies an ontological ejection beyond the familiar realm of being, beyond one's knowable "I." In fact, it is this presupposed loss of identity that has historically functioned as the punishment that an exile, banished from his or her community, was expected to suffer. If we express exile in terms of loss, such an understanding presumes that after she loses an "I," she necessarily needs to invent a new subject position for herself. However, Ewa's narrative complicates such an onward trajectory of subjecthood. Instead, while pondering her position as a "hybrid creature," we see that the residue of the previous "I" lingers in Ewa's written "exiled I." Living this hybrid self implies being doomed—or allowed—to quiver, as her rendition of an exile disrupts the dichotomy between the "I" and "non-I" and validates the space between the two.

The concept of uprootedness that Ewa discusses is particularly compelling in this context because in traditional immigrant discourse, the concept of uprootedness—the severing of roots—is often analyzed as both a physical and emotional transport from one culture to another. To be uprooted means not only to be physically dislocated but also to be thrown out of language and out of one's familiar body. Consequently, uprootedness is often coded with sentiment as a loss of one's stable communal ground and as a reason to mourn what has been lost and cannot be regained. Within the parameters of such a vision, the uprooted self is marked as a wandering, unanchored "I." To some degree, Ewa follows these conventions as she describes her life in Poland as a "Paradise." However, at the same time as her sense of the "I" quivers, she mobilizes the experience of uprootedness by refusing to obliterate her past.

The Borders of Language and Self: Language "Entering" the Body

The material familiarity that Ewa's uprooted self leaves behind results in pain, prompting us to consider how one's native language points to the presumably stable roots that underpin our identities. The roots signify home, affinities, and ties that situate us in language and its culture, granting the presupposed comfort of familiarity. Even though we may not always be able to point to the etymological roots of familiar words, we feel the connoted concepts in our bodies. Exactly how might we feel language in our bodies? In the beginning of "Exile,"

Ewa writes: "When my friend Penny tells me that she's envious, or happy, or disappointed, I try laboriously to translate *not* from English to Polish, but from the word back to its source, to the feeling from which it springs" (107; emphasis mine). The trajectory of literal translation moves from English into Polish but is clearly not adequate for Ewa's understanding of Penny's emotions. Instead, Ewa searches for a sensation that would reveal the meaning to her. In her search, she visualizes her body as a spring that generates meaning, emotionality. But at this point in her linguistic journey, the translation does not work: "I don't know how Penny feels when she talks about envy. The word hangs in a Platonic stratosphere, a vague prototype of all envy." What Ewa experiences is the discrepancy between the English concept of envy and the familiarity of envy in Polish. The English term appears abstract to her, away from materiality, merely a dry concept without "its colors, striations, nuances—its very existence." It is this universal model of envy that frustrates Ewa as she bears the disjuncture between the words and feelings they manifest. When she expresses this as "the loss of a living connection," she underscores the idea that our native language presumably wraps itself around us, envelops our bodies, allowing us to feel it (107). The devastation of a living connection is evoked in Ewa's body that cannot yet experience the English concept of envy.

The anguish that Ewa initially endures in Vancouver as she merely conceptualizes her exiled position is expressed by her feeling of suspension between the two languages. As Polish becomes irrelevant in the face of her new being, English is accessible to her merely on the level of words—sounds that have not yet located themselves in her body:

> Polish, in a short time has atrophied, shriveled from sheer uselessness. Its words don't apply to my new experiences; they're not coeval with any of the objects, or faces, or the very air I breathe in the daytime. In English, words have not penetrated to those layers of my psyche from which a private conversation could proceed. (107)

The fading of her native tongue means more than just a loss of the validity of Polish on Canadian ground; it also suggests the ontological discomfort of her self. Ewa feels the unavoidable slippage as Polish becomes obsolete, relevant only to the past, and the unstoppable shriveling of language affects her bodily self as well. The withering of Polish atrophies her "I," and because of this painful suspension, she senses how being is demarcated and experienced within the borders of language. The fading of Polish creates a barrier that does not allow her to embrace even such an unquestionable act as breathing. When Ewa contemplates how her "thread has been snapped," she reflects on her new predicament, which is marked by the fact that she can no longer make meaning out of the life and culture in which she is positioned (107–8).

English, on the other hand, has not entered her body yet, has not penetrated her consciousness. Even introductory cultural phrases like "You're welcome" pose a serious dilemma: "The very places where language is at its most conventional, where it should be most taken for granted, are the places where I feel the prick of artifice" (106). In other words, the very presumption that the most ordinary, supposedly the easiest phrases are the most natural to acquire, is problematic. Ewa's struggle tells us that, contrary to conventional assumptions, the most banal linguistic moments are, in fact, most constructed. She questions the belief that such everyday locutions facilitate our understanding more than, for example, more metaphoric and complex language. It is such conventional expressions that sit unquestioned and unchallenged within language, as we use them mechanically to satisfy social conventions, that are most ungraspable to the narrator. She perceives them as empty and useless not because she does not yet know English-speaking social conventions but because such phrases sound artificial and produce no bodily sensation for her. In fact, words that Ewa learns from books—like "enigmatic" or "insolent," "words that have only a literary value" as she comments—seem more palpable and produce less resistance (106).

The condition of suspension that Ewa illustrates traps her in a space where she cannot speak her experience to others or even to herself: "I have no interior language, and without it, interior images" (108). The concept of interior language suggests that language is not solely a system of semantic and syntactic rules that one learns in order to know how to speak and make meaning. Rather, we see how language is neither stable nor controllable. Even though Ewa still knows Polish, it nevertheless escapes her against her will. The intimacy of interior language gave her the resources of visualization itself, the ability to create "images through which we assimilate the external world" (108). Within this vision of absorbing the external world into herself through the imagery created by interior language, Ewa dramatizes herself as an active agent who wants to mediate meaning.

Ewa's desire to mediate her new cultural position manifests itself in the space of her diary that she receives from Penny as a birthday gift (121). The turbulent experience of writing the diary creates Ewa's "first jump" into her new subjecthood (121). However, the diary, which is meant to bring her pleasure and offer a protected space of privacy, poses a dilemma for her. She knows the cultural function of a diary as a place for daily musings and for the most intimate observations, but she does not know which language to choose as her diary language:

> Writing in Polish at this point would be a little like resorting to Latin or ancient Greek—an eccentric thing to do in a diary, in which you're supposed to set down your most intimate experiences and unpremeditated thoughts in the most unmediated language. *Polish is becoming a dead language, the language of the untranslatable past.* . . . Because I have to choose something, I finally choose English. *If I'm to write about the present, I have to write in the language of the present, even if it's not the language of the self.* (120–21; emphasis mine)

It is significant that writing becomes the place where this struggle to mediate Ewa's new subjectivity occurs. She reveals that, contrary to a traditional view that we simply speak the language through a command we have over it, her position is riddled with contradictions. The language of the self that she evokes is Polish, while the language of her present lives in English. Writing in Polish becomes impossible because her native tongue is dead; it has no relevance to the present moment and no cultural reference to her own immediate position. Her choice to write in English is not necessarily an easy one because "English is not the language of emotion" for her. Even though writing in English should work to anchor Ewa in the present moment, she instead experiences the splitting that underlies the writing dynamic. In her diary she uses English to try to imagine and write about the self that she might have been had she stayed in Poland. When she says that "the diary is about me and not about me at all," she expresses a sense of being torn by a paradox that underscores the quivering of her self (121).

Interestingly, what is revealed here is that the connection between the self and language is not a natural process, but a constructed one. We see how the presupposed comfort Ewa feels in her native language is only an illusory comfort we assume we have. Ewa discovers that the process of writing "gives [her] a written self": "This language is beginning to invent another me" (121). Since her first attempts to write happen to be expressed in her second language, Ewa becomes intensely aware of how writing in general (not necessarily in one's native language) works to produce the written self of the "I" that undertakes writing. Her written self is as much fictional as real, a self that lingers in the in-between space, between the "I" that writes and the "I" that is being written by language. Writing, thus, is a space of invention of her bifocal identity.

The cultural presumptions about diary writing that Ewa sketches suggest that a diary supposedly offers a most intimate, personal kind of writing where we are able to capture the most immediate experiences in the most unmediated language. Diary writing, in this sense, is thought to be a private, authentic articulation because it is writing addressed to the self. It is the "I" writing to its own "I," trying to apprehend and express its self. This idea of an inward-oriented writing, "entirely for myself," may suggest that the writing "I" is capable of creating a uniquely authentic discourse of the self (120). Ewa's experience, however, undercuts these assumptions as she sees how her own diary writing is and is not about her.

Ewa is initially unable to use the pronoun "I" in her diary. The difficulty of writing the "I" suggests a contradiction that shatters the very foundation of the diary as it undercuts the common concept of diary writing that supposedly rests on using the "I" in the first place: "I am unable to use the word 'I.' I do not go as far as the schizophrenic 'she'—but I am driven, as by a compulsion, to the double, the Siamese 'you'" (121). This doubling highlights the splitting that Ewa senses as she is locked between the two linguistic spaces. And the use of "you" is interesting because it suggests that she does not address herself, but somebody else instead. The "you" she uses is and is not her, accenting the splintering and estrangement of her self.

One such dialogue where Ewa positions herself as a "conversation" appears at the initial moment of writing the diary:

> But you would have been different, very different.
> No question.
> And you prefer her, the Cracow Ewa.
> Yes, I prefer her. But I can't be her. I'm losing track of her. In a few years, I'll have no idea what her hairdo would have been like.
> *But she's more real, anyway.*
> Yes, she's the real one. (120; emphasis mine)

What underlines Ewa's split subject position in these dialogues is the way in which her two different "I's" speak to each other. These discussions between the two selves mark the two contesting linguistic modes, Polish and English, and often take on an argumentative note at pivotal moments in Ewa's life, such as when she tries to make decisions about her career choices, her marriage to an American, and finally her divorce. But the relationship between these "I's" is not stable and does not maintain the same tone. Unlike in the first conversation, where we can detect a nostalgic tone surrounding the fading of Ewa's Polish self, the next dialogue, which takes place in the United States, features the space of a battle:

> If you don't satisfy me, you'll always be dissatisfied.
> Go away. You're becoming a succubus.
> I won't be easy to get rid of.
> I don't need you anymore. I want you to be silent. Shuddup. (199)

The Polish "I" is figured here as a hungry voice that demands to be heard, as it threatens to haunt the present "I" by disrupting its presupposed comfort that it strives to achieve. We can detect a sense that the Polish "I" needs to be expelled and silenced in order for the present "I" to simply be.

RESIDENT ALIENHOOD: TRANSLATING THE BODY

As an immigrant, Ewa is constantly reminded of her shaky and shifting status as an "I." The imagery of doubling and splitting registers on many levels and does not disappear even at the end of the narrative, as she explicates her position as a "resident alien" (221). A resident in an official immigrant discourse suggests one who has the *right* to occupy a cultural and social space. An alien marks a stranger, a foreigner, an other coming from the outside. Thus, logically, a resident alien—an insider-outsider—to some degree at least, seems to be an oxymoron, a contradiction difficult to negotiate internally and externally. And even though a resident alien eventually may go through a naturalization process, an official conversion from an alien to a citizen, the shakiness of the "I" formally marked by the status of a resident alien is never fully erased.

To "naturalize" means to invest an alien with the rights and privileges of citizenship. This act of naturalizing, performed by the nation-state, is an official baptism thought of as the highest privilege a foreign "I" may aspire to. In this context the very concept of the citizen—an "I" that is natural—is set in opposition to an artificial, "alien I." The close reading of a "natural I" reveals that the notion of citizenship rests on a natural order that the alien I threatens to disturb precisely because she comes from the outside of this presupposed orderly social coherence. And even if a foreigner is given a chance to become naturalized and acquires a legally sanctioned position in this natural order, often her body betrays her as nonnatural. This betrayal may be manifested by an accented speech, by skin color, by a difficulty in following accepted cultural patterns and conducts, or by a general linguistic awkwardness that reveals itself as an exile struggles to find her own place and voice in a new social realm.

In *Lost in Translation*, we witness such a cultural and linguistic battle as Ewa, suspended between the two languages and their different worlds, initially finds herself with no agency. It is significant that Ewa's passage into exilic subjecthood starts with the process of translating her body. Her process of becoming an "I" is facilitated by friendly old-émigré Polish women who are "well versed in native ways." They take on the task of revising Ewa's image and reenvisioning her "deficient" body so that she can become a desirable subject: "I've emerged as less attractive, less graceful, less desirable. In fact, I can see in these women's eyes that I'm somewhat a pitiful specimen" (109). In order to create her new self, Ewa is schooled in using shampoos and lotions, her armpits are shaved, she is given lipstick and high-heeled shoes: she is produced by a Polish-Canadian "elaborate packaging" (110). Even though she goes through the translation of her bodily self without protest, this act of producing a proper female subject does not quite work: "[M]y body is stiff, sulky, wary." She adopts socially imposed gender conventions appropriate for a female her age, but no matter how much she wants to belong, her body betrays her: "[M]y gestures show that I'm here provisionally, by their grace, that I don't rightfully belong" (110). It is easy to dress and paint the body so that it fits within the normative cultural decorum and becomes the proper body. But this superficial change is only cosmetic after all and does not penetrate the flesh. Ewa does not feel comfortable within this new package created for her, and in fact, her body rebels against this forced translation of her image. The women who acculturate Ewa's body assume that such a change is both indispensable and desirable for her. In fact, the assumption is that she should be grateful for being taken under the well-meaning wings of her Polish-Canadian benefactors. But only the surface of the body can be altered by fancy clothes and elaborate makeup; her gestures, her body language, do not correspond to the new image. To begin to translate the exiled body—to carry it across—means to painstakingly create the body in a new language in such a way that the exile can begin developing interior language.

Ewa's unease is registered on and in her flesh:

> My shoulders stoop, I nod frantically to indicate my agreement with others, I smile sweetly at people to show I mean well, and *my chest recedes inward* so that I don't take up too much space—mannerisms of a marginal, off-centered person who wants both to be taken in and to fend off the threatening others. (110; emphasis mine)

Her position on the cultural margin, on the contours of the social realm, is also manifested in the way she carries herself. She intuits that her off-centered "I" has no right to claim the social space in the same way that, for example, rightful citizens can. This social discomfort is visible in her posture as she cautiously positions herself spatially. The chest that "recedes inward" shrinks the bodily borders and makes Ewa less ostentatious, more modestly situated in the social realm. The Polish-Canadian benefactors draw Ewa's mother's attention to the fact that since Ewa's breasts are already visible, she should begin wearing a bra. Her introduction to the exiled subjecthood is thus simultaneously linked to her passage into heterosexual womanhood. The act of making her breasts less visible works on two levels: it attempts to conceal Ewa's changing body as she is taught how to be a woman, a marginalized position in any case; and it claims the assigned marginal position that she is expected to occupy as a foreign body.

The schooling of Ewa's proper subjecthood shows us that in order to be embraced by a new culture, she first needs to have the right kind of body, one that is not too ostentatious or noticeable, but merely agreeable and aesthetically pleasing. The fact that she hopes to "fend off the threatening others" with her receded breasts also tells us an untold story: this cultural transformation is not just about glorious improvement that will ease her entrance into the social stratum, as her benefactors would like her to believe, but also about the reduction of Ewa's body to the standardized form of an assimilated immigrant.

One of the most memorable moments of such a reduction happens shortly after the family's arrival in Canada. Ewa and her younger sister, Alinka, enter the school that provides classes in English for newcomers. They both are assigned new names, new immigrant identities that will be recognizable and translatable within their new English-speaking community. This quick and unsentimental baptism is performed by the English teacher and their Canadian benefactor, Mr. Rosenberg. Ewa's new given name is Eva. The irony of this linguistic transformation is that both names sound exactly the same in both languages, but the change is necessary because the Polish "w" (pronounced as the English "v") does not produce the same utterance in English. Thus, the first moment of translation happens on the intimate level of a letter, on the surface of one seemingly minute sign that nevertheless has a profound effect on Ewa's consciousness:

> We make our way to a bench at the back of the room; nothing much has happened, except a small, seismic mental shift. The twist in our names takes them a tiny distance from us—but it's a gap into which the infinite hobgoblin of abstraction enters. Our Polish names didn't refer to us; they were as surely us as our eyes or hands. These new appellations, which we ourselves can't yet pronounce, are not us. They are identification tags, disembodied signs pointing to objects that happen to be my sister and myself. We walk to our seats, into a roomful of unknown faces, with names that make us strangers to ourselves. (105)

The very first act of translation, or triangulation as she eventually calls it, is actually performed not by the narrator but by the people around her. It is she who needs to be translated first into the English word, the new signifier, that will make her readable. But what for those around her is a convenient and quite simple act, for the narrator it is a "seismic mental shift," a thrust into painful abstraction. The physical dislocation marked by exile is strengthened by the uprooting of her identity that, at this point in her life, she associates with her Polish name. The new identity—Eva—is a "disembodied sign" because it does not implicate the body; it is just an identification tag, marking the traditional gesture of assimilation.

This moment also undercuts the conventional dynamic of assimilation. Instead of taking and accepting the new name with the eagerness and fervor that would mark her passage into an American identity, Ewa feels like a stranger, not just in relation to the surrounding culture but also to herself. She is now not merely an other situated on the cultural margin but also an other to herself—doubly displaced. The first displacement is a more traditional one: she is an exile thrust into an unknown cultural landscape, an uprooted immigrant whose grounds of stable references have been shifted. The second displacement is more elusive, more perplexing. How does one become a stranger to oneself?[4] Because her new identity indicated by the name Eva has no bodily connection for her, she reads it as an empty sign. This translation of Ewa, which is really about translating her subjecthood, presumes, on the one hand, that she is "empty" and indeed has no subject position within the new cultural space. On the other hand, Ewa already occupies a place of exile that needs to be reconfigured so that she can be assimilated into the English-speaking community. Although she instinctively resists assimilation at first, by the end of the section "The New World," she no longer rejects the process of assimilation but instead reimagines it: "But if I'm to achieve this [translate oneself] without being assimilated—that is, absorbed—by my new world, the translation needs to be careful, the turns of psyche unforced" (211).

This ritual of identity formation speaks about the fact that the process of translation is not unidirectional. It is not just the newcomer who translates what is around herself; the culture in which the exile is placed performs the act of translation as well. Following Ewa/Eva's story, we see that this act is not only bidirectional but in fact tridirectional since the narrator needs to translate herself to herself. To complicate this process even further, the narrator also challenges an understanding of "otherhood" that appears triangulated here as the process of translation itself:

> But mostly, the problem is that the signifier has become severed from the signified. The words I learn now don't stand for things in the same unquestioned way they did in my native tongue. "River" in Polish was a vital sound, energized with the essence of riverhood, of my rivers, of my being immersed in rivers. "River" in English is cold—a word without an aura. It has no accumulated associations for me, and it does not give off the radiating haze of connotation. It does not evoke.

Ewa already knows the English word "river," and she understands which Polish word it corresponds to. She performs the literal translation well. But the process of translation does not end there. Clearly, she does not feel the word and the concept it is supposed to connote. The meaning of native, familiar words rests in her body; she experiences various degrees of signification with familiarity and ease. "River" in Polish is a vibrant sound that implicates her being as she imagines herself plunged into waters. "River" in English appears to Ewa as an other, ungraspable concept: "The river before me remains a thing, absolutely other, absolutely unbending to the grasp of my mind" (106). The imagined familiarity of rivers has been uprooted for Eva.

Thus, the triangulated concept of "otherhood" further complicates the process of translation. Traditionally, it is the foreigner who with her culture and linguistic baggage is perceived as an other in relation to a culture that she enters. The new culture, in this case both Canada and the United States, usually does not think of itself in these terms. Foreigners are outsiders who enter the inside of a cultural structure, threatening to contaminate its space with their otherness. Their strangeness is usually provisionally accepted as long as the foreigner is eager to undergo the smoothing out of her differences so that she fits within the already existing normative identity. In Ewa's case, both her translation into "Eva" and the alteration of her body smooth out her Polish-Jewish otherness. Ewa's body is figured here as a space that needs to be covered with an imaginary Canadian uniform, sewn for her by her patrons, that will match her new identity. This process of erasing difference may be hard to resist, as is the case with Ewa, because it is not quick and overt but subtle and ongoing.

The homogenization that threatens Ewa raises the question of the contamination by otherhood that the dominant culture fears. This contamination is not only the newcomer's foreign language, customs, traditions, and beliefs. More important, it is also the threat of the disruption of a supposedly clear cultural identity that the newcomer presents because she comes from a different cultural space. The normative model of cultural identity is the privileged model that the dominant culture guards, projecting this identity as homogenic and stable. The Polish-Canadian community that Ewa's family enters in Vancouver presumably already belongs to the dominant culture. In this community, the goal of moving from the status of an outsider to the position of a subject that can be taken in and approved of is perceived as indispensable for the well-being of immigrants. The idea that one may wish to resist this process and refuse its dynamic does not even register in the community Ewa's family encounters.

As Ewa reads the Polish-Jewish community in Vancouver, she sees how immigrants attempt to fend off the possibility of being perceived as subjects of contamination through their obsessive desire to promote themselves as clean. The perfectly manicured lawns and "meticulously made up" (140) attires serve only as manifestations of their immigrant appropriateness: "Sitting upright in their cars, in their immaculately pressed dresses, keeping their houses *more spotlessly neat than the natives*, they say to each other, 'I'm fine, everything is fine,' and they almost believe that they are" (143; emphasis mine). These newcomers hope to appear neat and tidy, worthy of acceptance. This fixation on cleanliness does not solely refer to their physical appearance and to their houses. For to be clean also means to be the proper "I" that fits within the preconceived orderliness of middle-class conventions. If we read the connotations of "contamination" closely, we can see that "to contaminate" suggests to bring in dirt, to pollute the tidily organized social structure.[5] Thus, the desire to manifest subjecthood as clean, even cleaner than that of the natives, is dictated not by the fact that immigrants need to prove themselves to be better than the natives, but rather by the idea that the mere status of the native supposedly grants protection against rejection from the established social realm.

In relation to contamination, it is significant that foreigners are usually allowed, even encouraged, to practice their own belief systems in the domestic sphere. Such a cultural dynamic creates the pretense that it is possible to have a genuinely multicultural society as long as these other cultures do not disrupt the already preconceived normative national identity. To be allowed to express one's otherhood only at home implies that even though a foreigner is permitted to practice her other identity at the private level, she understands that in public her "I" needs to conform to the rule of the norm. Ultimately, in order to control the threat of unsettling the uniform "I," the culture creates various coercive mechanisms that pull the foreigner toward homogenization. Either the outsider is willing to assimilate and cut off her previous selfhood or, if she resists this process, the label of foreignness brands her so that she cannot be easily taken in. As Ewa stresses her position between the past and the present, outside and inside, she not only complicates and subverts this understanding of foreignness but also explodes this binary way of comprehending the foreigner.

NARRATIVE GESTURES OF CONTAMINATION: IMMIGRANT RAGE

By frustrating the binary understanding of assimilation, Ewa, metaphorically, does contaminate the new cultural space in a variety of ways. First, her narrative unconventionally locates "Paradise" in Poland. This formal organization of the text is, of course, highly ironic given the fact that historically both the United States and Canada figure in immigrant imagination as lands of opportunity for a new beginning, as paradise for the newcomers. Moreover, "America" has always been proud of its status as the land of the new, a culmination of newcomers' dreams, the promised land that shelters the exiles. This status marks the United States as primary in the Western first world.

Ewa's writing Poland as "Paradise" is not simply a reversal of the established model. Rather, she reveals the need to question uncritical assumptions about these geopolitical divisions and suggests that the immigrant imagination is not necessarily uniform. Even though the picture she paints of her Poland is grim and hardly inviting, Ewa, upon exile, feels that she has been "pushed out of the happy, safe enclosures of Eden" (5). For her, this feeling of being catapulted out of comfortable familiarity is reinforced by the lack of a map with which she can imaginatively chart and visualize herself in a new world: "But I have no map or model in my mind as I stand at the railing disconsolately" (95). Not only the fear of the unknown destabilizes Ewa's "I" upon leaving, but also the fact that for her, exile means the end of her childhood narrative. However, the story of her childhood is not necessarily idealized as a carefree and rosy existence:

> The wonder is what you can make a paradise out of.... I grew up in a lumpen apartment in Cracow, squeezed into three rudimentary rooms with four other people, surrounded by squabbles, dark political rumblings, memories of wartime suffering, and daily struggle of existence. (5)

Even as an adolescent girl, Ewa is quite aware of the daily turmoil her family experiences. She registers the specific tension of what it means to be Jewish in postwar Poland, and she perceives the "daily struggle of existence" that affects both her Jewish and Polish friends. Moreover, Ewa's childhood narrative must be read in the context of the legacy of the Holocaust that looms over the entire country and shapes the dynamic of life in communist Poland.

Another narrative gesture of textual contamination is figured through Ewa's angry critical voice when she becomes a successful student at Harvard and in the end a vigorous professional writer, a New York intellectual. This is especially visible in her concept of immigrant rage, which she introduces toward the end of "The New World" section: "Much of the time, I'm in a rage. Immigrant rage, I call it, and it can erupt at any moment, and at seemingly minuscule provocation" (203). The transgressive force of this concept lies in the idea that a foreigner is not supposed to be openly angry, especially if she is lucky to receive the best education this country can offer. The two concepts—immigrant and rage—seem to be mutually exclusive. In fact, the inflammatory anti-immigrant discourse tells us that the mode of rage belongs exclusively to rightful citizens who continue to worry about the effects of immigrant contamination of this land and vehemently express their moral rage and anxiety aimed at foreigners. What often underlines this rage is the assumed difficulty of guarding the nation's borders from the flood of poor, uneducated, ignorant foreigners who are supposedly only waiting to get their foot in this country's door to drain its social benefits, such as welfare. Such an imagery of immigrants-as-vultures who want to usurp the place for themselves feeds xenophobic feelings and entices lawmakers to create more convoluted and severe immigrant laws.[6]

When the narrator of *Lost in Translation* emphasizes the notion of immigrant rage, she not only claims the right to have passionate, strong feelings like rage, but she also challenges our stereotypical assumptions about foreigners who are supposed to appease the climate of discomfort and fear surrounding immigrants by proving themselves to be subjects worthy of residing in this country. And to show herself virtuous and adequate, an immigrant is supposed to occupy a place of a voiceless subject because, after all, she does not have the natural right to speak up, especially as a cultural critic. To claim rage as an immigrant is an offense and violation of all these common assumptions made about foreigners. Moreover, the rage that Ewa expresses alters its tone and does not stay static. This rage is once directed at "'the Culture'—that weird artifice I'm imprisoned in—and at my closest friends. Or rather, it's directed at the culture-in-my-friends" (203). More important, it seems to be a rage at her own hybrid position as a foreign body:

> As for me, I want to figure out more urgently than before, where I belong in this America that's made up of so many sub-Americas. *I want, somehow, to give up the condition of being a foreigner.* I no longer want to tell people quaint stories from the Old Country, I don't want to be told that "exotic is erotic," or that I have Eastern European intensity, or brooding Galician eyes. I no longer want to be propelled by immigrant chutzpah or desperado energy or usurper's ambition. I no longer want to have the prickly, unrelenting consciousness that I'm living in the medium of a specific culture. (202; emphasis mine)

Ewa's battle with her own "I" is more difficult to win than the sophisticated arguments she has with her friends about, for example, "the subjection to collective ideology" or "bitter reflections on American individualism" (203). Her own struggle with the brand of "foreignness" is especially important because, even though she cannot simply erase "the condition of being a foreigner," she again draws our attention to the persistent feeling of heaviness that accompanies this condition.

In the above passage she rages against the romanticized notion of the foreigner, the exotic-erotic link that aestheticizes the foreigner's bodily self as a desirable, imported object who can entertain the English-speaking audience with "quaint stories." In a sense, *Lost in Translation* may itself be deemed such a quaint story told by a Polish-Jewish foreigner who wishes to reject her foreignness for a comfortable position of her new "I" in the promised land. I argue that despite Ewa's momentary desire to dissect her subject position as a foreign "I" and to give up "the prickly, unrelenting consciousness," she cannot cancel her hybrid self and lift the sensation of heaviness from her being. And even though she may be propelled by a justified longing to figure out where she really belongs, she remains till the end of the narrative in the space of quivering: "Of course, one of the shards sticking in my ribs suggests that maybe I'll never belong comfortably anyplace, that my sensibilities and opinions will always be stuck in some betwixt and between place" (216). Here Ewa again uses bodily imagery as a site of knowledge that foregrounds her shifting "I." The "shards sticking in [her] ribs" are a metaphor for a sense of her flesh being torn and fragmented, rather than unified and closed off to any permutation. Thus, the place "betwixt and between" is not some idealized moment of suspension, but rather a both painful and pleasurable, daunting and empowering lived experience.

In scrutinizing her place of quivering, Ewa does not, however, glamorize her own subject position as unique and singular. After all, she notes that "dislocation is the norm rather than the aberration in our time" (274), and "like everybody else, I am the sum of my languages" (273). But as she makes this statement in which she points to some shared cultural commonalities in postmodern times, she does not deny the specificity of her "I." As she gives us a sense of her hybrid self oscillating in the in-between space between different "I's"—past and present, Polish-Jewish and American—and between Polish and English linguistic systems, we see that, as she writes, "the gap cannot be fully closed" (274). When Ewa says that "the fissures sometimes cause me pain, but in a way, they're how I know that I'm alive," she points to the cultural cracks that mark an exiled "I" (273). Yet these fissures that cause pain give both vitality to her being and an awareness that the meaning of one's self is constantly under cultural negotiation: "Because I have learned the relativity of cultural meanings on my skin, I can never take any one set of meanings as final" (275).

Once again the narrator lets us know that the bodily self is not a coherent whole outside language and culture but a lived material and cultural construct "written in a variety of languages" (275). The insistent tie between cultural meanings and the skin implicates the idea that meaning is not produced by professional linguists in some abstract realm of dictionaries and encyclopedias but instead is always mediated through our material selves. Even the language of passion and love that we perhaps deem most intimate is not universal:

> In English, "man" and "woman" were empty signs; terms of endearment came out as formal and foursquare as other words. In that neutral and neutered speech, words were neither masculine nor feminine; they did not arise out of erotic substance, out of sex. How could I say "darling," or "sweetheart," *when the words had no fleshly fullness, when they were as dry as sticks*? (245; emphasis mine)

Ewa, of course, can say "darling" or "sweetheart," but in order for these concepts to carry erotic meaning, to "arise out of [her] erotic substance," they need to acquire "fleshly fullness." It is not enough to learn the word and to know its meanings and cultural connotations. At this level of knowing, her words are "as dry as sticks," concepts that she can clearly use but which have no power to speak her "erotic substance." On this level she cannot speak her erotic "I," and the language of desire is merely painted through an imagery of dryness, stasis, and the ascetic feeling of words.

The moment Ewa writes that "the language has entered my body, has incorporated itself in the softest tissue of my being," we see that the movement of words from "dry sticks" to their erotic "fleshly fullness" is a process, a journey of bodily translation through the meanders of culture and its symbolic systems that register on her skin: "'Darling,' I say to my lover, 'my dear,' and the words are filled and brimming with the motions of my desire; they curve themselves within my mouth to the complex music of tenderness" (245). This passage quite vividly articulates the "fleshly fullness" of words that Ewa was yearning for. The concept of fullness may seem problematic because on one level we may understand her desire for linguistic fullness as a desire for absolute meaning that an exile hopes to reach. But Ewa has already thwarted such an interpretation by indicating that she "learned the relativity of cultural meanings on [her] skin." Rather, her desire for "fleshly fullness" is figured here as a yearning for bodily feeling the language, for an intimate connection with meaning that goes beyond the knowledge of words listed in dictionaries. The physical movement of words entering the bloodstream that Ewa visualizes earlier may be read as an image that allows her mouth to "brim with the motions of desire."

QUIVERING "I": THE TRANSLATING BORDER

In locating *Lost in Translation* as a transnational narrative of exile that validates the critical importance of the in-between space by foregrounding the "quivering I" of the Polish-Jewish-American narrator, it is important to hear Ewa's voice in its specificity. When she writes, "I am a Jew, an immigrant, half-Pole, half-American.... I suffer from certain syndromes because I was fed on stories of the war" (198), she points to the position of transnational exiled subjects who come from the second world (198). This focus not only complicates the transcultural debates as it destabilizes the binary opposition between the West and the third world, but as we see in Ewa's critical reading of Canadian and American cultures, it also questions the very construction and numbering of these worlds. The textual complexity of *Lost in Translation* is underpinned by Ewa's journey of exile from communist, post-Holocaust Poland to her "life in a new language." Even by the end of the narrative, we are again reminded of the narrator's specific cultural location: "Does it still matter . . . that my version of reality was formed in Eastern Europe?" (211).

This question, in an important way, compels us to consider Ewa's quivering sense of being as precarious. Her subject position is threatening because it works to disrupt the privileged ontological status of the Western subject that still would like to write itself, Kristeva says, as "unitary and glorious" (1991, 2). At the same time, however, the narrator's quivering "I" is in danger because the lack of her presupposed stable identity leaves Ewa in a vulnerable cultural position. Although we see her as a critic of culture expressing such transgressive passions as immigrant rage, her uncertain position is marked by the continual danger of losing her voice (or a location within the symbolic structures) before she can even claim to have one. In fact, at the close of the narrative her voice—an expression of agency—"is still a highly unreliable instrument." She writes that "at the oddest moments, it betrays me, buckles, rasps, refuses to go on. It plays only in flat, shallow registers, and sometimes I literally cannot find it" (217). We see how Ewa's voice is more than an instrument of speech; it reveals itself as a medium of the possibility of being in the world with agency and passion. Feeling her way through the linguistic texture of her second language, the quivering of her voice makes her hyperaware of her shifting position in language as a medium.

Ewa expresses this concern when she writes that "perhaps I'm not quite equal to the challenge of postmodern uncertainty." She does not refuse the notion of postmodern uncertainty but rather suggests that we come to recognize and live it in different ways:

> It is well known that the System over there [in Eastern Europe], by specializing in deceit, has bred in its citizens an avid hunger for what they still quaintly call the truth. Of course, the truth is easier to identify when it's simply the opposite of a lie. So much Eastern European thinking moves along the axis of bipolar ideas, still untouched by the peculiar edginess and fluidity created by a more decentered world. (211)

Here we read the narrator's concern with an uncritically celebratory mode in which some embrace the postmodern critique of the subject without recognizing the specific cultural location of the speaking "I."[7] Ewa's illusive search for a center in a decentered world takes on a poignant tone if we remember the history of her Polish-Jewish "I." However, *Lost in Translation* is also a critique of a privileged Western subject that obsessively guards the borders of its "natural I." What seems to bridge the gap between the radical political tone of the text and its often surfacing impulses of the narrator to anchor herself is the emphasis on the task of translation as the mediating factor in this nuanced narrative.

To elucidate her complex position, Ewa draws on Theodor Adorno, who "warned his fellow refugees that if they lost their alienation, they'd lose their souls" (209). Even though Ewa understands and lives this warning, she also sees the difference between her own and Adorno's positions. She doubts that "Adorno could have maintained [his idea of alienation] over a lifetime without the hope of returning home" (209). For Ewa there is no one home for which she can yearn and hope. Even though she maintains her ties with Poland and her Polish friends, her Polish-Jewish "I" belongs to the narrative of her childhood. On the other hand, her "life in a new language," between Vancouver where her parents live and New York where she finds a place for herself, is more fluid, without one stable location that she can simply call home. The concern peculiar to her situation centers on finding a balance between sustaining her specificity without losing her soul. It is a complex and shifting dance between being a cultural critic with a dynamic voice and finding a place from which she can speak and write her quivering "I" without having it invalidated. In other words, it is a balance between fitting and simultaneously not fitting within the realm of a Western social stratum:

> The soul can shrivel from an excess of critical distance, and if I don't want to remain in *arid internal exile* for the rest of my life, I have to find a way to lose my alienation without losing myself. But how does one bend toward another culture without falling over, how does one strike an elastic balance between rigidity and self-effacement? How does one stop reading the exterior signs of a foreign tribe and step into inwardness, the viscera of their meaning? Every anthropologist understands the difficulty of such a feat; and so does every immigrant. (209; emphasis mine)

Of course, there is no single definitive answer to Ewa's questions regarding living "the difficulty of such a feat." But these questions are crucial for pondering the notion of immigrant meaning that is always locked within the dialectical space of translation. We see that while Ewa does not want to lose her critical eye, she also wants to be able to mobilize the condition of an "arid internal exile." As I have discussed, it does not mean that she wants to find a comfortable place for her "I." After all, she is the hybrid, the "I" of the border who lives the process of translation as an ongoing encounter with the production of meaning. It is this encounter that provides the challenge of living her "bifocal vision" through the triangulated process of translation: "We are called upon to travel so far beyond our borders. These borders are not only literal geopolitical boundaries but also physical and metaphorical 'borders of our skin'" (213). To live the body in translation often means to question the familiar borders of our materiality.

As Hoffman's narrative shows, to be "lost in translation" does not necessarily suggest the mode of mourning for that which is gone and cannot be regained. Rather, to be "lost in translation" as an exiled "I" is about both losing and gaining meaning; it is about quivering on the translating border while paradoxically and painstakingly carrying oneself across.

Monsieur Trelkovsky (Roman Polanski) "becoming" Simone Choule in *The Tenant*. Courtesy of British Film Institute.

4

CLAUSTROPHOBIC EXILE: *THE TENANT* AND OSTRACIZING LOGICS OF DIFFERENCE

> The flesh is intrinsic to the cinematic apparatus, at once its subject, its substance, and its limits.
>
> —Steven Shaviro, *The Cinematic Body*

> These women have the most beautiful music; the glitter of spotlights is theirs. Adoration and sublimation, a formidable love that must forever be conquered and danger that is absolute are theirs. And the act of falling, the final gesture is theirs as well—and the voice in its death agony. When the men die or are defeated, it is because they have some unremarked traits deriving from a femininity unerringly detected by the opera. The ones defeated are the weak sons, the lame, the hunchbacks, the blacks, the foreigners, and the old men—those who are like women. The triumphant ones are the fathers, the kings, the uncles, the lovers. . . . The defeated are the forces of the night, the forces of darkness, the forces of the weak and underprivileged.
>
> —Catherine Clément, *Opera, or The Undoing of Women*

Roman Polanski's films have fascinated and provoked viewers and critics since his first film études such as *Teethful Smile* (1957), the award-winning *Two Men and a Wardrobe* (1958), and his graduate film, *When Angels Fall* (1959).[1] Even though these short films were only student productions, they attracted attention as intriguing and original cinematic experiments, quite stunning and provocative in the artistic landscape of postwar communist Poland. It is interesting, for example, that while Polanski's feature debut, *Knife in the Water* (1962), garnered several prestigious awards in the West, including the very first Polish Oscar nomination in 1963, Polish critics in communist Poland hailed the film as incomprehensible, posturing, or even outright dangerous. This is how one of the film theorists writes about the reception of the film in Poland: "Because the film was considered an attack on the established social norms, it had to be denounced to protect the ideological principles it threatened. The critics reprimanded the depiction of characters and the portrayed reality as well as the main issue of the film, foreign influences, and the representation of a young generation."[2]

The unnerving content displayed in Polanski's first feature film, its assault on conventional cinematic vision, and his own experience of exile seem to permeate almost all his work. His internationally produced films, such as *Repulsion* (1965), *Rosemary's Baby* (1968), *The Tragedy of Macbeth* (1971), *The Tenant* (1976), and *Death and the Maiden* (1994), have established his artistic reputation and, perhaps more important, articulated the cinematic fascination not necessarily with sensationalized violence but with the terror of a more subtly poignant nature: the horror of enclosed spaces that create an intense mood of claustrophobia. Even though Polanski himself has always refused to discuss the connection between his personal experiences and his films, thus allowing the viewers to treat his films as cinematic texts open to interpretation, critics have consistently noted the correlation between his childhood history as a Jew during the Nazi occupation of his native Poland and his films' acute preoccupation with self-contained spaces, which seem to evoke the Holocaust ghetto experience.[3]

This chapter focuses on *The Tenant*, a cinematic text that is largely unknown and untheorized, even though Polanski's other films have received considerable critical attention.[4] I argue that *The Tenant* is a cinematic narrative of exile, which allows us to analyze this film as a passionate critique of phobic nationalism and the obsessive desire to guard national borders against strangers-foreigners, coded as undesirable intruders and stigmatized as others. I read *The Tenant* as a filmic narrative of abjection by focusing on two critical moments in the film: the screams that open and close the narrative sequence. Drawing on Julia Kristeva's notion of the abject—"the in-between, the ambiguous, the composite"—I examine the positions of two important figures in the text: a second world foreigner-exile and a ghostly lesbian, both abjected by the community in which they live (Kristeva 1982, 4). By investigating this repudiated location of abjection, I inspect *The Tenant* as a film that dissects distinctly different mechanisms of abjecting both "strangers"—the foreigner and the lesbian—to disclose the phobic model of community, which coheres and "cleans" itself through expelling the bodies of others. I also draw on Catherine Clément's argument about the historical representation of women and other "others" in opera who are always condemned to die "operatic deaths." Since I argue that the protagonist performs such an operatic death, Clément's point about the expulsion of historically borderline subjects beyond the privileged realm of signification is especially important to my study.

What is particularly arresting in *The Tenant* is the cinematic employment of tight, restrained spaces—the claustrophobically restricted mise-en-scène—which envelops the figure of the foreigner and represents and comments on the very position of exile. If we treat *The Tenant* as a narrative preoccupied with the cinematic expression of exile and the meaning of being foreign, we may begin to see that the formal experiment of situating the story in a tightly composed and closed space is not merely a stylistic exercise in aesthetic expression. Rather, the insistence on creating and sustaining the claustrophobic horror of stifling space becomes a way to express the painful suffocation created by social oppression and ostracism that the foreigner endures in a new culture. In the film, the apartment itself is not a static place of comfort that we might associate with the idea of home; in an eerie way, it becomes an almost living organism that envelops, tortures, and consumes the protagonist. This ravaging sense of torture, heightened by the paranoid surveillance by neighbors-informers and the protagonist's desire to hide from the never-ending oppressive and destructive scrutiny of others, especially in the context of Polanski's life in the ghetto, evoke the politics of abjection under the Holocaust. Furthermore, the film's emphasis on the dynamics of denunciation, voyeurism, inspection, and continual suspicion might be interpreted as a commentary on French xenophobia and the anti-Semitism that prompted French collaboration in the deportation of Jewish neighbors during the Nazi occupation.

If we accept this interpretation, we may see how *The Tenant* and other Polanski films, most interestingly *Death and the Maiden* and *Repulsion,* reinvent, or reconfigure, the horror genre. The horror that permeates the visual universe of *The Tenant* and his other films often seems to rest in the human eye, in the vision itself, rather than in the creation of formidable monsters whose images abound in many classical horror films. Already in *Repulsion*, we see experiments with the employment of and focus on the "screen eye" that arrests viewers with its intensity (Clover 1992, 166–67). The opening of the film offers no traditional establishing shot that would readily help the spectator understand the spatial or temporal relations of the narrative. We see only a close-up of a human eye. Curiously, the credits and the big sign "Repulsion" roll diagonally out of the eye, coming from under the eyelid. At first, the eye is static, but eventually, it slowly starts to move, looking around. Finally, within the same shot, the spectator's curiosity is satisfied through an emerging close-up of the female face, which is revealed as the possessor of the eye's gaze.

Repulsion opens with the intense image of a female eye; the narrative of *The Tenant* ends with the shot of the male foreigner's moving eye, desperately trying to see how he is perceived by others. As in *Repulsion,* this eye demands its right to see, its right to vision. The final image, guided by the subjective point of view of this eye, offers as an answer only the ominous darkness of the foreigner's screaming mouth. The depiction of the moving eye and the sound of the scream become a stylistic means by which this cinematic text tries to engage the social struggle of people positioned on the cultural margins. Here, given the figure of the foreigner, the screen eye becomes a foreign eye: one that defamiliarizes vision itself and forces the viewers to become foreign as they perform an act of identification with the protagonist.

The Tenant, which takes the form of art-cinema narration, tells the story of Monsieur Trelkovsky (Roman Polanski)—a Polish immigrant in France—who moves into a Parisian apartment that belonged to a lesbian, Egyptologist Simone Choule. Simone's suicidal leap from the window of her apartment functions as an arresting point of entry into the film's narrative. Captivated by the information that Simone is still alive in a hospital, Trelkovsky visits her just before she dies, and while he is there, he witnesses her horrifying scream whose *sound-image* terrifies and haunts his sensibility. Although her tightly bandaged body, barely human at this point, features only a darkened eye socket and the gaping hole of her mouth, it insists that it is alive and marks that insistence by a scream. Even after we learn that she has died, her scream becomes an unforgettable expression of a fragile boundary between still living and almost dead. Thus, the scream marks Simone's position—an unthinkable site of being neither fully alive nor fully dead.

The enigma of her death puzzles and unsettles Trelkovsky, as haunting signifiers of Simone's being slowly invade his own subjectivity to the point that he "becomes" her. We watch him gradually slipping into insanity; he moves from a mere fascination with Simone's clothing and the cosmetics he finds in the apartment to the active appropriation of her possessions that eventually destroys him. In an important narrative complication, we learn that *him-becoming-her* is not entirely locked within the sphere of his hallucination, for other characters in his apartment building obsessively insist on identifying him with Simone as well. Eventually, like Simone, Trelkovsky throws himself out the window, and the film's closure features his scream, which evokes Simone's last uncanny howl.

The film's plot coheres around Trelkovsky, who is figured both as an agent and as the anticipated psychological subject of the narrative. However, his metamorphosis, his character-in-process, and his final "splitting" call into question the notion of a unified, coherent subject posited by the narrative of psychological realism. The destabilization of the securely positioned rational subject frustrates the traditional narrative order and space that we ordinarily conceive as knowable. The process of defamiliarizing conventional narrative practices is also visible in the disruption of the boundaries of genre as the film plays off the horror film, drama, ghost story, and tragicomedy. Because of the permeability of genre borders, the narrative of *The Tenant* is remarkably demanding in asking the viewer to make sense out of multiple narrative ambivalences, episodic series of events, disjunctions in temporal order, and narrative contingencies. Commenting on art cinema in general, David Bordwell suggests that the very construction of film art depends on questioning the classical mode of telling the story:

> Like classical narration, art film narration poses questions that guide us in fitting material into an ongoing structure. But these questions do not simply involve causal links among fabula events.... In the art film... the very construction of the narration becomes the object of spectator hypotheses: how is the story being told? *why tell the story in this way*? (1985, 210; my emphasis)

This question seems especially significant for analyzing *The Tenant* because answering it allows us to assess the ideological weight of the film's narrative design. One way to understand this narrative complexity may be through conceptualizing *The Tenant* as the cinematic narrative of abjection and its foregrounded difficulty of reading the position of the foreigner-stranger.[5] Thus, in an effort to represent the abject—an unwanted wavering of being that is readily pushed into the abyss of nonbeing in an attempt to construct a clean and coherent "I"—the film calls for a reading of the site of the abjection—the foreigner's body. While challenging dominant concepts of the "I"/non-"I" dualism, the film invites viewers to read the way the foreign body speaks the injustice it encounters.

Consequently, rather than proposing the usual abstraction or erasure of the abjected flesh, the film insists on performing a difficult process of reading a specific abjected body. The narrative impulse to de-aestheticize and read this body in pain is visible in the final sequence that features the protagonist's last scream after his operatic suicide. The focus on Trelkovsky's final scream shows that the anguish of the screaming body needs to be addressed as a social commentary on pain that refuses to separate aesthetic and political realms. By analyzing the scream closely, we may probe the subversive energy of the abject, which works on several levels simultaneously: it points to the fragility of the symbolic order and its anxiety to construct and reconstruct itself through the logic of purity; it helps to desublimate the flesh, that is, to save it from the aesthetic of the sublime and its transcendence of materiality; it examines the specific structures of oppression that produce abjection, while, concurrently, it underpins the way in which abjection—what falls outside the privileged system of order—gives space for an articulation of oppression.[6]

Kristeva, who describes the abject as the "jettisoned object" placed in opposition to the "I," conceptualizes it as a third category that complicates or blurs the boundaries between the traditional subject/object division (1982, 2). In fact, it may be useful to consider the abject as a porous bar—a wavering slash—between subject and object that destabilizes this conventional split. Given the fact that Trelkovsky, a somewhat shy and lonely foreigner, is continually confronted with a hostile, aggressive, and xenophobic community, we may look at his scream as the expression of abjection. The scream—not quite language and not quite not-language—quivers on the border of intelligibility. In other words, Trelkovsky-as-abject wavers between being and not being a culturally sanctioned "I," thus questioning the construction of the privileged subject itself. His scream may thus be conceptualized as a poignant articulation of this quivering: to scream implies voicing the impossible position between life and death, being and not being, the heterosexual and the homosexual, and he and she. The link between different gender positions is especially significant because, especially in the last moments of the film, Trelkovsky's abjection is signified through the poignant image of ejection of his cross-dressed, cross-gendered body (literally out the window, and metaphorically outside the privileged realm of signification). This foreign body, heavily painted through excessively vulgar makeup, resembling a stereotypical prostitute, unmistakenly evokes the scandal of the suicidal spectacle of a fallen woman.

Thus, the closure of *The Tenant* offers perhaps one of the most extravagantly remarkable suicide scenes in the history of art cinema. Trelkovsky, a foreigner in Parisian middle-class society, dressed as a woman, dies in a way that resonates with the way prima donnas die in the world of opera. The whole apartment building is transformed into a theatrical mise-en-scène overpowered by the surrounding color of redness. The courtyard washed in red not only signifies the ambience of opera but, more importantly, foreshadows the bleeding body of the protagonist. The balconies become opera booths; the ordinary tenants become opera spectators looking at the suicidal spectacle through opera glasses, cheering the performer before his self-destructive leap. In an unnerving way, this spectacle is enacted twice, dramatizing the foreigner's exile and the spectacle of the dying female body. After his first jump, the performer is still alive. Through his subjective point of view, we witness the grotesque figures of the tenants-viewers, whose bodies seem deformed and demonized. Through his eyes, we watch their snake-like-tongues that seem to condemn him once again. When, while jumping, he cries, "I am not Simone Choule! I am Trelkovsky!" we see his final struggle to affirm his "damned" identity.

Operatic Suicide: Expelling the Foreign Body

In *Opera, or The Undoing of Women*, Clément looks critically at the realm of opera as a product of bourgeois culture, an argument that helps examine the ideological weight of Trelkovsky's operatic suicide. Refusing to separate art from ideology, Clément demystifies opera as a signifying practice historically situated on the pedestal of high culture that insists on the continual spectacle of women dying operatic deaths. Importantly for my reading, she also suggests that opera features not only the death of women but also the dying of "those who are like women," i.e., "the weak and underprivileged" (1988, 22). The sentenced-to-death underprivileged foreign body necessarily needs to be expelled from the narrative so that the traditional telos can neatly seal the closure, allowing the Parisian community to come together again, intact and undisturbed. Since Trelkovsky's feminized death clearly evokes the unrepresented death of Simone, the lesbian whose apartment he takes over after her unexplained suicide, the examination of his death—the final act of abjection—becomes especially important.

Traditionally, when the punished woman or an underprivileged other who takes her place dies in the opera, we do not hear their voices beyond the death scene. The final aria *is* their last moment of speech. The narrative of *The Tenant*, however, allows the abjected body to speak beyond the traditional telos, defying the privileged design of narrative signification and closure. The closing scream is the disruptive moment in the narrative precisely because we hear the voice of the foreigner's body *after* the suicidal spectacle. The only form of language accessible to Trelkovsky is the act of screaming. His screaming body, crying in the darkness and seclusion of the hospital bed, does not lend itself to an uncomplicated act of interpretation. The meaning of the scream and its origins are neither easily knowable nor clearly localizable. Instead, the scream's vibrations upset the narrative design because they undercut the pleasure of an effortless construction of the story. The scream calls into question both the stable position of the spectator and traditional interpretative practices and marks the final dissolution of boundaries between madness/sanity or reality/hallucination. It also blurs the boundaries between a coherent and a fragmented subject and between the visible and the concealed, undermining the spectatorial desire for revelation of the presupposed end of signification and the final disclosure of truth about the protagonist.

In this sense, the screaming body thwarts an easy comprehension of the film's closure. Ultimately, even the spectator familiar with the art-cinema narration must feel puzzled by the ambiguity that does not allow us to say what the scream means. Because the position of Trelkovsky-as-foreigner is continually emphasized throughout the narrative, he himself as an excluded "citizen" occupies the place where "meaning collapses" (Kristeva 1982, 2). Although he owns a French passport and can rightfully proclaim himself a French citizen, he is marked as an alien, a figure that does not quite fit within the community he enters. For example, early in the film, when the police inspector learns about Trelkovsky's Polish ethnicity, he immediately emphasizes Trelkovsky's otherness, hinting that the protagonist does not really belong to the French social structure and its symbolic configurations.[7]

The closing scene comes after Trelkovsky's jump from the window, a jump preceded by a comment by the policeman about "being reasonable." Trelkovsky's body flies from the apartment window into the pit of the courtyard. The next shot offers the hoisted, injured, bandaged body, as if packaged for death. The provocative pools of darkness and their sharp contrast to the constrained body wrapped in white bandages implicate the aesthetic conventions of expressionism, that is, the interest in a poetic and expressive mise-en-scène rather than in telling a story, and the emphasis on mood rather than on plot through the use of expressive camera angles and lighting. These conventions also signify the horror genre, and we may read these marks as a stylistic means to underscore a terror of the social structure that excludes the protagonist on the basis of his ethnic difference.

When the final scene opens with an image of a bandaged body, we can only hypothesize that it is Trelkovsky who, like Simone in the opening of the narrative, is trapped in a hospital bed. Eventually, within the same shot, the spectator's curiosity is satisfied through an emerging close-up of Trelkovsky's mouth and one eye that looks out in horror. The close-up is achieved through a zoom-in that forces us to witness the bloody stains on the bandage, the swollen, open mouth, and the moving eye. The movement of the camera is accompanied by the nondiegetic sound that, as in classical expressionist film, echoes emotional turmoil and horror. The rhythmic pulsation of the sound punctuates the unsettling picture of the body and anticipates its final transgression. Since this music has been repeatedly associated with Simone, its sound functions as her theme, reminding us that even when approaching the closure, the solution to the enigma of Simone's suicide has not been revealed and that the causal gap created by her suicide is not healed. As in the beginning of the film, when Trelkovsky visits Simone in the hospital and is mortified by her dying, we are confronted again with the screaming body. It is through his subjective point of view that we have access to the vision of the moving eye.

Looking through Trelkovsky's frightened eye, we see, as he does from the perspective of his hospital bed, his own figure standing and talking to Simone's friend, Stella (Isabelle Adjani). This is an unusual doubling of vision and almost an explosion of seeing: Trelkovsky looks at Trelkovsky. In other words, Trelkovsky-the-victim carefully scrutinizes Trelkovsky-the-visitor. We are confronted with the dying exile who sees too much, who, in a sense, is blinded by his own acute perception.[8] The eye sees Trelkovsky and Stella engaged in the same dialogue we heard in the opening of the film when they visited dying Simone in the hospital. Thus, when Trelkovsky sees himself talking to Stella, we are offered an ominous moment, clearly reminiscent of the scene when he and Stella stood in shock over Simone's bed. This moment destabilizes the film's closure by confusing the temporal and spatial order of the narrative and by producing two different yet simultaneous subject positions for the protagonist. When Trelkovsky looks at himself addressing his own position, saying, "I hardly know her," his comment marks the radical blurring of boundaries between self and other. When the body finally screams, after Stella has posed a series of questions about recognition and knowing, the camera zooms in and moves us into the darkness of the screaming mouth. The unsettling image of this cinematic intrusion into and penetration of

Stella (Isabelle Adjani) and Trelkovsky after their visit to Simone Choule at the hospital. Courtesy of *Camera Obscura*.

the body creates a vision of the permeability of the borders of the flesh. At this moment we gain access not only to the character's emotional interiority but also, quite literally, to his physical inside. More important, this cinematic move seems to suggest that by performing an act of identification with the protagonist, the presupposed stability of the spectator is threatened as well. The fact that the film offers an identification with a fragmented and tormented subject, whose identity cannot be easily figured, prompts the viewers to "become" foreign themselves.[9]

What does it mean for spectators to experience the condition of foreignness? How does the dynamic of the scream invite this identification? And how does this potential identification undo the supposedly stable position of a spectator? In films constructed according to the Hollywood classical narrative model, the viewers are usually offered an identification with a protagonist-agent who is typically goal-oriented. The hero's goal tends to conflict with the aspirations or actions of other characters, thus creating a conflict that needs to be successfully resolved by the end of the narrative.[10] Even when the Hollywood narrative depicts marginalized groups, the spectators are hardly ever offered an identification with such characters, which allows the viewers to be safely positioned as spectators and does not call into question typical viewing practices. By contrast, in *The Tenant,* through various cinematic techniques such as extreme close-ups and zoom-ins, the spectator is constantly visually tied to the figure of the foreigner. This anchoring of the spectatorial vision works as an unnerving mechanism that does not allow the viewers to dismiss the foreigner's pain. And Trelkovsky's scream, when the dark inside of his mouth becomes the very last image of the film, yet again mobilizes the spectatorial gaze and binds it to the foreigner's flesh.

Given the fact that *The Tenant* uses some features of the horror genre, the representation of the scream does not seem unusual. Typically, horror films thrive on screaming figures, usually female, who, pushed into terror, express their distress or fear in a shriek. In such scenarios, the purpose of showing the scream often works to heighten the narrative tension and to scare the spectators, to make them feel the terror of the frightened character. But in *The Tenant* we are confronted with a different kind of apprehension. Trelkovsky's scream is not so much an expression of fear as an illustration of emotional anguish and frustration at the point of contact between the living and the dead. Confronted with the scream, the viewers are not likely to close their eyes, which often happens when watching horror films. This act of forcing the spectators to shut their eyes—to escape the experience of panic—seems to lie at the heart of the stylistics that guides the horror genre. Usually, the moviegoers perform this act of shutting down vision to flee the images of escalating violence or to avoid the rising tension that precedes a brutal encounter between victim and attacker. Here, because the approaching terror is not created by some easily identifiable external factor (after all, there are no cruel attackers or monsters), we are faced with the notion of violence that comes from *within* the protagonist's vision, violence created by a suffocating sense of escalating surveillance from scrutinizing neighbors. The scream itself—the unruly shrieking body that refuses to be ejected beyond the realm of representation and into oblivion—seems to come from "the edge of nonexistence and hallucination" (Kristeva 1982, 2).

Because of the numerous references in *The Tenant* to the stylistics of expressionism, Trelkovsky's scream also evokes Edvard Munch's 1893 expressionistic painting *The Scream*. Expressionism, which began around 1908 as an avant-garde style in painting and a reaction against nineteenth-century realism, found its most profound manifestation in German cinema.[11] Some of the important cinematic expressions of this aesthetic style—such as the closed-frame composition, which confines and draws the viewer into the world of the story, and the carefully constructed mise-en-scène, which seems to parallel the emotional state of the screen character—inform Polanski's film. Significantly, one of the crucial stylistic achievements of expressionist cinema is the fact that expression itself comes from dual elements: mise-en-scène *and* the human figure. Unlike a classical Hollywood film, in which the self-contained human figure is the most expressive element, in expressionist cinema the human body extends itself into the mise-en-scène to the point that, as in Munch's painting, we cannot quite distinguish between the definite boundary of the screaming body and the surrounding background that envelops the anguished figure.

By recognizing the visual parallel between the screaming foreigner in *The Tenant* and Munch's *The Scream*, which influenced expressionist cinematic aesthetics, it becomes possible to read Trelkovsky's scream as an expression of his desire to fit into the ocular universe of the film, his longing for blending with the surrounding world. In Munch's painting, the scream upsets the traditionally stable background, and the dynamic of the scream seems to vibrate throughout the entire frame. In other words, the mise-en-scène of the painting seems to be screaming as well. Fredric Jameson argues in his reading of *The Scream* that the "gestural content already underscores its own failure, since the realm of the sonorous, the cry, the raw vibrations of the human throat, are incompatible with its medium."[12] In this sense, we can view and hear Trelkovsky's cry, thanks to the cinematic audiovisual expression, as a moment that represents those "raw vibrations of the human throat" that the painting allows us only to imagine.

If *The Scream* can be understood as an anguished expression of the inner self, as an attempt to collapse the border between the inside and the outside in order to expose the emotional reality of the human subject and to dispute the presupposed seamlessness and neatness of the human body, then Trelkovsky's scream foregrounds two elements: his painful rejection beyond the visual universe of the story and, simultaneously, the subversive potential of his scream, which shakes the stability of the visual representation. As in *The Scream*, we see how the mise-en-scène vibrates, haunted by the upsetting shriek, which gives us a sense of the explosion of the human self. Since the darkness of his screaming mouth is the very last moment of the film, *The Tenant* is an open-ended narrative that does not attempt to resolve the explosion performed by the scream itself. We are left on the border of intelligibility and unresolvable tension that forces us to ponder the torment of the screaming protagonist.

Trelkovsky's problem is that his identity differs from that of other characters we encounter in the story. The narrative does not provide any details about his past; we are permitted to know only that he is an immigrant who hopes to

Monsieur Zy (Melvyn Douglas) warns Trelkovsky about too much noise in *The Tenant*. Courtesy of *Camera Obscura*.

find a place for himself in middle-class society. But this search for a space where he can function like any other member of the Parisian community becomes an ongoing struggle since he is barely tolerated as somebody "other." In the very opening of the narrative, as he enters the apartment building where he tries to rent a room, he is attacked and almost bitten by a small but viciously barking dog that belongs to the concierge (Shelley Winters). She treats Trelkovsky with disdain and an air of superiority, and the ferocious dog that keeps snapping at him foreshadows various future attacks the protagonist will encounter: his unpleasant confrontations with the apartment owner, Monsieur Zy, who, knowing that Trelkovsky is foreign, imposes absurd conditions on renting an apartment; daily dealings with his colleagues at work, who often take advantage of his shyness and awkwardness; and his ultimate hallucinatory confrontation with the apartment tenants, who, as opera spectators, will watch his suicidal act with manifest pleasure, pleased that they are finally getting rid of this unwanted intruder.

In a significant way, the narrative also foregrounds the presence of garbage in the apartment building. Many times in the film we watch Trelkovsky carrying trash to the garbage bin, or we repeatedly see other tenants around the garbage bin. Similarly, the narrative emphasizes the watchful presence of other tenants in the bathroom whose window is across from Trelkovsky's, highlighting the expulsion of bodily waste. Thus, the narrative subtly accentuates the process of throwing away waste and disposing of unwanted and dirty trash, drawing our attention to the importance of cleaning the apartment building. Given the fact that by the end of the film Trelkovsky himself feels like a throwaway, a disposable character like Simone for whom there is no space among the rest of the tenants, the narrative seems to underline the parallel between the images of trash and the unwanted presence of the foreigner in the respectable and clean French community.

Being discriminated against, often only in subtle ways, Trelkovsky tries to escape to the supposedly sheltered realm of the domestic space. But in an ironic narrative twist, his apartment comes to life and its out-of-balance, shrinking walls begin to enclose and haunt him. In this claustrophobically restrained space, the protagonist loses his sense of time and space, in a sense even loses himself, and the viewers, too, lose an orderly perception of coherence. Trelkovsky attempts to hide in his apartment, but the domestic instead intensifies the terror he dreads, suggesting that in this community there is no space where he can reside.[13] What we witness here is the curious reversal of the social dynamic. Traditionally, it is society that fears the foreigner and often rejects him or her on the basis of this fear. This fear of and scorn for Trelkovsky as an immigrant are highlighted in the narrative as other characters continually read his figure as clumsy, troublesome, and too different from everybody else. We may understand this anxiety over what is marked as foreign as a fear of an identity that poses a threat to the supposedly already sanctioned "national identity."[14] But in *The Tenant,* although the social phobia is emphasized, it is Trelkovsky who ultimately fears everybody else.

In this sense, the spectatorial identification the film offers with the haunted figure of the foreigner and the claustrophobic space he occupies produces a sense of visual discomfort. And because the foreigner's eye anticipates the eye of the viewer—Trelkovsky's eye and the eye of the spectator are linked through the experience of his terror—we necessarily participate in the endurance of the ocular horror as well. Together with Trelkovsky, we are locked in the apartment that lives and absorbs his identity. The uncannily oppressive aura of his room as an animated space ready to consume him is sharpened by the sound track filled with eerie, foreboding sounds; unexpected, menacing noises; and creepy voices. In short, a sense of ever-present surveillance is expressed as if through aural terror as well, manifested in the film's continual emphasis on overhearing, monitoring, eavesdropping, restrictions on noise-making, and general amplification of diegetic sound.

One may argue that this nauseating feeling of suffocating in the enclosed interior compels the spectators to feel the pressure of social ostracism. Thus, understanding *The Tenant* as an ocular narrative reveals the dialectical relationship: the enacted horror on the screen and that of the spectator who both constructs and reads this cultural phobia, or horror. In other words, as the viewer's perception is arrested by the aural anxiety and bound to the image of the crumbling walls in the protagonist's apartment, the menacing shadows lurking in the corners, and Trelkovsky's own reflection in the mirror as a man-who-becomes-woman, the film challenges stereotypical notions of immigrants who are coded as "others," not like the supposedly uniform "us," the legitimate members of community. In a sense, we, the spectators, watching and viscerally feeling Trelkovsky's slippage into the suicidal abyss, gain a glimpse of how it feels to be "other" in this film.

Kristeva, in her discussion of foreignness, is involved in reinterpreting the figure of the foreigner in order to reenvision contemporary social communities as dynamic sites that do not ostracize or flatten heterogeneity, rather than as closed, self-contained entities. She scrutinizes "the absorption of otherness proposed by our societies" and probes the question of living with others "*as others, without ostracism but also without leveling.*" The analysis of the figure of the foreigner, she claims, which "turns [the homogenized] 'we' into a problem" appears crucial for confronting both xenophobia and the assimilation that works to produce uniformity in the name of cultural sameness. The foreigner, she suggests, the exile—historically perceived as a stranger, the other, or the enemy "responsible for all the ills of the polis"—already lives *within* the "I," an insight that is an invitation to a new epistemological model that does not lead either to the homogenization of foreignness or its abjection. This model insistently questions the privileged ontological status of the subject who likes to write itself as, she says, "unitary and glorious," while burying its incoherences and "strangenesses" (1991, 2, 1).

Such an understanding of the foreigner may help us see how the fear of foreignness has historically arisen out of a phobic model of community that wants to secure its own coherence and purity by projecting otherness onto the body of the foreigner.[15] Moreover, this projection of otherness is an act of aggression that marks the stranger's body as an object of violence. The foreign body—the abject—needs to be expelled beyond the realm of privileged symbolic representations so that the community may proclaim itself clean and unaltered. It is precisely the foreigner's alien ontological status, his or her quivering sense of being, that disturbs the presupposed stable and coherent identity of the community.

The Film's "Haunting Secret":
Teasing the Realm of the Perceptible

Even though one could argue that the film's final scene provides a space of fusion between Simone's and Trelkovsky's screams—the last scream evokes the opening howl in an uncannily similar way—it is important not to homogenize and level the difference between those two critical narrative moments. Since the film focuses on the ontology of the abject, with Simone-lesbian and Trelkovsky-foreigner marked as others, one might be tempted to perceive them as abjected in the same way, through similar mechanisms of power. We may be further tempted to universalize their pain when we remember that Trelkovsky, by the mere fact of occupying Simone's space, is not only readily identified with her and with her incomprehensible flight from the window, but he is also openly invited to organize his life according to Simone's past practices. The examples of Trelkovsky's identification with Simone are countless: he becomes the recipient of Simone's mail; Simone's old friend returns her book to him; the waiter in a nearby café continually serves Trelkovsky Simone's favorite drink and cigarettes, openly neglecting his orders; and finally, he becomes Stella's companion-lover, as if taking the position that once belonged to Simone.

However, if we work from the assumption that Trelkovsky's and Simone's experiences of abjection are different, we may be able to recognize the shifting positionality of abjectness and to defy the potential equation of the two tormented bodies. The most obvious difference between the two characters is the fact that while Trelkovsky's abjection *is* represented in the narrative and becomes the film's central interest, Simone merely occupies the narrative edge, forcing the spectators to hypothesize her posture. The gender difference, the distinctly unique social positions of Simone's implied lesbianism (we hear Stella saying in an offhand comment, "She didn't like men"), and Trelkovsky's foreignness together with his cross-gendered, conspicuously ambivalent sexual identity figure in the narrative as signs of difference that do not let us conflate their oppression. Although it is clear that neither has a stable position within a traditional configuration of middle-class Parisian society, they are nevertheless oppressed by different structures of power. If we read their screams carefully, side by side, we can see the gender- and sexuality-specific pain and counter the potential erasure of their specificity.

The sequence that features Simone's scream at the onset of the narrative opens with Trelkovsky walking into the hospital and learning that in order to find Simone, he needs to locate bed 18. Simone is thus coded as a numbered body, suggesting an obliteration of her identity. Trelkovsky enters a big room, with many patients trapped in their beds, sharing one space. It is clear that this space does not offer the patients privacy and comfort: the pain of healing and the pain of dying are exposed to the public eyes of visitors. As Trelkovsky walks through this room, we see, through his subjective point of view, Simone's friend Stella standing over her bed. Soft lighting exposes the ugliness of the hospital setting and the ordinariness of the suffering patients. As Trelkovsky sits by Simone's bed in shock, we share his vision of her body, which is explicitly marked as different: her figure, enveloped in the tangles of white bandages, is positioned in contrast to the bodies of other patients around her. Simone's abjection is specifically underscored through her mummified flesh, which renders her immobile and faceless. Simone-the-Egyptologist—an almost successful suicide—is transformed into an Egyptian mummy, covered in a shroud-mask from under which only her dark and glistening eye stares at the visitors. Through a close-up, we see her bandaged head exposing this staring eye and an open mouth with a visibly missing tooth. (Later on in the film when Trelkovsky finds a tooth in a wall of his new apartment, we can hypothesize that it is Simone's missing one.) Through a shot-reverse-shot that links Trelkovsky's vision with Simone's eye, we witness the gaping hole of her mouth and the darkened eye socket, which terrifies Trelkovsky. The stillness and bewilderment of this scene are interrupted by Stella's question, "Are you a friend of hers?" This is the earliest foreshadowing of his link to the abjected female figure.

As Trelkovsky and Stella stand over Simone's bed, Stella poses a haunting question that never finds a narrative solution, "How could she do anything like that?" When Simone's body finally screams in pain, both visitors are asked to leave. Right before they exit, Trelkovsky looks at Simone one more time, and once again through his eyes, we gaze into the darkness of the screaming mouth. As Trelkovsky and Stella walk through the hospital hallway, the sound of Simone's scream bridges the gap between the two separate spaces, creating an ominous sense of the power and persistence of the scream. It is as if the scream does not want to fade into the oblivion of hospital darkness, and it reminds us in a poignant way that Simone is still alive. The scream-as-sound bridge that refuses for a moment to vanish from the audio track of the film is a haunting challenge to the entire narrative. As Trelkovsky and Stella become enveloped in the scream's dynamic upon their exit, the narrative universe becomes a space troubled by Simone's insistent shriek that demands to be heard.

The screaming body remains in offscreen space, only its howling reminding us of its existence. Considering that this is the only time we see Simone as a human subject (there are other moments in the film when she appears as somewhat ghostly), this narrative moment carries special significance. Not only does this sequence prefigure Trelkovsky's tragic end, but it also situates a lesbian female character on the fringes of the narrative. Simone's presence in the offscreen space functions in a way that is subversive because it calls into question the coherence of the narrative space whose cohesion rests on her exclusion, and is simultaneously problematic because she is eliminated from the privileged system of representation. Although we do not see her as a living character past this moment, Simone's scream teases the realm of the perceptible, reminding us of her abjected position. Thus, conceiving of Simone's presence in an offscreen space, or in what Teresa de Lauretis calls the "space-off," raises the complex question of representability of female agency, a question that is further complicated by Simone's status within the narrative as a lesbian who commits unexplainable suicide.

De Lauretis uses the notion of the space-off to reflect on "a view from elsewhere," a place of discourse from which it may be possible to transform dominant cultural narratives that privilege masculine desire and agency. Dissecting cultural productions that are based on "male narratives of gender," de Lauretis suggests that the creation of new discursive spaces remains an ongoing feminist task: "what we [women, feminists] have produced is not recognizable, precisely, as a representation." She locates the space-off within the ideology of present discursive practices:

> For that "elsewhere" is not some mythic distant past or some utopian future history: it is elsewhere of discourse here and now, *the blind spots,* or the space-off, of its representation. I think of it as spaces in the margins of hegemonic discourses, social spaces carved in the interstices of institutions and in the chinks and cracks of the power-knowledge apparati. (de Lauretis 1987, 25; my emphasis)

Although these "blind spots" belong to the space that is unseen in dominant discourses, they are implied, and their very position on the margins helps to cohere the authority of controlling discourse and, at the same time, draws attention to the fragility of the center. De Lauretis suggests that classical cinema tends to erase the space-off so that the conventional rules of narration can remain intact. On the other hand, art-cinema narration often emphasizes the offscreen space, asserting that the so-called film space is constructed through the employment of both onscreen and offscreen spaces simultaneously.

The narrative of *The Tenant* gives special attention to the offscreen space because it blurs the boundaries of the two film spaces. This destabilization of the tight construction of the image's border, imposed on the frame in classical narration, signifies the conscious expansion of cinematic vision through a disruption of spatial limitations. The transgression of the limited cinematic borders has serious implications for our comprehension of the film's representation, allowing us to conceive of what is traditionally concealed by and contained within the onscreen space. Simone's character can be seen as an agent working in the space-off, an abjected subject who unsettles the realm of the visible. Her presence on the outskirts of the narrative is unruly; she disturbs the narrative smoothness and haunts the narrative, refusing to disappear from the film's text.

While it is important to recognize Simone's unruliness, the offscreen position of the female abject cannot be seen solely as the desired liberatory space of power. Clearly, Simone as a desiring agent is not represented in the film. We can only feel her ghostly presence in the space of her apartment that is marked by the unsettling music, by her clothing and cosmetics, by Egyptian hieroglyphs, and by the tooth that Trelkovsky finds hidden in the apartment wall. Although Simone is expelled from the narrative at its onset, she does not quite disappear and eventually returns to us as a spectral apparition in the Egyptian episode in the bathroom vis-à-vis Trelkovsky's apartment.

This narrative episode takes place right before Trelkovsky's gradual slippage into the hallucinatory realm where he imagines he becomes a woman. Even

Trelkovsky looking at himself as a woman in *The Tenant*. Courtesy of British Film Institute.

before that moment, there are several times when, while watching the communal bathroom from his window, he sees different immobile, as if frozen, faces staring at him in an unexplainable way. Intrigued by the eerie presence of those various motionless faces, Trelkovsky uses binoculars to enable his and our vision. This ongoing spectacle of reciprocal voyeurism emphasizes the importance of being watched in the film. Even when he is the one who watches, he is always watched back and scrutinized. One day, when he goes into the bathroom, the place is revealed to us as an enclosed space whose walls are covered with Egyptian hieroglyphs. The enigmatic signs cover every inch of the walls. From there, Trelkovsky looks into his own window and, to his surprise and horror, sees himself looking through binoculars watching himself. This unexplainable duplication of his flesh terrifies him, and at the same time, it signals to the audience his approaching transformation and the multiplication of his identity. The unnerving music that accompanies his mysterious discovery escalates, increasing the narrative tension. When he goes back to his apartment, staggering, dizzy from the experience, once again he approaches his window and looks back at the bathroom. This time he sees a moving mummy, Simone, who unravels her bandages, disclosing her face to us. We presume it is Simone because the uncovered face shows a mouth with a missing tooth.

This moment is the climax of all the numerous Egyptian elements that we have seen in the film so far: Simone, we learn in the beginning, was an Egyptologist; the first time we see her trapped in the hospital bed and enveloped in white bandages, she unmistakably resembles an Egyptian mummy; the close scrutiny of the mise-en-scène of Trelkovsky's apartment reveals various Egyptian artifacts; the postcard addressed to Simone that Trelkovsky receives shows a photograph of an Egyptian sarcophagus; the bathroom walls are cloaked in hieroglyphs; and finally, the dying Trelkovsky himself will look like a mummy at the end, resembling Simone's wrapped body. One way of understanding the Egyptian trope, specifically the repeated figure of the mummy, is the foregrounded link between the living and the dead.[16]

The mummy itself constitutes a place of ambiguity, for it has neither a human nor a nonhuman status; it is neither alive nor quite dead. Similar to the process of embalming the dead body of a human being, the impulse to preserve the body as a mummy suggests the insistence on remembering that person and defying the passing into nothingness. In other words, the mummy challenges the conventional understanding of life and death and the human and nonhuman categories. Also, in a curious way, the unclear nature of the mummy corresponds to the ambiguous status of the screams, which are neither language nor nonlanguage but linger in the site of ambivalence between the two.

This emphasized ambiguity suggests the narrative puzzle that coheres around Simone, who, as the film's secret, remains an unexplainable core, a sign-hieroglyph, of the narration. Lynda Hart argues that the historical position of lesbians functions as a haunting secret, a concept that helps us grasp Simone's unusual location in the film. Hart draws on Diana Fuss's contention that lesbian and gay theory is preoccupied with the rhetoric of hauntings: "this striking, repetitive fascination with the specter of abjection, a certain preoccupation with the figure of the homosexual as specter and phantom, as spirit and revenant, as abject and undead." Hart theorizes the lesbian-as-secret as a "discursive *act* performed by the hierarchical ideology that systematically reconstructs the hetero/homo binary" rather than "some hidden, mysterious, or esoteric *content*."[17] Seen in this light, Simone, returning as a ghostly mummy that comes alive for a moment in Trelkovsky's vision, implicates the narrative need for the systematic reconstruction of the fragile binary Hart conceptualizes. Simultaneously, however, because of her unruliness, Simone evokes the desire to deconstruct this binary that sustains the stability of the traditional narrative pattern that relegates her and her sexual difference to the margins in the first place. Besides, Trelkovsky-as-Simone, at least to some degree, also becomes a somewhat ghostly, hallucinatory presence toward the end of the film. Especially in the film's last scene, which features his doubling, one might argue that he is a specter, or at least that the image of the two Trelkovskys again makes us question the thin line between mirage and tangibility. Since both Trelkovsky and Stella are deemed unwanted figures by the neighbors, both of their characters, continually wavering between life and death and hallucination and reality, haunt the oppressive model of community that the film critiques.

After Simone-ghost reveals her face in the Egyptian bathroom episode, the sequence ends abruptly. In the following shot, we see Trelkovsky in his bed and hear loud, rhythmic pounding outside his window. Trelkovsky wakes up (was the encounter with Simone a real narrative event or was it merely his hallucination?) and sees the workers fixing the broken glass that resulted from Simone's suicidal fall. As he looks to locate the source of the unnerving pounding, the workers laugh at him. When he moves away from the window, we can see that Trelkovsky, still dressed as Trelkovsky, is now wearing somewhat exaggerated makeup. Next, he looks at himself in the mirror, and we can see his fingernails covered with nail polish. We, the spectators, and Trelkovsky himself, are surprised to see him transformed into a woman. It is not just a transformation into a generic woman; he uses Simone's cosmetics and eventually puts on her dress that he finds in her wardrobe. He is becoming Simone, a lesbian.

From that moment on, the narrative rapidly relates Trelkovsky's metamorphosis. It is as if after seeing Simone's ghost casting off the bandages, he is now expected to become her. Her unveiling becomes an invitation to Trelkovsky's veiling. Simone sheds the constraining bandages so that he can put them on. He buys a woman's wig, high-heel shoes, wears Simone's dress, hosiery, and makeup. Until his operatic suicide, when he will die dressed as Simone, he changes himself into a female persona only inside his apartment; outside the confining walls of his space he is still "old" Trelkovsky-foreigner. Inside, we see him numerous times dressed as a woman, looking at his new image in the mirror with astonishment. His voice changes too as he practices womanly lines such as "I think I'm pregnant." His change seems to be almost complete when he discovers, touching his bloody mouth, that he too, like Simone, is missing the same front tooth. What is most surprising for the spectators may be the fact that this transformation is not an entirely conscious act of cross-dressing and gender-bending, but rather a hallucinatory and compulsory alteration that terrifies Trelkovsky because he has no control over it.

At such moments we, together with the protagonist, experience most intensely the suffocating enclosure of the haunting and oppressive mise-en-scène: the apartment is filled with strange voices and noises, the unnerving dripping of water from the faucet intensifies with each moment, the curtain is fluttering sinisterly, we see a hand crawling from outside Trelkovsky's window, the ominous shadows envelop the apartment's space, and we hear foreboding knocking at his door. Even during those somewhat hallucinatory instants, Trelkovsky attempts to protect himself. He barricades his door with furniture to defend himself against the knocking at the door; he tries to stab the crawling hand with a knife. Even if we regard those moments as his delusions, the absurdly oppressive treatment from his neighbors feels very real. Monsieur Zy's "Why are you bringing women around here?" warns him yet again that he will be evicted if he does not follow the rules of the rental agreement.[18] Monsieur Zy's question is, of course, highly ironic because at this point in the film Trelkovsky does not bring any women to his apartment. It is he who performs the figure of a woman, and his surprise at Monsieur Zy's accusation is genuine.

Trelkovsky's last attempts to save himself from Simone's suicidal fate even drive him to rent a hotel room. But the enclosed space still feels claustrophobic to him, and his search for a room of his own reveals to us the brutal condition of his being: there is no place for a foreigner in this community just as there is no space for a lesbian. In a desperate move, he seeks Stella's help and confesses his burden: "It's them. They are trying to kill me. Drive me to a suicide. She is dead because of the neighbors. It was a plot. They forced her to commit suicide, and they are trying to do the same to me. It's so appalling, so incredible that I can hardly tell you. They've been trying to turn me into Simone Choule." Even though Stella is sympathetic to his plight, she does not treat him quite seriously, and her response, "You are strange," once again underlines his unrelenting difference.

At this point, Trelkovsky's seeing becomes even more acute. In one of his most memorable visions, which directly precedes his tragic end, we see him motionless in a chair watching the window. Outside, a ball bouncing in the air eventually changes into a cut-off head draped in a wig with Trelkovsky's face. As petrified Trelkovsky looks outside, he witnesses the ostracism of Madame Gadérian and her little daughter by some of the tenants. Madame Gadérian, bound and being poked with sticks by the tenants as if she were a dangerous witch, is unable to help her daughter. Behind her, we see a French policeman who guards her with a club. As Monsieur Zy holds the girl, other neighbors transform her into a courtly jester. They cloak her in a red robe and put a mask on her face. The mask resembles Trelkovsky's face. The girl, transfigured into a Trelkovsky-clown, recognizes Trelkovsky in the window and shouts in an accusatory tone, "It's him! He's there!"

How can we read the feminized foreigner who witnesses this spectacle of ostracism and in the end is turned into the hunted one himself? And why in Trelkovsky's vision does Madame Gadérian's daughter become Trelkovsky behind a jester's mask? Earlier in the film, one of the tenants, Madame Dioz, collects signatures in the apartment building for a petition against "this dreadful Madame Gadérian." The accusation against her is supposedly the noise she makes in her apartment: "The unspeakable, uncivilized Madame Gadérian. We have to do something about it. She is making life impossible for the other tenants." The encounter with Madame Dioz unnerves Trelkovsky as she openly and meticulously scrutinizes his place when she comes inside. When he refuses to sign the petition, saying he does not even know Madame Gadérian (we learn later that he is the only one in the entire apartment building who does not sign this petition), Madame Dioz threatens to remember his refusal: "I shall make a note of your attitude. I can see what we are dealing with here. I know your type exactly!" Later, Madame Gadérian comes with her daughter to reveal to him the real reason why the tenants would like to get rid of her. She shows Trelkovsky her daughter's handicapped leg, revealing the girl's disability that she believes prompts the neighbors to try to evict her. This event links Trelkovsky-foreigner with the disabled girl and her "unspeakable" mother. All three, for different reasons, are unwanted by the "normal" neighbors.

The accusation of being noisy is another factor that ties him to the banished mother and daughter. Trelkovsky is accused numerous times of being noisy, and when he finds himself at the police station where he goes to seek help after his apartment has been plundered, he learns about a series of complaints against him. In another ironic twist, despite the fact that he is there to ask for protection and help, he is accused and branded by the chief policeman as a "troublemaker disturbing the peace," and the surprised Trelkovsky undergoes an interrogation about his citizenry:

> POLICEMAN: "Trelkovsky. Is this a Russian name?"
> TRELKOVSKY: "Polish, Polish."
> POLICEMAN: "So, you are not French?"
> TRELKOVSKY: "I am a French citizen."
> POLICEMAN: "Let me see your identity card."

This inquisition into the legality of his identity prompts him to leave the police station in disbelief. Even as he is about to exit the room, we hear the policeman's warning: "Just make sure I don't hear anymore about you." This statement quite explicitly suggests that as long as the foreigner occupies the space of silence, he may be benevolently tolerated by the French authorities.

Undoubtedly Trelkovsky's alliance with Madame Gadérian and her disabled daughter is based on their shared abjection. The episode with the petition against Madame Gadérian confirms that the narrative focus on social persecution, intolerance, and a phobia of otherness is not simply a product of Trelkovsky's tortured imagination. The social world inside the apartment building does not accept those who are somewhat different: Simone and her implied sexual difference, whose dealings with the tenants we can only imagine; Madame Gadérian and her physically different, weak daughter; and eventually, Trelkovsky, who as a naturalized citizen is not French enough to be treated as a legitimate Parisian inhabitant. This list of social misfits undeniably identifies Trelkovsky with the position occupied by women. The film does not suggest that the prejudice Trelkovsky endures is an exceptional experience that involves him alone. As a foreigner-exile who timidly seeks a space for himself in a new culture, he echoes the already existing social phobias that, as we see in the film, mainly target female characters who, for various reasons, do not reflect the normative subjectivity.

So how can we perceive Trelkovsky's location as a feminized other? Alice

Jardine suggests, "The space 'outside of' the conscious subject has always connoted the feminine in the history of Western thought—and any movement into alterity is a movement into that female space." In other words, the *space* of otherness—and we can understand it as both a social space and a textual location "over which the [master] narrative lost control"—has been historically marked as feminine.[19] Thus, Trelkovsky, a stranger upon his entrance into Parisian society, is "put into a discourse of 'woman.'" In this context, the process of him-becoming-Simone cannot be seen simply as his hallucinatory usurpation of her location. Rather, he is one of, as Clément writes, "the defeated . . . the weak sons, the lame, the hunchbacks, the blacks, the foreigners, and the old men—those who are like women" (1988, 22). This likeness, without dismissing the importance of gendered identity, refers to a sociocultural place, a position historically deemed as a space of weakness and deprivilege.

THE LOGIC OF IMPOSSIBILITY: WHERE CAN THE FOREIGNER GO?

> In an empty suburban parking lot, setting the hand brake,
> he wonders what it actually was that brought him here
> and why on earth he was never able not to succumb
> to the clichés of sorrow, familiar to all who practice
> the invisible craft of exile.
>
> —Stanisław Barańczak, "Setting the Hand Brake"

"The invisible craft of exile" stressed in Barańczak's poem is also portrayed in Andrei Tarkovsky's *Nostalghia* (1983), one of the most visually stunning and powerful films about exile and memory in international film history, a film that in many ways echoes Polanski's film.[20] *Nostalghia* opens with an intense image of fog. The spectators can barely see the figure of the protagonist, Andrei, a Russian intellectual-in-exile, and his Italian female companion-translator, Eugenia, getting out of a car and stepping into the Italian countryside. Impenetrable fog, which tightly envelops the protagonist and inhibits clear visibility of what is on-screen, is the film's very first image. During the course of a long opening sequence, the Italian translator enters a nearby church to look at a famous painting of the Madonna, while the man stays outside, merged with the dark. The sequence ends with an arresting juxtaposition of conflicting imagery. After we see flying and screeching birds springing from the Madonna's altar, the next shot reveals an immobile and brooding protagonist, still in the mist, who observes a delicate white feather slowly falling on his body.

In the course of the film, we watch as Andrei is continually haunted by self-doubt stemming from leaving his homeland ("How could I?" "Why?") and by the burden of a newly acquired freedom, and we witness his contradictory location, which has already been emphatically captured at the end of the opening sequence. The weight and darkness of exile is juxtaposed with the lightness associated with the feather and the freedom and movement of flying birds. Living outside the Soviet Union, he is supposedly free to enjoy various Western pleasures, but the heaviness and complexity of this freedom is continually emphasized throughout the film with the images of darkness, unbearable stillness, gloomy mise-en-scène, heavy rain, and long takes that feature the protagonist staring into the twilight. At one point, we hear Eugenia's attack on Andrei's paradoxical position: "You all seem to want freedom, but when you get it, you don't know what to do with it." Thus, *Nostalghia* foregrounds the idea that even though the experience of exile may be liberating, it is nevertheless always also painful and arduous. Above all, as the opening image of a foggy landscape in Tarkovsky's film tells us, the condition of exile is about disorientation, instability, confusion, and issues of visibility.

While his Italian companion is often filmed in well-lit places, Andrei's figure is usually surrounded by shadows and pools of darkness. This lighting technique works on a double level: the viewers often cannot see Andrei clearly because he is not quite visible to the rest of the Italian community he encounters. The spectators may feel frustrated with so many murky images that do not allow for an easy perception of the protagonist, but this seems to be exactly what the film wants us to experience: the condition of being partially invisible although a member of the community. The idea of a foreigner who is not quite a full subject like everyone else, and the contradictory position of an exile located between the mobility of freedom and the heaviness of being, links Tarkovsky's *Nostalghia* and Polanski's *The Tenant* as films preoccupied with the complex dynamic of displacement. *Nostalghia*'s emphasis on representing the stranger's paradoxical social location—a space barely visible because it is immersed in intense fog—further helps to elucidate the way we may read Trelkovsky's location of contradiction.

Examining *The Tenant* in this context of foreignness shows how its narrative works as a critique of the discriminatory logic of exile that locks the stranger in the location of impossibility. On the one hand, leaving one's country requires the utmost courage, a perplexing leap of imagination. But such a decision is often met with the scorn and critique of fellow citizens who are quick to reprimand an exile for leaving his or her place, for abandoning the country where they should stay, where they rightfully belong. On the other hand, the acceptance of the foreigner in a new place is usually painfully earned, if at all, as she or he struggles to find a space for her or his transported identity. *The Tenant* neither romanticizes the position of the exile nor calls for a quick or smooth acceptance of a stranger's otherness. Rather, the film comments on the need to focus on rereading the specificity of the abjected foreigner in order to dissect generalities about immigration and authentic citizenry.

The Tenant may thus be best understood as a cinematic narrative of exile.

Robert Sklar notes, the cinematic expression of exile holds a special place in the history of cinema:

> Though border crossings by filmmakers had been common in cinema history, the experience of exile—of separation or expulsion from one's home country—nevertheless held a special meaning. Filmmakers had been forced into or had voluntarily chosen exile from Russia after 1917, from Germany and other European countries under Fascism, and from Czechoslovakia after 1968. (1993, 492)

The experience of filmmakers' border crossings is crucial for a twofold understanding of cinema: as a transnational medium that has always defied rigid notions of national borders, and as an art form of a moving image with a subversive potential and power to comment on social and political issues. Historically, for many religious and political forces, cinema's ability to cross linguistic, cultural, and geographical boundaries, and often to circumvent political restrictions, has been the source of anxiety associated with the fear of contamination by unwanted influences and foreign otherness.[21]

Understood in this context, *The Tenant*, a film about exile, joins a long tradition of films that comment on the experience of being out of place, of being homeless.[22] The film's demanding formal complexities are thus dictated not solely by the art-film tradition, but also by a necessity to thwart the constraining boundaries of traditional narrative structure in order to reflect on exile with passion and sensitivity.[23] The film sets up this argument by the paradoxical expression of an exiled position: the idea of the movement and potential freedom often associated with border crossing juxtaposed with countless images of enclosure and suffocation.

Further complicating the narrative design of *The Tenant* is Trelkovsky's very place of ambiguity. An abject, he can be defined only according to the paradoxical image of an indefinite border. He simultaneously is and is not a man; he is and is not French. Trelkovsky's masculinity is problematized from the very opening of the film when we meet him as a timid stranger without confidence or manly bravado. He stands in contrast to his fellow office mates who are assertive, loud, articulate, and domineering. Madame Dioz's nosiness offends and paralyzes him. He tries to avoid the concierge who patronizes him and scrutinizes his comings and goings. The owner of the building, Monsieur Zy, is an authoritarian voice constantly threatening him. And Trelkovsky's Frenchness is not natural but artificial.

Moreover, Trelkovsky enters the West from the position of a second world citizen. He comes from the space behind the Iron Curtain, a geopolitical realm at once repudiated (because it is dangerous to the ideology of the West) and marked as somewhat mysterious (because it is outside the system of Western representation). In a sense, his figure of an intruder connotes an aura of ambivalent otherness historically attached to the communities behind the Wall. It is interesting to note here that this derogatory ambivalence continues even in the current postcolonial and transnational critical debates that often obliterate the existence of the second world by focusing solely on the first and third world dichotomy as a legacy of imperialist and colonialist discourses. In these debates, the space that belongs to the second world is itself a space of ambiguity, a fuzzy in-between that escapes orderly categorization.[24] Given all those factors that underline Trelkovsky's position of ambiguity, we should also remember that the experience of exile itself creates the space of uncertainty; an exile is always suspended between his or her old and new identities. And this in-between location is constantly under negotiation, never quite stable. I do not claim that a special epistemic privilege is granted to those who make an often painful decision to become exiles; such an idea romanticizes the foreigner, erases the exile's struggle to survive, and ultimately and quite mistakenly puts the foreigner on top of the power hierarchy. So I do not suggest that Trelkovsky possesses some secret knowledge accessible only to foreigners. Each case of exile has its own cultural and historical specificity, but given the film's narrative, Trelkovsky, whether he wants it or not, occupies the space "outside of the conscious subject," as Jardine (1982) puts it. And this position of abjection—this ontological otherness—defines him as an unrelenting alien, one who, like Simone, haunts the oppressive model of the Parisian community. Trelkovsky's position in *The Tenant* may be better understood as a position of epistemic difference, which is precisely what makes him inadequate, deficient, and lacking the natural link with French soil.

The acute emphasis on and attention to Trelkovsky's epistemic difference ultimately makes Polanski's film poignant and moving. But it is most unusual that in *The Tenant* the foreign body is represented onscreen without any attempt either to redeem and appropriate it into the existing social structures in France, or to dismiss the protagonist as simply an insane character who in his hallucinatory apprehension suddenly decides to become a woman. The film refuses to simplify the notion of exile or to reduce the figure of the foreigner to a comforting single category. Instead, *The Tenant* sets up the protagonist's scream—an expression of the agonized human body—as a passionately desperate cry against nationalism and the obsessive desire to guard national borders against outsiders.

In creating such an un-Hollywood ending, the film offers a different kind of cinematic pleasure, one that has nothing to do with happy endings and the ease of being absorbed by the seamless Hollywood narrative. This pleasure does not come from passive spectatorship, from an effortless understanding of the narrative design, or from being a safe distance from the screen events, which allows the audience to be simply entertained. Instead, *The Tenant* mobilizes the notion of spectatorial involvement and the viewers' identification with the onscreen characters to show the need to reimagine the concept of the cinematic body itself (Shaviro 1993). It is precisely this cinematic body—the dialectical relationship between both the spectator's own flesh and its affective responses *and* the performance of the foreigner's body on the screen—that asks us to recognize, as Kristeva envisions, the foreigner's foreignness within us. We who watch this film, like the phobic Parisian community the film critiques, become haunted by the figure of the foreigner. His position continually reminds us of the vehemently imposed artificial rigidity of the national borders that are meant to protect the fragile boundary of the native "I" that sees itself as an authentic and rightful citizen. And Trelkovsky's final scream, the ambiguously haunting shriek, remains till the very end a challenge to the common nationalistic concept that to be a rightful citizen, one's body must necessarily have a natural connection with one's nation.

The Wall—Sarajevo, Postcards from the War series, 1993. This image, designed during the war in the former Yugoslavia by the TRIO Sarajevo group, functioned as a comment on the new symbolic wall separating Europe from the war-torn communities in the Balkans. Courtesy of Goran Sipek.

5

ANATOMIES OF ABJECTION:
ETHNIC CLEANSING AND LIMINALITY
IN *BEFORE THE RAIN*

> It was all planned. None of it was coincidental. All along the goal was ethnic cleansing. Better said, genocide: ethnic cleansing is a gentle term.
>
> —Nusreta Sivac, comment about Omarska Detention Camp, organized by the Serbs in 1992 in Bosnia, in *Calling the Ghosts*

In an article published in a *Screening Europe* collection, Stuart Hall reflects on the political reconfigurations of Europe at the time of its critical changes marked by the fall of the Berlin Wall in 1989 and the collapse of the Soviet Union and Yugoslavia in 1991:

> There is nothing to be said, in this day and age, for being nostalgic about the cold war, but the cold war did at least give Europe a kind of arbitrary stop. The Berlin Wall, monstrosity that it was, did set up a kind of barrier, real and symbolic. Its awesome brick visage carried a message: "Beyond this frontier is another kind of Europe, another system, another world." In a way this reinforced certain old European preconceptions, for the "real" Europe has always imagined over there as elsewhere, other, the beyond: the frozen wastes, wolves roaming the icy slopes, the mysterious east, barbarians clamouring at the gate of civilisation. (1992, 46)

Certainly, many scholars, such as Dina Iordanova, Maria Todorova, and Slavoj Žižek, have argued that the Balkan conflict has been frequently understood and represented in the West precisely in those terms: the less civilized part of Europe erupting beyond control, the barbarians mercilessly and impulsively acting out the eye-for-an-eye philosophy, "the mysterious east" consumed by old, deep-seated ethnic conflicts that set the peoples of the Balkans apart from the true European community. Although Todorova argues that Balkanism is a discursive strategy that has worked to produce the idea of the Balkans as a "repository of negative characteristics against which a positive and self-congratulatory image of the 'European' and 'the West' has been constructed" (1994, 453), Iordanova pushes this kind of critique further to suggest that many Balkan intellectuals participate in what she terms "consenting self-exoticism" (2001, 61). She writes:

> [T]he "orientalisation" of the Balkans cannot be declared a purely Western project, as it is a process which has been embraced, internalised and partially carried out by many consenting Balkan intellectuals. It is not just "the West" which constructs the Balkans as compliant to Western stereotypes, to a large extent this construction is taken up and carried further by "the Rest," and in our case by Balkan writers and film-makers themselves. The result is a specific voluntary "self-exoticism," which becomes the preferred mode of self-representation for many Balkan film-makers. (56)

Considering this foreclosure of representation, I am specifically interested in the formal challenges that cinema faces in order to perform the Balkan conflict without reproducing the familiar impulse to binarize Europe (the civilized West versus the barbaric East). How can a critical tribute be paid to the region without falling into the predictable pattern of portraying the Balkans as "the Other of the West" and "the madhouse of thriving nationalisms" (Žižek 1994, 212–13)? What textual strategies might be effective in subverting either a xenophobic or xenophilic illustration of the Balkan struggle or in representing violence against the usual scheme of sexualized entertainment or sublimated, sentimentalized brutality? How to enunciate the workings of the logic of ethnic violence without either demonizing or exoticizing the inhabitants of the Balkans? These are important questions because they involve opening up representational practices that would allow for more complex registers of cinematic signification. In this context, these registers might give voice to the critique of the logic of ethnic cleansing, propelled by the idea of privileged and authentic citizenry.

With these concerns in mind, I analyze the discourse of national purity in Milcho Manchevski's 1994 directorial debut, *Before the Rain,* which focuses on the dynamics of ethnic anguish between Macedonian Christians and Albanian Muslims in Macedonia, close to the Albanian border in the early 1990s. The film constructs a compelling interrogation of the cultural mechanisms fostering the growth of oppressive nationalism: the policing of ethnic boundaries and the pursuit of an ideology of purity in the service of national homogeneity.

Macedonia, a part of the former Yugoslavia, with its difficult and conflicted history of nationhood, is certainly a compelling ground for an inquiry into the mechanisms that instigate religious and racial violence. The country declared its independence in November 1991 after the collapse of Yugoslavia, and in April 1993 it was finally admitted to the United Nations as the Former Yugoslav Republic of Macedonia.[1] According to the last census in 1994, about 66 percent of the country's multiethnic population consists of Orthodox Slavs, who consider themselves Macedonians, and about 22 percent are Muslim Albanians, who wish for a separate state of their own. The remaining 10 to 15 percent are Serbs, Turks, Vlachs, and Gypsies.[2]

Another film that is well-known in the West about the Balkan conflict is Michael Winterbottom's *Welcome to Sarajevo* (1997), which focuses mainly on the experiences of Western characters. But Manchevski's film, like the recent Oscar-winning *No Man's Land* (Danis Tanovic, 2001) and, to some degree, *Beautiful People* (Jasmin Dizdar, 1999), gives space to the Balkans' point of view. The film dissects the sociocultural mechanisms that produce phobic nationalisms in a way that self-consciously seeks to resist the aestheticization and sublimation of abjection. Additionally, the narrative refuses to present the Balkan conflict in terms of predictable binaristic hierarchies such as victim/victimizer, hero/villain, or interpreter/interpreted and opens up a space for a more dialectical representation of ethnic cleansing. It is the film's focus on the exilic status of the protagonist, Aleksandar Kirkov (Rade Serbedzija), that mobilizes the need to question these traditional dichotomies.

Aleksandar's quivering subjectivity, his status as a liminar who does and does not belong to his nation, enables us to examine the normative idea of the "I," the self historically conceived within the parameters of ethnic sameness and stable national territory. I argue that the film uses Aleksandar's liminality to critique the logic of national purity. Interestingly, what is unconventional about Manchevski's film is that, unlike many well-known films of exile, which often focus on the struggle of a foreigner-stranger within the space of his or her nonnative culture, *Before the Rain* foregrounds the challenge Aleksandar ends up facing in being reincorporated into his native place, in being reaccepted by his own people upon his return.

Furthermore, the film invites us to reflect on the urgency to reconfigure the *privileged* notion of the nation-state based on a claustrophobic paradigm of pure, homogeneous community that has historically repudiated otherness in all its various forms. On this level, *Before the Rain* speaks not only to the spectators from the former Yugoslavia but to the Western audience as well, including, of course, an American audience whose national history is not by any means exempt from ethnic violence.[3] Thus, what the film asks of us is quite difficult: to recognize the problematic doubleness embedded in the concept of national identity. I mean that either glorification of one's origins or their denial can be equally dangerous because both, fueled by the logic of ethnic purity, may instigate xenophobic nationalisms.

TRANSNATIONAL EXILIC CONTEXT

The film won numerous international awards and initially received little critical attention in the West until 2000 when the journal *Rethinking History* devoted an entire issue to *Before the Rain*.[4] Andrew Horton, who interviewed Manchevski, argues that *Before the Rain* "is, by far, the most important movie to appear from the war-torn Balkan republics that once constituted Yugoslavia since the current war began in 1991."[5] To call this film a "border crossing text," as Horton does, is indeed pertinent because the film resists the "purity" of traditional categories defined according to national origins. It is interesting that Manchevski, born in Macedonia and educated in the United States, does not really consider himself a Balkan filmmaker. Asked about this, he replied, "I have had the luck of living in New York, although I don't see myself as an American, but I also don't see myself as a Balkan. I think I am a filmmaker across the oceans" (Horton 1995, 45). His refusal to situate himself and his work within a single national category and the fact that *Before the Rain* foregrounds exile as a narrative concern allow us to conceptualize the film as belonging to transnational exilic cinema. As such, the film enacts its transnationality thematically and formally: national and ethnic border crossings lie at the heart of this three-episode dramatic feature whose triptych structure is bound by Aleksandar's diegetic movement as a Macedonian exile—from Macedonia to London, and back to Macedonia. His crossings—reminiscent of Manchevski's own transnational and transcultural condition—punctuate the film's overlapping three parts, "Words," "Faces," and "Pictures."[6]

It is relevant to contextualize *Before the Rain* within the category of transnational exilic cinema, especially because this classification is an important one when we approach the global diasporic filmmaking of the late-twentieth-century liminars, transnationals, and exiles. As Hamid Naficy writes, this exilic genre "cuts across previously defined geographic, national, cultural, cinematic, and metacinematic boundaries" (1996, 119). Naficy's work on "accented cinema" has been extremely influential in drawing attention to the sustained theorizing of "cinema *of* exile and cinema *in* exile," specifically as it pertains to the work of filmmakers in the postmodern era of the post-1945 massive displacements of peoples.[7] These exilic dispersals, in part due to the complex processes of global decolonization, resulted in the transcultural movements of economic and political refugees, exiles, and immigrants, mainly from the non-Western spaces coded as second or third world, to the industrially advanced Western nation-states.[8] His notion of "accented cinema," Naficy argues, "emanates not so much from the accented speech of the diegetic characters as from the displacement of the filmmakers and their artisanal production codes" (2001, 4). As I suggested in the introduction, the category of transnational exilic filmmaking is not simply the latest current terminology, but rather an effort to open up the often reductive and condescending markers of immigrant, minority, and ethnic filmic subcategories that, although historically valid, tend to group diasporic work into what Naficy calls "discursive ghettos" (1996, 120). Furthermore, these traditional labels often work to code specific cinematic texts as of ethnic interest, as if ethnicity inherently belonged to the so-called minority discourse.[9]

When addressing transnational exilic cinematic texts and their frequent emphasis on the multiplicity of national belongings, it is important not to homogenize transnational locations; each needs to be analyzed in its specificity, with attention to the heterogeneity of gender, racial, and ethnic modalities. Clearly, *Before the Rain* is a product of Manchevski's authorial vision, his political and ethnic affinities, his own exilic longings and nostalgia, and his transcultural positionality as an artist "across the oceans"—that is, neither quite fully Macedonian nor fully American in terms of the traditional logic of national identity.[10]

Manchevski has commented that the script for the film came into being in 1991 when he went back to Macedonia after a six-year absence. He writes that the emotionality of this visit was intense; he experienced "a sense of heartfelt homecoming and a sense of impending doom." The historical moment of his visit was marked by the twofold sensation of endings and beginnings: while Yugoslavia, the country in which Manchevski was raised, was disintegrating, Macedonia was one of the new nations emerging out of the war. He describes the sensation of impending changes and the aura of uncertainty: "It felt sort of like the pressure you feel on the inside of your mouth before it rains." While *Before the Rain*'s diegesis is largely set in Macedonia and was inspired by the political events in the Balkan region, Manchevski insists that the film "is not about a particular country. It is about people caught on the verge of wider violence that is about to erupt around them."[11]

Within this context, *Before the Rain*'s attempts to grapple with the aesthetic and political concerns that I sketched out in the opening of this chapter produce significant tension. As others have already argued, the film may be read as performing Balkanism, that is, recycling familiar stereotypes about the "otherness" of the Balkans.[12] Simultaneously, however, due to its "carefully designed quirk in the [narrative] chronology," to use Manchevski's words, the film appears to be mindful of normative representations of the Balkan conflict, specifically the popular Western notion of the circularity and timelessness of Balkan ethnic violence (2000, 129).

Using the tradition of art-cinema narration, the film's formal arrangement is indeed complex, self-consciously dislodging chronological time by telling the story as if out of sequence. The nonlinear, fragmented, intricately tangled narrative appears to mimic the linearity of the circle except, as the old monk says in the film, "the circle is not round" because its seemingly cyclical nature is thwarted and filled with temporal and logical paradoxes. As Robert A. Rosenstone succinctly puts it, the narrative "incorporates a temporal sense that is, literally, disjunctive and impossible" (2000a, 124). The film's formal experiment with the illogic of its narrative becomes, I suggest, a means of performative *critiquing* of the stereotypical portrayal of the Balkan violence as a permanent historical construct in this region. This critiquing is crucial for two reasons: it does not locate ethnic violence solely in the Balkans, and it does not allow for the representation of Western Europe as a superior, civilized space that has already overcome its ethnic dilemmas.

In the remainder of this chapter, I focus on *Before the Rain*'s representation of the workings of the logic of ethnic purity within the context of the interlocked diegesis and transnational crossings between London and Macedonia. I discuss Aleksandar's location of what I term "quivering ontology," which ruptures a privileged vision of a nation; I examine the haunting positioning of female characters; and I conclude with the explication of the "violence of vomit." The narrative performance of such violence invites reflections on the complexities of a transnational location, which, as evoked by Manchevski's film, contest celebratory conceptions of transcultural identity.

Narrative Illogic/Logic of Purity

The first episode of *Before the Rain*, "Words," which opens with the stunning image of an ancient monastery and the surrounding Macedonian countryside, introduces us to Kiril (Grégoire Colin), a young Orthodox monk committed to a vow of silence. The clash between this segment's title and Kiril's muteness becomes apparent when he finds a young Albanian Muslim, Zamira (Labina Mitevska), hiding in his cell from armed Christian villagers who are hunting her. Kiril has no words to give her because of his vow; besides, they have no language in common. The villagers seek retaliation with no pardon, believing that Zamira killed their local shepherd, but thanks to Kiril's silent collusion in concealing her, the vengeful militants do not find her. Kiril's interest in helping Zamira leads him to a crisis: he abandons the monastery and breaks his vow of silence and tries to escape with her. The sudden conclusion of "Words" comes in an image of gory, heart-wrenching violence: both Kiril and Zamira are caught—not by the terrorizing villagers, but by Zamira's own Muslim relatives, including her grandfather and brother. Before Zamira is killed—shot many times by her own brother—and Kiril is told to run away, we witness the shocking abuse of Zamira by her grandfather, a man who holds the highest position of authority in the family.

The conflict in "Words" revolves around not only the suspicion that Zamira may be the killer of the shepherd ("Blood calls for blood. You'll start a war now. You slut.") but also the fact that, as a Muslim, she has been helped and rescued by a Christian, a man from an antagonistic culture. As Zamira is kicked and

Kiril (Grégoire Colin), a monk, is committed to maintaining his vow of silence in "Words," the first section of *Before the Rain*. Courtesy of Milcho Manchevski.

punched before she dies, the grandfather's words reveal the history of her treatment within the family: "I never hit you. I locked you up in the house. I cut your hair. Should I shave it off?" The painfully ironic twist in this closing is that the audience has been led to believe that Zamira is in danger from the Christian villagers, not from her own Muslim family. But hatred of another culture is evidently stronger than affinity with one's own brothers and sisters: because Zamira runs after Kiril, in the eyes of her brother she has betrayed her family, her heritage, her culture. She has betrayed her blood.

The most significant point that "Words" establishes is that ethnic groups in Macedonia are committed to the destructive logic of ethnic purity. On the surface, the film appears neither pro–Albanian/Muslim nor pro–Slavic/Christian; both communities are caught up in the destructive paradigm of ethnic superiority. We hear the rhetoric of hate articulated strongly by characters from both ethnic groups. Zamira is called an "Albanian whore" by angry Christian villagers; Kiril is labeled "Christian scum" by Zamira's Muslim grandfather. Both groups display cruelty and ruthlessness; both believe in their special entitlement to the land they share. The film thus seems to be critical of both cultures and each group's dogmatic claim that the heritage of its blood is superior to that of its neighbors. The narrative does not excuse either culture from perpetuating ethnic hatred. One of the Christian villagers, addressing the monks who try to resist the search of the monastery, asks emphatically: "Remember five centuries of Muslim rule? An eye for an eye." The statement is supposed to serve as a reminder of hatred grounded in specific historical circumstances. We witness a similarly vehement attitude from Zamira's grandfather and brother, both ready to punish Zamira for having crossed an imaginary ethnic border and for the betrayal of her Muslim roots by having associated herself with a Macedonian Christian.

Manchevski has acknowledged that *Before the Rain* is a "very emotional story" presented through a deliberately complex structure whose purpose is to critique war and ethnic cleansing without taking sides in the conflict (Horton 1995, 45). Despite these conceptual intentions and an attempt to present a balanced critique of both communities, the film, through its emotional pull and its point-of-view filming, does seem to imply that the land that is being ravished by violence putatively belongs to the Christian majority.[13] "Words" clearly anchors Orthodox Christianity as historically rooted—hence privileged—within the Macedonian land. The aesthetics of the mise-en-scène does not evoke emotional proximity to the Albanian Muslims the same way it garners spectatorial attention when it comes to the representation of the Christian nation. Also, the narrative offers a compassionate look at various rituals within Christian culture: visiting family graves, paying respect to the dead, performing burials and liturgies, celebrating weddings and family gatherings, sheep raising, farming. In short, through all these diegetic moorings, the audience is invited to believe in the ethnic authenticity of the Christian majority.

The monastery plays an important role in the process of authorizing Christians and creating the impression that they rightfully belong to the land. The monastery is portrayed as the site of the ancient sanctuary, a place of spiritual purity and metaphysical reverence. Monks walking under the starry skies, imagery of almost fairy-tale quality, the monks' chants, the solemnity of their prayers, and shots of the monastery situated against the remarkable blueness of Lake Okhrid create a nostalgic aura and underscore the emotional and historical significance of Christian Orthodox aesthetics.

When the narrative gives us an agonizing-to-watch sequence of violence and destruction—a game of protracted torture of turtles—its dramatic impact metaphorically argues that the looming conflict on the larger scene threatens to erase the historic beauty and the uniqueness of the Christian nation. In this sequence, we see the monks say their prayers amid the ancient paintings of their sanctuary while a group of village boys plays with turtles outside. The first shot of the children shows two boys fighting with turtles turned tanks: "Go, Ninja Turtle! Kill him!" Through parallel editing, we witness the monks praying and the children outside building a circle around the turtles with wooden sticks and setting it on fire. This kind of editing intensifies the pressure of the approaching violence, juxtaposing the sacred litany with the cruelty of destruction. In an eerie way, the chanting of the monks intensifies the strangely defamiliarized image of violence. The narrative movement back and forth between the monastery and the children aurally accentuates the monks' prayers as the sound bridge carries their voices and estranges the children's cruelty.

At the end of the sequence, the shots cut rapidly between the prayers, Kiril's awed perception of the grandeur of the frescoes, and the cruelty of the turtles' final explosions in the fire. The last shot gives us a close-up of a turtle lying on its shell, dying. This closing moment mobilizes a metaphorical connection between the dying turtle and the monks, who, we may deduce, are also symbolically threatened with violence and extinction. The idea is further emphasized when Kiril, the only young novice among the elderly monks, leaves the monastery, crushing the community's hope for the survival of the spiritual tradition among future generations.

While "Words" pulls the audience gradually into the excruciating-to-see dynamic of violence in Macedonia—the explosion of the turtles and then the shooting of a cat that foreshadow Zamira's violent death—it is clear by the end of the middle section, "Faces," that both "Words" and "Faces" are symbolically interlocked. In "Faces," at first we seem to be moving away from the events in Macedonia. This part opens with an image of a woman sobbing in a shower—Anne (Katrin Cartlidge), a photo editor in London whose personal dilemma is sketched quickly for the audience (Anne has already appeared briefly in "Words"). She must choose between her estranged husband, Nick (Jay Villiers), and an impulsive lover—a Macedonian photojournalist, Aleksandar. Nick comes across as a stable British husband while Aleksandar, an exile, is a tempestuous, world-traveling artist, the acclaimed author of prize-winning photography documenting the war in Bosnia. We are led to believe that "Faces" will narrate Anne's personal conflict, and although it does so to some extent, it also shows that a London photo editor who studies pictures of war from a seemingly safe distance is not that far from the conflict in former Yugoslavia after all. Within minutes after she meets Nick at a restaurant to resolve their relationship, a shoot-out initiated by a stranger, presumably from the Balkans, who has come to settle a score with one of the waiters, leaves Nick dead, implying that no one is free from the erupting violence, not even in an elegant London restaurant.[14]

The connections that emerge between "Words" and "Faces" foreground the notion that distant and seemingly very different cultural locations, Macedonia and London, are interconnected through violence. The purpose of this accentuated bonding, I suggest, is to question the binary understanding that stereotypically privileges the "normal" West over the "barbaric" non-West. Thus, several overlapping images of transnational crossings underscore metaphorical connections between the first two narrative parts: the words "Time never dies. The circle is not round," spoken by a monk in the first part, appear in "Faces" as graffiti on the London street, as if written into the mise-en-scène of the city; in the restaurant where Nick dies, there are turtles again, this time swimming in a restaurant aquarium, also constrained and trapped as in "Words"; in her photo studio in London, Anne examines the war photographs that document Zamira's killing.

These photographs, especially in the hands of a Western editor, hold a crucial significance: we are shown how the tragedies materially experienced in the ethnic war in the Balkans are transported to the West via visual representations in order to be studied, examined, and published. Although it is not clear how Anne obtained these photographs or who took them (although we may deduce that she gets them from Aleksandar), the friction between Anne's position as a scrutinizer and the horror the pictures represent is striking. Anne analyzes photographs of war with a magnifying glass, dissecting the visual records of the tragic events. In her white darkroom gloves, she looks like a scientist who contemplates people's faces in the photos; she carefully observes the photographic sequence featuring Zamira's death and a collection of random photographs depicting the Bosnian war and its victims. The slickness of the photo studio and Anne's white gloves suggest that she is engaged in a safe analysis; she is privy to tragedies going on in the Balkans through photographic illustrations. The underlying assumption here, foiled by the end of "Faces," is that ethnic violence belongs to faraway places.

The eerie visual clash between Anne's sterile high-tech editorial room and the "dirty" horror shown in the pictures is additionally underscored when we see a series of glossy, color pictures of Western models and pop stars placed next to the Bosnian pictures. The unnerving, rhythmically pounding sound further heightens the tension and the apparent contrast. The photographs Anne reviews are shown in close-ups so that the spectator's gaze, too, is implicated in the scene. The austere black-and-white pictures give us an uncanny collage of terror: a man standing without a shirt, exposing his starved, bony torso, his gaze empty and barren, as though he were deprived of sight; a child whose forehead is tattooed with a number; a person wearing a gas mask; an old woman crying over a grave; corpses of children lying against a wall. There is also a picture of a young man wearing a swastika band on his arm, an image that constructs a link between the war in former Yugoslavia and the Holocaust.[15] When the second episode ends with Anne's broken voice, whispering in disbelief—"Your face, Nick. Your face. Your face"—the audience is invited to associate Nick's violent death in a London restaurant with the haunting faces of the Bosnian people in the photographs.

Quivering Ontology:
Paradoxical Estrangement/Exilic Return

"Pictures," the last section of the triptych, focuses on the homecoming of the already introduced Aleksandar and thematizes the dialectics of exile, calling into question a traditionally stable understanding of the ideas of self, home, nation, and cultural belonging. The unsettling incongruity the film creates about Aleksandar's status is that the condition of being an exile implies continual quivering between the worlds of the native and adopted cultures. The emphasis on Aleksandar's difficulty in anchoring his identity to a single place is not simply an invitation to deplore the perceived compromise of his native roots. Nor is it an encouragement to sentimentalize the exile's often painful antinomies or to celebrate his hybridity as cosmopolitan. Rather, his homelessness opens up the space for questioning the logic of privileging one's origins. In fact,

Though a native Macedonian, Aleksandar (Rade Serbedzija) is a stranger in his native village in "Pictures," the third section of *Before the Rain*. Courtesy of Milcho Manchevski.

Aleksandar's in-betweenness turns him into a stranger, and his return to his native Macedonia exposes his unclassifiable status—it is as if at the same time he is and yet is no longer Macedonian. It is precisely this uncertain location of what I call quivering ontology that underlines the condition of liminality experienced by the protagonist.

"Pictures" shows Aleksandar's return from London to his childhood village in Macedonia, the place we already know from "Words." His arrival is ridden with contradictions: he hopes to reconnect with his people, but seems unaware that the very idea of who "our" people are in the village has become a contested ground. He confronts a foreboding tension between Albanian Muslims and Macedonian Christians who treat each other no longer as neighbors in one community but as enemies. The disharmony, intolerance, and sectarian violence he encounters painfully remind him of the past that he nostalgically recalls as a time of Muslim/Christian harmonious coexistence before the latest ethnic cleansing. Aleksandar's problematic desire to reclaim the home in which he grew up underlines his exilic longing: his impulse to recover the past, to restore a prelapsarian moment, to go back to the "original" communal unity. Ironically, although he had escaped death as a photographer on the front, he is caught in the deadly crossfire in his native village. By the end of "Pictures," like Zamira who was killed by her brother, he, too, is shot dead by one of his own people, his cousin Zdrave.

As Aleksandar returns to his homeland, his liminality invites a critique of nationalist rhetoric. The film unveils the loss of affinity with his people, suggesting that once the "I" becomes an exile and steps beyond the realm of "one's own," this "I" becomes curiously foreign to kin. Even though his relatives and old friends are touched by his return, they do not quite know how to relate to him since he eludes the usual categorizations along the axis of a native/foreigner. Through the experience of exile Aleksandar has lost his status as a person who unequivocally belongs to his native place and its people; he has become estranged from them and has turned into a paradoxical mixture, a hybrid, both a foreigner and a native at once, both an insider and an outsider, or in Salman Rushdie's words, "at once plural and partial" (1991, 19). It is obvious that his presence creates a sense of discomfort in the village because his cultural loyalty is perceived as ambiguous. The seemingly contradictory notion that Aleksandar is no longer a native, even though he was born in Macedonia, is emphasized by one of his relatives who tries to warn Aleksandar about his involvement in the conflict: "Keep out of this. You are not from here." He is indeed a phantom; a provisional, tenuous "I"; a being who has returned to reclaim its old self that no longer is.[16]

This idea of Aleksandar as a foreigner among his own people is further dramatized when he visits Hana, his romantic interest from the past, whose home is on the Albanian side of the village. (This episode also underscores how both communities vehemently police their ethnic boundaries.) While Aleksandar is greeted somewhat affectionately by Hana's father, her son (Zamira's brother and killer) is openly hostile: "Why is he here? He doesn't belong here. I'll slit his throat." This comment about belonging is ironically reminiscent of an earlier scene. When Aleksandar first approaches the village, he is immediately accosted by a young Macedonian whose job is to guard the village borders (and whom we have already seen among angry villagers searching for Zamira in the first episode). When Aleksandar addresses him in his language, the young man relaxes slightly: "Ah, you are one of us." The above contradictory perceptions of Aleksandar expose that the notion of belonging or not belonging, and being or not being "one of us," is the underlying philosophy of the village the film wants to critique. Of course, the difficulty of Aleksandar's position lies in the fact that he both is and is not one of them.

Aleksandar's encounter with Hana's family also foregrounds the important issue of Albanian women's social position and oppression in the village and provokes the reading of women's patriarchal entrapment in both communities.[17] The ethnic war within the diegesis concerns only male characters; they are always the agents performing violence. All positions of authority in the village—doctors, monks, group leaders—belong to men. Men patrol and protect the borders. Macedonian and Albanian women are relegated to serving food, taking care of children, providing sexual services to men, tending the wounded, and lamenting the killings. And although they are not portrayed performing violence, they, the Albanian women especially, are the ones whose bodies endure male violence: before her death, Zamira is assaulted by her grandfather—called a "slut," a "whore," and beaten; Hana is locked up in her familial, multigenerational home.

Not surprisingly in this context, in order to greet Aleksandar Hana must first receive her father's permission to enter the room. She appears cloaked in dark clothing; her head is tightly wrapped; her eyes are cast down, confirming her subdued position in the house. She walks into the room only to serve food and drinks, and before she finally does look up, she looks at her father for permission to make eye contact with Aleksandar. She hardly speaks; she has no power to gaze and therefore no power to assert her subjectivity. As Aleksandar walks away, we see Hana's solemn face in the window, watching him. The window is barred, her face positioned behind the grates, underscoring her entrapment by the familial dynamics of patriarchy. Aleksandar's and Hana's eyes convey their affection for each other, and their looks manifest that they are both, in different ways, outcasts of the village. The difference between their positions, however, is crucial: he is entitled to mobility; she is not.

Female Hauntings

If women like Hana and Zamira are shown as controlled and tyrannized by their families, they are, at the same time, sites of critical possibilities. Given the context of the violence they experience—Zamira is killed, Hana bereaved—they obviously do not occupy liberatory positions. Nor does their resistance readily project a new model of "nation" that would contest phallocentric social structures. Still, aside from Aleksandar, the two women are the only ones who risk crossing the ethnic boundaries: Zamira because of her connection with Kiril; Hana because of her visit to Aleksandar's house, as she searches in desperation for her missing daughter. Even though they are narratively punished for their transgressive acts, through their actions both women point to the urgency of critiquing the intersection of patriarchal hegemony and the logic of ethnic violence. Their affiliations with men outside of their blood signal cross-cultural, cross-ethnic openings—cracks in a circle.

Interestingly, the women—like Aleksandar, who is marked by a sense of unsettling instability—set the temporal paradoxes in motion; they appear in the narrative at moments when, logically, their appearance should not be possible or seems least likely to occur. For example, during Aleksandar's visit at Hana's house we briefly see Zamira, even though she has been killed by her brother in the first section of the film, "Words." Also, at the opening of the film, we see Anne as a peripheral participant of a funeral in Macedonia. But we cannot understand her presence here until we find out who she is in the second part, "Faces," and then learn of Aleksandar's death at the end of "Pictures." Only at the closing of the narrative does the spectator realize that Anne comes to Macedonia because Aleksandar is dead and that the funeral that opens the film is his burial.

These narrative complications continually stress the tension between aesthetic expression and the way such an expression comments on politics, and

Zamira (Labina Mitevska) before the fatal confrontation with her Muslim relatives in "Words." Courtesy of Milcho Manchevski.

they lead us to consider the larger argument the film interrogates: the correlation between art and violence. Even before Aleksandar comes back to Macedonia, we hear his "confession"; he is experiencing an ethical crisis. "I killed. I killed," he tells Anne. This comment refers to Aleksandar's last trip to the front as a photojournalist during which he complained that there was nothing for him to photograph. The letter he writes to Anne from Macedonia reads in part:

> Dear Anne... It's gonna rain.... This place is the same as before, but my eyes have changed like a new fit on the lens. Last week I told you I killed. I was friendly with this militia man and I complained to him I wasn't getting anything exciting. He said, "no problem," pulled the prisoner out of the line and shot him on the spot. "Did you get that?"— he asked me. "I did." I took sides. My camera killed a man.[18]

As Aleksandar's voice-over narrates the letter, we see, shot by shot, detail by detail, the photographic sequence he is describing. From the moment a militia man points a gun at the back of the victim's head, through the slow motion of his falling down, Aleksandar's camera captures the killing of an anonymous man in Bosnia.[19]

While *Before the Rain* problematizes Aleksandar's position as a photojournalist and artist committed to his work, even through the involuntary instigation of the killing, the film's point is not simply to critique a single individual like Aleksandar. Instead, Aleksandar's ethical crisis regarding the aesthetic exploitation of death points to the way the West (specifically, in this context, photo editors in London) has used images of abjection, isolation, and destruction in the former Yugoslavia to transform them into an often sensationalized expression that becomes, as Žižek writes, "good fodder for hungry Western eyes."[20] Aleksandar's statement about killing with his camera invites us to consider whether, indeed, photography and, more generally, art can "kill." The answer the film gives is quite complex, one that forces the spectators to contemplate the very politics of representational practices. If art can be used as a political critique of war and violence (the position that *Before the Rain* appears to take), the film seems to suggest that there is a difference, however fragile, between art done for the sake of capturing and exploiting the morbid "beauty" of abjection, and a self-conscious art that foregrounds desubliminatory examination of abjection and the complexities of representing, in this context, the interethnic destruction.

The most compelling example, I think, of how *Before the Rain* desublimates abjection is figured through a series of black-and-white photographs representing Zamira's killing. In the second part, "Faces," as I have already mentioned, Anne studies photographs showing Zamira's final moments and death. The film implies that she receives the photographs from Aleksandar, yet, if he took the photographs of the killing and gave them to Anne in London, this would mean that he himself survived Zamira's death. However, by the end of the narrative we know that Aleksandar dies *before* Zamira is shot. In fact, he dies because he tries to save Zamira.

Some critics have argued that the end of the film suggests that the narrative has created a full circle.[21] While on the level of imagery, the spectators might have the impression of a return to the opening scene (we again see Kiril in the tomato garden and a running Zamira), the narrative chronology has been foiled, especially by use of the photographs with Zamira. It is the haunting appearance and reappearance of these still photographs that prompts a series of questions: Who took these photographs? How is it logically possible for them to materialize at different diegetic moments? Where is their stable place in the narrative? Why do they weigh on the film with their insistent reoccurrence? It is clear that the photographs are the site of ambiguity, an ontological puzzle of the film. Their frequent insertion into the narrative has altered the film's temporality, impeded its narrative rhythm. The photographs have created yet another temporal space that is interjected into the film's larger space—a frame within a frame, or time within time, of fragments of transitory and shifting moments. These moments ask us to think about the way we experience narrative time, so-called screen time, and to contemplate how such time differs in its dynamic from the way we might "feel" time created by the still photographs.

These formal complications are important, I believe, not because they underline an aesthetic experimentation and sophisticated formal "play," but rather because they stress the need to foreground the difficulty embedded in representing violence. Specifically, what is at stake here is the problem of the aestheticization of death and the erasure of violence done to Zamira. Because the presence of the photographs within the narrative design is disjunctive, they create a sense of discomfort and confusion, suggesting that there is indeed no fixed place for them within the diegesis. It is as if they symbolically refuse to be contained by the narrative and instead, like Zamira who also appears and reappears, disrupt the narrative movement and haunt the spectatorial vision.

BODILY EXPULSIONS/VIOLENCE OF VOMIT

Although Manchevski's film depicts a crisis of national identity engendered by the discourse of authenticity—that is, a claim to legitimate ownership of a place—the reconceived idea of a nation as a multicultural community that can recognize and respect a multitude of otherness *within* itself becomes the film's haunting. This effect results from the cracks, the small splinters that, as the formal arrangement of the narrative demonstrates, interrogate the circularity of ethnic violence. I have suggested that these narrative cracks are performed by Aleksandar's transnational status and by the liminality of the main female characters, whose actions, while restrained by the patriarchal logic of their communities, point to the need to challenge the phallocentric dynamic of violence that implicates men as fighters/killers and women as their submissive, quiet servants. Thus, the temporal disjunctions in the film, which make our comprehension of the narrative at times frustrating, might be interpreted as performative sites calling into question the violently revolving hatred of otherness. In this sense the film calls for the need to loosen the violent and unyielding conceptual rigidity of the idea of national identity, to conceive of the "I" dialectically: "against origins and starting from them" (Kristeva 1993, 16).

To show how the issue of national identity, nationalist logic, and what Robert Burgoyne terms "the emotional pull of ethnic modes of belonging" (2000, 161) always necessarily involves one's body, *Before the Rain* continually assaults its audience with repeated images of blood and sounds of vomiting—the visual-aural motifs that underline the narrative theme of violence and bodily reactions to it. These acts of vomiting signify more than the bodily need to cleanse one's self at the sight of horrible brutality; these moments are acts of awakening, acts of solidarity with the ones who die, who are, in fact, brutally expelled out of being. The vomiting—sounds of bodily excess—parallels the ejection of the unwanted people, those who need to be expelled beyond the validated realm of cultural intelligibility. In other words, the very performance of vomiting is a gesture toward an identification with the abject zone, a space without which the subject cannot call itself a subject and, simultaneously, a space historically repudiated because it points to the very materiality and negation of the self.[22]

Arrested by the hollow gazes of the war victims in the photographs, Anne vomits. Her response parallels Kiril's earlier reaction to the brutal killing of a cat by one of the Christian villagers, whose gunfire shreds the body of a cat to pieces. Unlike Kiril and Anne who shiver in pain at the sight of violence done *to* others, Aleksandar's act of bodily expulsion is more about himself when he recognizes that he has performed an act of violence with his camera. The moment of destroying the highly troublesome photographs documenting the death of a Bosnian man and expelling them from representation signals an awakening mobilized through the painful experience of an encounter with horror. All three characters, in different ways, respond to violence bodily. An experience that one cannot simply intellectualize shatters the body. Vomit—an expulsion of the unthinkable, the horrible—is presented as a defense of the flesh against death and abjection. These bodily responses to violence suggest that the film wants to make a visceral appeal by binding the spectator's gaze to the expelled bodies of those who fall victim to the logic of racial hatred.

Within this conceptual framework, *Before the Rain* shows a self-conscious awareness of the difficulties embedded in representing violence with the purpose of critiquing it yet without glamorizing it as a staged spectacle. The film is conscious of analyzing violence without falling into the dangers of reinscribing it as it tries to refrain from exploiting images of gratuitous brutality. At the same time, however, the film appears to function concomitantly on two clashing levels. On the one hand, the spectators are lured with the appealing images of the

Macedonian landscape, the aesthetics of the Orthodox liturgy, poignant music, the tragic beauty of Zamira and Kiril. On the other hand, the film hopes to elude spectatorial comfort zones through its metaphorical attention to blood and vomit, preventing us from feeling that the impending war the narrative represents is a conflict that does not involve us. This implication of the audience is, certainly, hard to achieve, given the fact that most of the narrative is located in a distant Macedonian village, seemingly far away from the Western culture that, Page duBois writes, often likes to believe that "barbarism resides elsewhere, in the other, that other world, unenlightened, steeped in medievalism and bloody cruelty" (1991, 155). Critiquing first world cultures for the displacement of torture into the non-Western world, duBois comments:

> Rather torture has become a global spectacle, a comfort to the so-called civilized nations, persuading them of their commitment to humanitarian values, revealing to them the continued barbarism of the other world, a world that continues to need the guidance of Europe and North America, a guidance that is offered in the form of a transnational global economy controlling torture as one of the instruments of world domination. (157)

DuBois's critique of the way the first world likes to preserve its projected superiority reveals a Eurocentric ideological positioning: Western nations like to maintain that they are protected from "the continued barbarism," that the horrors transpire beyond their limits in "the other world," but also wish to sustain their role as rescuers and leaders in maintaining the world's order under the slogans of humanitarian concerns.

Manchevski's film exposes the logic of such "discursive colonization," to use Chandra Talpade Mohanty's words, by refusing to create a space where the audience can feel safely positioned outside the discourse of ethnic cleansing (1995, 260). Frequent use of close-ups after Aleksandar enters Macedonia does not permit the spectator to feel emotional distance or to perceive the characters of the village as depersonalized masses. The camera's attention to details exposes the pain written into the mise-en-scène of the region. Old women's tired, wrinkled faces; their bent backs; bony donkeys; malnourished, exhausted dogs hardly able to walk—all these images enunciate the specificity of pain. And as the narrative movement of each episode binds our gaze, the audience experiences a "history of what has not yet happened"—the foreboding sense of the impending destruction, the heaviness of the mise-en-scène, the moments "before the rain" (Rosenstone 2000b, 191).

Sounds of thunder and remarks by various characters about rain frame the narrative. In the beginning of "Words," the monk's comment establishes the narrative space: "It will rain. It smells of rain." Later Hana's father tells Aleksandar, "Blood is in the air. It should rain." And finally, Aleksandar's last words—"It's going to rain"—cue us to the impending eruption of conflict. Indeed, the concluding scene, which leads us back to the beginning of the narrative, takes place amid heavy drops of rain and lingers on the image of the exile's corpse, drenched in blood and abandoned. And so we are left to ponder the cruelty of bodily expulsions and the moment of dreaded identification with the site of abjection.

New Europe: Eyes Wide Shut, 2004. Copyright Kamil Turowski. All rights reserved.

Afterword
The Last Immigrant

> The border experience can happen whenever and wherever
> two or more cultures meet peacefully or violently.
>
> —Guillermo Gómez-Peña, "Bilingualism, Biculturalism, and Borders"

As I end this project, I reflect on the curious fact that, especially in my days of becoming a resident alien, it did not occur to me to consider myself a transnational, much less a cosmopolitan. Even without a critical-theoretical apparatus, I instinctively sensed that such categories typically apply to people like my American professors and colleagues who, while traveling professionally, for example, under faculty exchange programs from the United States to France or Hungary, liked to speak about their multicultural experiences as cosmopolitan adventures. I grasped that cosmopolitanism is a matter of nationality, race, and privileged class discourse. But just recently, in a somewhat paradoxical twist of fate, as I was teaching my Transnational Narratives/American Contexts senior seminar (under the rubric of "world literature"), one student openly expressed her relief over seeing me as the instructor for this class: "I am glad to see you as our professor, as I believe we can trust someone so 'cosmopolitan' to teach us about world literature." The student did not know my personal history of origins and displacements; what prompted her to make this observation was my accented speech, indicating that I am from elsewhere. Hence, my presumed cosmopolitanism was translated in this pedagogical context as a position of authentic authority and epistemological privilege.

Why then is it so hard for certain aliens, even of the resident kind, to exchange their exilic, in-between selfhood for a supposedly comfortable cosmopolitan identity as a citizen of the world? Before I offer a possible answer, I turn again to Julia Kristeva:

> Beyond the *origins* that have assigned to us biological identity papers and a linguistic, religious, social, political, historical place, the freedom of contemporary individuals may be gauged according to their ability to *choose* their membership, while the democratic capability of a nation and social group is revealed by the right it affords individuals to exercise that choice. *Thus when I say that I have chosen cosmopolitanism, this means that I have, against origins and starting from them, chosen a transnational or international position situated at the crossing of boundaries.* (1993, 16; my emphasis)

The notion of conceptualizing the "I" "against origins and starting from them" feels immediately astute and provocative. It forcefully speaks about the need to rethink the self according to a different logic, one that contests monocultural, historically oppressive nation-state narratives of identity. That is, such a new paradigm contests the idea of a straightforward and transparent relationship between the self and the nation: it inspects a nation's "ownership" over the self; it interrogates unquestioned discourses of belonging; it probes the issues of legitimacy and authenticity in relation to the very notion of national identity.

However, although Kristeva's is certainly a seductive proposition, the stress on choosing one's national affiliation and a transnational position presupposes that one has access to such a choice and ignores a whole array of specific experiences of those whose agency and mobility are frequently severely limited: refugees, migrants, and displaced people; those without proper papers; the deported ones; the stateless ones; the noncitizens confined to sweatshop factories or refugee camps. As my readings have shown, mobility for aliens is always conflicted because of legal restrictions. Passports, visas, and green cards navigate aliens' lives with a particular intensity, and an access to a cosmopolitan identity is often an unattainable luxury. In the contemporary era of globalization, the choosing appears to belong to, in Zygmunt Bauman's words, "the world of the globally mobile," while those without admission to the freedom of mobility remain impoverished, barred from entering this new site of privilege (1998b, 88).

Not long ago, for example, entire communities east of the Berlin Wall were forcibly confined within the boundaries of their countries. An option to leave the second world could be exercised by only a few in the privileged elite; ordinary citizens did not even own passports. When it was finally possible to apply for a temporary passport, one had to go first through a series of interrogations, explaining and documenting one's desire for mobility as well as signing declarations promising one's prompt return. Nowadays, in the post-Wall period, exit and entry visas and border customs in Europe are being abolished, contributing to the celebratory rhetoric of globalized mobility, particularly in the former Soviet bloc. In Poland, for example, media routinely feature ads with well-known public figures proudly proclaiming: Yes, I am a European.

The subtle irony about this newfound political climate is manifold and

Afterword

"Certainly, everyone who lives in Poland knows what it means to be a European.... Now the time has come to be in this collective Europe, not only for beautiful ideas, but for very specific benefits as well."

nuanced. Such euphoric acknowledgments about finally being able to own a truly pan-European status speak to a certain self-awareness of one's abjected position and to a desire to move beyond the painful legacy of the Wall that once literally as well as metaphorically divided the two Europes. Furthermore, this euphoria about belonging to one unified Europe foregrounds the larger unspoken point here: that post-Soviet countries, exhausted by the legacy of communism, pursue Western-like identity, while Western Europe, through a benevolent gesture of inclusion, may now allow its poor cousins to participate in the grand narrative of the New Europe.

Despite this critical shift, a shift that not long ago seemed unthinkable, one wonders to what extent the climate of unification is illusory in its privileges, especially since the asymmetries in the economic, political, and military powers in the new European Union remain intact. In fact, the process of East-West engagement has been very uneven, and Western Europe dominates it as the center of authority and control for the entire continent, more so now than ever before. Western European countries are now free to invest in and take advantage of East European markets previously closed off to foreign investors. At the same time, because of their economic inferiority, Eastern and Central Europeans are left with only token privileges like travel visas (for those who can afford them) and what effectively amounts to a minority vote in the European Parliament. Considering these asymmetries, Bauman, for example, argues that the new regulations promoting mobility and their celebratory tone of freedom are, indeed, highly deceptive:

> Progressively, entry visas are phased out all over the globe. But not passport control. The latter is still needed—perhaps more than ever before—to sort out the confusion which the abolition of the visas might have created: *to set apart those for whose convenience and whose ease of travel the visas have been abolished, from those who should have stayed put—not meant to travel in the first place.* (1998b, 87; my emphasis)

These new stratifications—the differences between those who may have validated access to mobility and those who may not—and their sustenance testify to the fact that contemporary movement across the borders is a symbolic and material benefit enjoyed only by a few select groups, beyond the advantages of most.

Since my book puts in dialogue narratives from Latin American and Caribbean American contexts and situates them next to second world voices, it allows us to consider parallels between different border regions. Mexicans, for instance, have had a different, but similarly conflicted relationship with the U.S. border in the sense of coping with a powerful and expansive neighbor whose culture usurps control of the entire continent. In a manner analogous to the post-Wall communities labeled as "the other Europe," Mexicans are cast as Latinos, not Americans, even though they live on the continent of the Americas. The irony, of course, is that, geographically at least, post-Wall communities *are* European as much as Mexicans *are* North Americans, but neither group has historically been able to claim this appellation fully. Playing with these notions of identity, belonging, and ownership, some Mexican-American "border artists" embrace the liminal space they occupy by flattening the hierarchy between the two cultures.

I am particularly reminded of Gómez-Peña's performance art and writing dedicated to the ongoing formulation and reformulation of a border identity. As a Mexican-American artist, Gómez-Peña has been engaged in the creation of what he terms an "aesthetics of fusion and juxtaposition," that is, a conscious mixing of Anglo and Spanish cultures, motivated by his own upbringing in both Mexico and the United States. In his performance art, he refers to himself and his collaborator, Roberto Sifuentes, as "experimental linguists," "activist artists," "iconoclasts and provocateurs," and "border citizens" devoted to experiments with identity (*A World of Art,* 1997). He writes:

> Many "deterritorialized" Latin American artists in Europe and the U.S. have opted for "internationalism" (a cultural identity based upon the "most advanced" of the ideas originating out of New York or Paris). I, on the other hand, opt for "borderness" and assume my role: My generation, the *chilangos* [slang term for a Mexico City native], who came to "el norte" fleeing the imminent ecological and social catastrophe of Mexico City... became Chicano-ized. We de-Mexicanized ourselves to Mexi-understand ourselves, some without wanting to, others on purpose. And one day, the border became our house, laboratory, and ministry of culture (or counterculture). (1988, 127)

In choosing "borderness," Gómez-Peña is certainly critical of the notion of international identity as a somewhat snobbish formulation validating once again an aesthetic and cultural importance of Western first worldness. At the same time, his comment compellingly evokes Kristeva's remark about positioning one's self "against origins and starting from" in that it points to not just the philosophical possibilities but also the material necessities of living a border, nonsingular identity. At stake for him is, he argues, "the creation of alternative cartographies, a ferocious critique of the dominant culture of both countries [United States and Mexico], and ... a proposal for a new creative language" (130).

Such an "alternative cartography," figured through what Gómez-Peña calls an "extreme aesthetic behavior," is forcefully represented in "The Last Immigrant," an installation component of a performance titled *The Temple of Confessions* (*A World of Art,* 1997). I focus on "The Last Immigrant" in my conclusion because it synthesizes many issues I have been theorizing in this book: alien body, consumption of difference, and social processes of abjection directed at immigrants.

Recorded on video and performed in collaboration with César Martinez, "The Last Immigrant," as Gómez-Peña puts it, was born of a critique of post-NAFTA United States: "NAFTA means open markets and closed borders, especially for Mexico. It's such a paradoxa." The performance features the process of homemaking of the "last immigrant": mixing Jell-O ingredients and creating a mold shaped like an adult human being. The mold is filled with the quivering gelatin mix, and, the artists comment, "an Aztec Jell-O man is born"—garnished with strawberries and whipped cream and ready for consumption. What follows is an invitation to the audience at the Corcoran Gallery of Art to an all-you-can-eat buffet where "The Eating of the Corpse of the Last Immigrant" is performed by the artists as well as audience members.

The conflictual provocation of "The Last Immigrant" is played out on many levels, anticipating visceral responses. The ingredients out of which the immigrant is created are very familiar, connoting pleasurable dessert. Yet the context of this serving—a human figure that is being dug into and scooped onto plates—inevitably evokes feelings of repulsion, even nausea and disgust. In short, we watch the performance of abjection: abjection of an immigrant being literally consumed by the audience, a creepy spectacle of destruction and absorption of the flesh. The creepiness is underlined by the fact that the immigrant, in his posture with arms folded over his chest, simulates a dead body, though uncannily quivering through its substance.

The power of abjection is such that the one who does the abjecting solidifies his or her own being through the expulsion of the one who is repudiated, unwanted. "The Last Immigrant," playing on antialien sentiments and fears, proposes a radical form of abjection: Let's consume the immigrant, thus assuring that his ejection is complete and final. Let's literally possess an immigrant's body. Coco Fusco, an interdisciplinary artist with whom Gómez-Peña collaborated, makes an interesting statement that sheds further light on how to read "The Last Immigrant." She claims that the prevailing mode of experiencing other cultures on the part of Anglo-Americans is through commodification and consumption. Referring to shopping, or eating ethnic food, Fusco argues that "ethnicity and otherness become a vicarious experience of sentimentality and emotion, and a reassertion of power through the act of consuming" (quoted in Sawchuk 1992, 29). Such a critique exposes subtle operations of the logic of difference that Western culture, through its powers of representation, instills in all of us: always teaching palatable and safe encounters with otherness, validating experiences of other cultures with the purpose of enriching our own multicultural education.

The conceptual twist offered by "The Last Immigrant" is the investigation of this presumed safety. That is, through the consumption of the quivering body of an immigrant, the audience not only actively instigates abjection but is peculiarly abjected in the process as well. By "possessing" the immigrant, the audience invites metaphorical and literal contamination of their own flesh. Shrewdly, thus, within the polite mise-en-scène of a buffet-party gathering, the performed violence is bidirectional, undermining the power and pleasure of the consumers. Simultaneously, however, the ritual of consumption, "The Eating of the Corpse of the Last Immigrant," inevitably also is a eucharistic simulation, evoking the Christian ritual of incorporation. The artist who invites the audience to a buffet is dressed in a priestlike robe; he speaks from behind the pulpit; the installation refers to "the corpse" of an immigrant. Considering this iconography and the particular context of the buffet, "The Last Immigrant" calls on the Christian notion of the sacred while also making it profane, taking it out of its dominating position. Thus, we may read the possession of an immigrant's body as a conflicted symbolic union with the other, an unsettling oneness with the alien body.

Notes

Preface

1. For an overview of historical reconfigurations of "transnationalism" and its meanings, see, e.g., Guarnizo and Smith 1998; Tölölyan 1996; Shohat and Stam 1996; Schiller 1999a.

2. See, e.g., Hoffman 1999. Eva Hoffman argues that "exile used to be thought of as a difficult condition. It involves dislocation, disorientation, self-division. But today, at least within a framework of postmodern theory, we have come to value exactly those qualities of experience that exile demands—uncertainty, displacement, the fragmented identity. Within this conceptual framework, exile becomes, well, sexy, glamorous, interesting. Nomadism and diasporism have become fashionable terms in intellectual discourse" (44).

As a complication of this point, see Ali Behdad's discussion, which, in the context of new directions for postcolonial theory, argues: "Postcolonial discussions of diaspora have problematically privileged literary and artistic expressions of displacement. Thus, they have constructed salutary models of exile that conflate the experience of the cultural elite with the everyday struggles of the ordinary immigrants—models that fail to address the historical specificities of immigrant lives" (2000, 407).

3. Bhabha 1996, 204; my emphasis. Gayatri Chakravorty Spivak makes a similar point, claiming that the diasporic underclass, the rural poor, and the urban subproletariat are the worst victims of transnationalization of global capital, which uses women in dominating and exploiting ways. Her larger argument

is that "transnationality is shrinking the possibility of an operative civil society in developing nations" (1997, 90–91).

4. For discussions of transnational feminist practices, see Grewal and Kaplan 1994, 1999.

5. Ella Shohat explains this notion in opposition to the simplistic idea of multiculturalism as merely evoking the existence of multiple cultures: "Unlike a liberal-pluralist discourse, polycentric multiculturalism entails a profound reconceptualization and restructuring of intercommunal relations within and beyond the nation state" (1998, 2).

6. For a concise critique of the "other Europe" notion, see Zaborowska 1995, ch. 1, 11–37. See also Stuart Hall's discussion of the "other" Europe as "elsewhere, other, the beyond . . . the mysterious east, barbarians clamouring at the gate of civilisation" (1992, 46).

7. For a discussion of the problematics of the three worlds theory, see, e.g., Ahmad 1987; Shohat 1992; Stam 1991.

8. *Toll v. Moreno*, 458 U.S. 1 (1982); http://laws.findlaw.com/us/458/1.html (accessed June 28, 2003).

9. *Harisiades v. Shaughnessy*, 342 U.S. 580 (1952); http://laws.findlaw.com/us/342/580.html (accessed June 28, 2003).

10. As Dorothy E. Roberts argues, "the regulation of membership in the national community does not only involve patrolling our borders to prevent disfavored groups from entering. The present nativism also includes efforts to restrict who may give birth to citizens within the nation's boundaries. Two types of legislation currently proposed accomplish this end: laws that prohibit certain immigrants from using reproductive health services and the elimination of automatic citizenship to U.S.-born children of undocumented aliens. . . . Denying dark-skinned immigrants the right to give birth to citizens perpetuates the racist ideal of a white American identity" (1997, 205). The case, for example, of the Nisei, second-generation Japanese Americans, citizens of the United States by birth, sent to internment camps during World War II, is another poignant instance that confirms that citizenship by birth is not an absolute guarantee of one's inclusion in the community. See Chang 1997.

11. *Harisiades v. Shaughnessy*.

INTRODUCTION

1. See, e.g., Jude Davis and Carol R. Smith's reading of the multiculturalism of *Independence Day*: "In *Independence Day*, it is a multicultural (white, black, Jewish), male and female, though softly heterosexual USA that succeeds in repelling alien invasion. However, these multiculturalist credentials are established by acts of cultural imperialism, in the USA's assumption of global preeminence and . . . by refashioning world history and identity into that of the USA" (1997, 148–49).

2. Jay Carr, "An Avalanche of Aliens," review of *Men in Black*, *Boston Globe*, July 1, 1997, E1.

3. My thinking about the logic of dirt and the logic of purity has been influenced by Mary Douglas (1966), who discusses the ideological and historical meanings of such concepts as purity, cleanliness, disorder, and pollution. I am also influenced by Kristeva's discussion of filth, defilement, and abjection in which she argues that casting off that which is "dirty" or "improper/unclean" is the very premise of the existence of the "I"; "what I permanently thrust aside in order to live" (1982, 3).

4. Carr, "An Avalanche of Aliens," E4.

5. Kuhn 1992, 13. Kuhn provides a useful discussion about the historical distinction between the notion of an alien as a foreign-born person and an alien as a science-fiction creature. She writes that the term "alien" has been employed to name the extraterrestrial only within the last fifty years or so; in the nineteenth century the word "alien" was used to name foreign-born residents, a shift that supposedly aimed at grounding the term within legal parameters: "Apologists for this shift point to a tendency in earlier times to look upon the alien as an enemy and to treat him as a criminal or outlaw. Now, though, the alien could enjoy legal protection from such barbaric treatment. Under the aegis of a liberal state, the alien was no longer to be the eternal outsider: armed with a passport, the alien could expect to travel freely among us: might even—given naturalisation—become one of Us. In this process, the documented alien, if no longer an outcast, is made visible, subject to observation and regulation as to protection."

6. See Louis Sahagun, "Immigration Sweep Stirs Cloud of Controversy," *Los Angeles Times,* September 1, 1997, A5.

7. "Chinese-American Rep. Denied Entry," *New York Times* on the Web, May 25, 2001.

8. I quote from a letter I received from Representative Wu. The letter included a copy of a transcript of his May 25, 2001, speech in the House of Representatives.

9. Dale Russakoff, "N.J. Secrecy Rule Keeps Arab American in Jail in the Dark," *Washington Post,* January 3, 2003, A1.

10. The Enhanced Border Security and Visa Reform Act of 2002 and the Patriot Act of 2001 were signed into law with the main objective to identify and eliminate potential terrorists from entering the United States or from residing in this country undetected after entry. However, as George N. Lester, a member of the American Immigration Lawyers Association, indicates, these changes affect all noncitizens traveling to or living or working in the United States in a variety of ways. Under these acts, all visa applicants from countries designated "state sponsors of terrorism" require a special background security check; all male visa applicants aged sixteen to forty-five, regardless of nationality, are now obliged to submit new forms providing extensive background information; students and exchange visa applicants are expected to be under the additional scrutiny of their academic institutions through an online system for electronic verification; automatic revalidation of visas for temporary visitors to the United States is

now severely restricted; visitors previously allowed to come to the United States without a visa under the Visa Waiver Program (mainly Western Europeans) will also be subject to heightened passport requirements. George N. Lester, "Survey of Post-9/11 Security, Travel and Visa Related Changes in U.S. Immigration Law and Procedure," *Boston Bar Journal* 46, no. 5 (November–December 2002).

11. Mary Louise Pratt, "Waking to the Dinosaur," President's Column, *MLA Newsletter* 35 (2003): 3.

12. Sapiro 1984, 9. This situation began to change with the Cable Act of 1922, an act that marked the shift toward independent citizenship for women (though a woman's citizenship was still conditional on her husband's), and finally, with the 1934 Citizenship Act, which "granted women the same rights as men to gain, hold, and transmit citizenship to their children" (15).

13. Smith 1998, 146. Smith explains that after 1902 U.S.-born citizen women could lose their citizenship if they married alien men: "Most of these women subsequently regained their U.S. citizenship when their husbands naturalized. However, those who married Chinese, Japanese, Filipino, or other men racially ineligible to naturalize forfeited their U.S. citizenship" (148).

14. Chang 1997, 247. Citing specific citizenship cases, Chang notes that the Court held "in essence that Asian immigrants could not become naturalized; they could not become full members of the national community, even if they wanted to become citizens" (ibid.).

15. See, e.g., Haney-López 1996; Ignatiev 1995; Guglielmo and Salerno 2003.

16. On the discussion of eugenics and the history of immigration, see Roberts 1997. Zolberg's quotes come from a brochure I obtained at the Ellis Island Immigration Museum in December 2000. The brochure was developed as part of the Millennium Program by the Statue of Liberty National Monument/Ellis Island Immigration Museum through the support of the national Ethnic Coalition of Organizations. Aristide R. Zolberg, "Why Can't Those Immigrants Be More Like Us? A Century of Immigration in America, 1900–2000," brochure (New York: Ellis Island Immigration Museum, 2000).

17. I quote here from the exhibition materials obtained from the Ellis Island Immigration Museum, December 2001.

18. I quote here from an e-mail distributed among Ohio University faculty by University Communications and Marketing, December 20, 2001.

19. I quote from an e-mail sent by the Center for International Studies to the English Department faculty at Ohio University, June 28, 2001.

20. For a discussion of these issues, see, for example, the section "The World in the Classroom: Women Teaching Diaspora," *Women's Review of Books,* February 2002, 3–18. See also Shohat's argument about multicultural feminist pedagogy in her introduction to *Talking Visions* (1998), especially the section "Missing Links: Beyond National and Disciplinary Borders," 38–46.

21. See, e.g., Sharpe 2000; Rutherford 1990; Schiller 1999b.

22. I do not suggest that the discussions of aliens in relation to immigra-

tion, diasporic experiences, and border crossings never appear in transnational feminist cultural studies. Even though the notion of alienhood is not necessarily foregrounded in their work, such scholars as Chandra Talpade Mohanty, Ella Shohat, and Gayatri Chakravorty Spivak all explore ideological valences of being coded as aliens. See Mohanty 1998; Shohat 1998; and Spivak 2002.

23. For a succinct overview of these issues, see Singh and Schmidt 2000.

24. See special issue of the *Women's Review of Books,* February 2002.

25. Regarding the definition of "flexible citizenship," Ong argues that "in the era of globalization, individuals as well as governments develop a flexible notion of citizenship and sovereignty as strategies to accumulate capital and power. 'Flexible citizenship' refers to the cultural logics of capitalist accumulation, travel, and displacement that induce subjects to respond fluidly and opportunistically to changing political-economic conditions. . . . These logics and practices are produced within particular structures of meaning about family, gender, nationality, class mobility, and social power" (1999, 6).

26. I draw here on Ursula Biemann's video essay, *Performing the Border.* Biemann focuses on the Mexican–U.S. border town, Ciudad Juárez (across from El Paso, Texas), where U.S. multinational corporations assemble electronic and digital equipment, employing large numbers of Mexican women from the area. Focusing on the growing feminization of the global economy, her fascinating essay posits the notion of the border as both a discursive and material space linked to the practices of economic, sexual, and labor violence that govern the lives of the employed women.

27. Pierrette Hondagneu-Sotelo, "Transnational Motherhood," http://www.pbs.org/itvs/thecity/immigration4_1.html (accessed August 1, 2002).

28. I use Mandy Jacobson's and Karmen Jelinčič's *Calling the Ghosts,* a documentary reconstruction of war events involving two women who grew up together in Prijedor, Bosnia. In this poignant narrative, Nusreta Sivac, a civil judge, and Jadranka Cigelj, an attorney, grapple with representing their past in Prijedor after the Serbian takeover on April 29, 1992. The film narrates experiences related to their torture and atrocities they witnessed at Omarska Camp and their activist work afterward in Croatia. One of the central points of the documentary involves the issues of silence and speech, that is, what it means for women survivors to speak (and hence expose themselves) versus what it means to be engaged in the narration of lived traumas. As Cigelj puts it, commenting on her work recording various women's stories: "The crime has not been filmed with a camera; it is only recorded in the memory of the witness. In order to expose the crime, you violate the witness." Sivac, too, comments on the pain of retelling experiences of torture: "I always say, it's a new shock every time you talk about it. . . . But I feel some kind of obligation toward all those women, friends of mine who are now gone, who were killed in the camp, toward all those people who were dear to me. . . . If the story is not told, then no one will know about it, right?"

Another important point the film raises is the issue of representation of the atrocities during the Balkan war by the Western media and ethical responsibility that comes with those practices of representation. One woman in the film, addressing Western journalists who are eager to speak to "raped women," says, "If you are going to help us—film us; if not, don't shoot us." For an important critique of representation in this context, see Kesić 2002.

29. I refer here to, for example, Shohat and Stam 2003; and Grewal and Kaplan 1994.

30. "Singapore on My Mind: Fiona Cheong, Lydia Kwa, and Shirley Geok-lin Lim Compare Notes," *Women's Review of Books,* July 2002, 25.

31. This point is especially important for my analysis. When I present my work on exilic alienhood in front of audiences, I typically hear a variation of this comment: "So, you argue that we are *all* exiles, right?" I am always stunned at such comments because no matter how hard I try to situate my discussions within specific historical, racial, sexual, and ethnic contexts, the old push toward seeing exile as an existential, universal condition inevitably surfaces, erasing the contextual frameworks I discursively set up.

32. Shohat's discussion of ethnicity is of special importance here. In the context of American cinema, she argues: "The disciplinary assumption that some films are 'ethnic' whereas others are not is ultimately based upon the view that certain groups are ethnic whereas others are not. The marginalization of 'ethnicity' reflects the imaginary of the dominant group which envisions itself as the 'universal' or the 'essential' American nation, and thus somehow 'beyond' or 'above' ethnicity" (1991, 215).

33. I am indebted to Kristeva's conceptualization of the figure of the foreigner, specifically to her shift to recognize the foreigner's foreignness within the "I" itself. When she writes "the foreigner is within us" (1991, 191), she does not mean that we are all foreigners. Rather, she refuses to locate otherness and difference somewhere else and calls for the disruption of the binary logic of the "I"—privileged native and "other"—unwanted intruder–stranger, a call that invites us to rethink the historically sanctioned self.

1. BECOMING TRANSNATIONAL

1. Speaking of transnational exilic cinema, Hamid Naficy expresses an idea pertinent for my discussion: "By being historically situated and culturally specific, and by paying attention to the inequality of power relations at the borders, the best of border films avoid being recuperated into the hegemonizing and homogenizing celebratory discourses of border crossing and globalization" (2001, 243).

2. Annette Insdorf, "'El Norte': On Screen and in Reality, a Story of Struggle," *New York Times,* January 8, 1984, 17.

3. The effort to preserve the firsthand recollections of immigrants is part of the Ellis Island Oral History Project. Begun in 1973, the project has accumulated over 1,700 interviews. My data is from the brochure "Ellis Island Library

and Oral History Project," which I obtained during my visit to the Ellis Island Immigration Museum in December 2000.

4. Reeves notes that as many as 2 percent of immigrants were sent back home each year (2000, 51). As many testimonials describe, the medical examination was the most dreaded part of the inspection process. On average, 15 to 20 percent of the newcomers were literally marked for further examination with chalk and coded: Ct for trachoma, L for lameness, Pg for pregnancy, K for insanity (59). Also, until 1911, all immigrants had to climb a flight of stairs leading to the examination room on the second floor. Doctors carefully watched the climbers to detect any deformities that might disqualify them.

5. Insdorf, "El Norte," 17.

6. See, e.g., Benamou 1988; Fregoso 1993; List 1989; and Barrerra 1992.

7. Naficy emphasizes this reading, arguing that while the first section of the film is marked by openness and immensity, the second is coded by closedness and claustrophobia (2001, 157).

8. As Chris List explains, the notion of disappearing within a Guatemalan context is marked by a specific historical meaning: "In Guatemala, when someone is kidnapped by the army, they are often tortured and their body is hidden. The practice is referred to as 'disappearing.' Since 1954, when the C.I.A. orchestrated the overthrow of the democratically elected government of Guatemalan President Arbenz, more than 10,000 people have been disappeared in Guatemala" (1996, 120).

9. Fregoso reads such a marking of Rosa as highly problematic: "Whereas the filmmakers intended to render a neo-Mayan (alternative) vision of an indigenous worldview, *El Norte*'s representation follows the conventional Western division of Nature/Culture, positing female subjectivity in the unknown, Mystery, nature, and woman as the ground for cultural reproduction and maintenance" (1993, 110).

10. Fregoso presents a useful discussion of the ambivalent status of coyotes: "Coyotes' livelihoods depend not just on their ability to live on the border of two cultures, but more precisely on the fact that they exist beyond the legislative frontiers of both" (1993, 85).

11. Rosa's remodeling is prompted by Nacha whose overall function in the narrative is to instruct Rosa in proper ways of inhabiting the world of *el norte*. Importantly, Nacha's comments about the need to cover up Rosa's Indianness are not meant to patronize Rosa. Nacha already knows what kinds of bodily visions are acceptable in the reality they occupy. Furthermore, Rosa's eventual transformation is not necessarily represented in an eroticized way. This suggests the narrative's conscious destressing of stereotypical representations of Latina women historically propagated by Hollywood productions. Hence, the normative portrayal of Latinas as hot-blooded, luring, exotic "objects" is clearly foiled here. For more on this subject, see, e.g., Fuentes 1992.

2. Accented Bodies and Coercive Assimilation

1. See, e.g., Behdad 1993, 2000; Guarnizo and Smith 1998.

2. Even though the category of "immigrant literature" has a historically validated presence in the United States, its sanctioned deployment inadvertently creates a sense of marginalization, even ghettoization, and marks "immigrant" texts as if of special ethnic interests. I am thinking here, for example, about a 1999 anthology on immigrant writing, *The Immigrant Experience in North American Literature* (Payant and Rose 1999). The title of the book suggests the impulse I am discussing, that is, conceptualizing immigrant texts as worthy of being given a niche within the canon of American literature. In their introduction, the editors argue for this kind of literature in the following way: "First, our approach is thematic and we see no problem with discussing immigration as a theme in American literature. Second, we would argue that much of the literature discussed in these essays is of high aesthetic quality, fit to stand alongside writing by 'mainstream' American writers" (xxvi). What is troubling in these formulations is the way the immigrant texts are coded as second-class citizens for whom a special plea needs to be made based on their aesthetic literary merits.

3. Basch, Schiller, and Szanton Blanc 1994, 8. As many would point out, this is a debatable idea. For example, given the vast body of filmic work produced in the second half of the twentieth century within the category of what Hamid Naficy (2001) terms "transnational exilic cinema," this statement could be just as valid when we approach the analysis of "in-betweenness" in transnational filmmaking.

4. See Grewal and Kaplan 1994 as one of the important books in this area.

5. This is, of course, not an exhaustive list. I purposefully chose the authors whose narratives give a sense of the range of the heterogeneity of transnational identities in relation to American citizenry: Arab, Cuban, Dominican, Haitian, Indian, Korean, Polish, to name just a few. The issue of immigrant literature and its insufficient parameters to contain the work of the authors I am mentioning needs further clarification. While evaluating the positioning of the texts I am discussing in relation to American literature, the category of "immigrant writing" is the one typically evoked. For example, Alvarez, Danticat, Divakaruni, Garcia, Hoffman, Mukherjee have all been classified as immigrant authors. But such a rendition of these writers and their work seems only partially fitting. Alvarez, Danticat, and Garcia, for example, were born outside U.S. borders, but were mainly raised and educated in the United States while maintaining connections with their respective originary places of belonging—Dominican Republic, Haiti, Cuba. Mukherjee, for instance, consciously rejects the label of an immigrant author, defiantly seeing herself as an American writer, a position for which she has been widely criticized: "I view myself as an American author in the tradition of other American authors whose ancestors arrived at Ellis Island" (Carb 1988, 650). Even though she is often classified as an Indian-American writer, she

refuses the hyphen as well: "I choose to describe myself on my own terms, that is, as an American without hyphens. It is to sabotage the politics of hate and the campaigns of revenge spawned by Eurocentric patriots on the one hand and the professional multiculturalists on that other that I describe myself as an American rather than as an Asian-American" (Bharati Mukherjee, "Beyond Multiculturalism," *Des Moines Register,* October 2, 1994, 2C).

6. Carole Boyce Davies uses the interesting notion of migratory subjectivities to discuss "cross-cultural, transnational, translocal, diasporic perspectives" that allow for the redefinition of "identity away from exclusion and marginality." Her focus is the category of "black women's writing" (Davies 1998, 996).

7. In 1991, the novel won the PEN Oakland/Josephine Miles Book Award for works that present multicultural viewpoints. Reviewers and interviewers refer to *How the García Girls Lost Their Accents* as semiautobiographical, or loosely autobiographical. Given the history of Alvarez's family exile from the Dominican Republic to the United States as political refugees in flight from Rafael Trujillo's dictatorship, the connections between her life and the lives of the fictional characters in the novel seem obvious. Alvarez was brought up in the Dominican Republic and came to New York as a ten-year-old girl in 1960. In numerous interviews, she acknowledges that what she writes comes out of her experience, but it is also fictionalized, altered, expanded: "So I think definitely my story is part of that first novel. But not only my story, the stories of my people, Latinos who were also Americans, a hybrid. I was especially interested in Latinas who were also dealing with gender issues, issues about being 'nice girls' from Latino families who had to deal with the rough and tough new world to which they had come. This story, the story of women like us, was one I had never read before. That's why I felt it was necessary for me to put it down on paper." "Citizen of the World: An Interview with Julia Alvarez," in *Latina Self-Portraits: Interviews with Contemporary Women Writers,* ed. Bridget Kevane and Juanita Heredia (Albuquerque: University of New Mexico Press, 2000), 26.

8. See, e.g., Saadawi 1997, for a powerful explication of dominant "uses" of multiculturalism that become "an exhibition, a spectacle for the pleasure of others to see, to consume" (122).

9. Alvarez 1992, 160. Page numbers for further references to this novel appear in parentheses in the text.

10. For an important discussion on the way contemporary American nativism manifests itself in multiple efforts to regulate and restrict reproduction within the national boundaries, see Roberts 1997. She comments on laws that seek to control birthing of legal subjects-citizens: "Laws restricting the birth of citizens attempt concretely to control the demographics of the country. They are designed to reduce the actual numbers of disfavored groups in population, but their broader impact is mainly metaphysical. They send a powerful message about who is worthy to add their children to the future community of citizens.

Denying dark-skinned immigrants the right to give birth to citizens perpetuates the racist ideal of a white American identity" (205).

11. Susan Miller, "Caught between Cultures," review of *How the García Girls Lost Their Accents*, by Julia Alvarez, *Newsweek*, April 20, 1992, 78.

12. Heather Rosario-Sievert, "Conversation with Julia Alvarez," *Review: Latin American Literature and Arts* 54 (spring 1997): 33. In *Something to Declare*, Alvarez, who now lives in Vermont, includes "A Vermont Writer from the Dominican Republic," a response to a query asking how she defines herself as a writer: "Jessica Peet, a high-school student, read my first novel, *How the García Girls Lost Their Accents*, in her Vermont Authors class and wanted to know if I considered myself a Vermonter" (xiv). In her essay, Alvarez stresses her doubleness: "So, yes, although I am from a tropical island, I am also a Vermont writer" (195). She mentions that, as a Vermont writer, she joins the company of such well-known authors as Jamaica Kincaid and Aleksandr Solzhenitsyn, among others, who, like her, defy the logic of monocultural belonging. She says, "Certainly none of us are Vermont writers in the way my old-time Vermont neighbor defines the term" (187). See also "Doña Aida, with Your Permission," in *Something to Declare*, an essay in which Alvarez further explains her hybridized identity that is "of neither world" (174) as a "pan-American, a gringa-dominicana, a synthesizing consciousness" (175).

13. Karen Castellucci Cox comments on the condition of the exilic in-betweenness explicated in the novel: "Thus, living between two cultures creates its own kind of 'dis-ease'—a discomforting consciousness of things missing, neither a language, nor a culture, nor an extended family within which to position oneself" (2001, 135).

14. Alvarez mentions that, although one could see *Yo!* as a continuation of the García family story, the novel is more about the process of writing and debunking the myth of an artist as the sole source of the creation of the story: "*[Yo!]* suggests that the idea of the artist as an elite who has exclusive rights to the story is wrong.... And part of the novel is what price the people in an artist's life have to pay. We're always hearing about the anguish and the pain of the artist but not about the people who have to put up with the artist" (1998a, 141–42).

15. Roberta Rubenstein makes a good point in reading the significance of "Yoyo": "The narrator is 'Yoyo,' a nickname for the child Yolanda with a double meaning that encompasses her eventual predicament as an exile moving back and forth between two cultures" (2001, 75).

16. Donna Rifkind, "Speaking American," review of *How the García Girls Lost Their Accents*, by Julia Alvarez, *New York Times Book Review*, October 6, 1991, 14; Judith Freeman, "A Powerful Move Back to Ethnic Roots," review of *How the García Girls Lost Their Accents*, by Julia Alvarez, *Los Angeles Times*, June 7, 1991, 4.

17. For important critiques that interrogate the discourse of multiculturalism, see, e.g., Chicago Cultural Studies Group 1994; Goldberg 1994; Sharpe 2000; Shohat 1998; Wallace 1994; and Žižek 1997. Goldberg's essay is particularly valu-

able for sketching out the history of multiculturalism, which arose as a response to monoculturalism, understood as both an intellectual ideology and an institutional practice of the first half of the twentieth century. Of interest to my project is his discussion of the "homogenizing, assimilative thrust of conservative multiculturalism" (26). Other critical terms used are "corporate multiculturalism" (Chicago Cultural Studies Group critiques); "liberal multiculturalism" (Sharpe); "liberal-pluralist multiculturalism" (Shohat); multiculturalism based on "monological identities" (Wallace); and "Western liberal multiculturalism," or Eurocentrist "racism with a distance" (Žižek).

18. Some time ago my department discussed the need to hire a specialist in non-Western literature. The conversation emphasized how much we would profit from having a special person whose work would promote diversity. The unspoken assumption that underlined our discussion was that all the rest of us, the regular faculty, simply teach literature, and hence we do not need to be preoccupied with the issues of diversity. Diversity within this discourse is marked by specialness; an attractive bonus nowadays that, traditionally, is attached to scholars of color who are marked as multicultural specialists.

19. I discussed these ideas with my students in a world literature course, and my predominantly white students were interested to hear a black female student's comment that she routinely receives e-mail notes from the Office of Multicultural Affairs on our campus. The white students never received any notes from this office.

20. Ella Shohat and Robert Stam take up this issue in *Unthinking Eurocentrism*: "Eurocentric thinking, in our view, is fundamentally unrepresentative of a world which has long been multicultural. At times, even multiculturalists glimpse the issues through a narrowly national and exceptionalist grid, as when well-meaning curriculum committees call for courses about the 'contributions' of the world's diverse cultures to the 'development of *American* society,' unaware of the nationalistic teleology underlying such a formulation. 'Multiculturedness' is not a 'United Statesian' monopoly, nor is multiculturalism the 'handmaiden' of US identity politics. Virtually all countries and regions are multicultural" (1994, 4–5). My thinking on this subject is informed by my pedagogical experiences, especially when it comes to the formulation of world literature syllabi. The predominant assumptions made by curricula committees come from the idea that the literary texts placed on such syllabi should emphasize the benefits of learning about other cultures, supposing that students do not need to scrutinize their own cultural positions. Hence, my students are often surprised to see on my syllabus such American transnational novels as Garcia's *Dreaming in Cuban* or Alvarez's *How the García Girls Lost Their Accents* because these texts, largely positioned within the American context, do not fit the traditional category of world texts.

21. I thank Donna Perry for drawing my attention to this point.

22. Ibis Gomez-Vega makes a similar point about Yolanda's encounter, suggesting that "having been raised on American television and the American fear

of everything that is different, Yolanda learns to associate her own people with the negative stereotypes that she absorbs almost unconsciously as she becomes an adult in the United States" (1997, 238).

23. Deborah Sontag and Celia W. Dugger, "New Immigrant Tide: Shuttle between Worlds," *New York Times,* July 19, 1998, sec. 1, 1, 28A.

24. Ibid., 1.

25. Sontag and Dugger, "New Immigrant Tide," 30.

26. Jenny Sharpe's caution is pertinent here: "Instead of treating transnational diasporas as homogeneous groups, we need to exercise vigilance about locating their members within specific racial formations" (2000, 112).

27. I am indebted to Shohat's discussion on the inadequacy of "the single-hyphen boxes" when it comes to the delineation of hyphenated Americanism. See her introduction to *Talking Visions* (1998, 7).

3. The Dialectics of Exile

1. Hoffman 1989, 245. Page numbers for further references to this novel appear in parentheses in the text.

2. Fjellestad 1995, 136. For other critical readings of *Lost in Translation* see, e.g., Bartkowski 1995; Hirsch 1994; Seyhan 2001; Zaborowska 1995.

3. For a discussion of an exilic condition as being "catapulted out of history," see Miłosz 1988; for an examination of a critical intersection between the process of translation and the position of exiles, see Rushdie 1991.

4. My own reading of *Lost in Translation* is influenced by Kristeva's discussion of "foreigners" and "strangers" (1991).

5. See introduction, note 3.

6. California Proposition 187 (also known as the Save Our State initiative), for example, is a well-documented illustration of how this rage has the potential to be transformed into formal discriminatory immigrant laws. Proposition 187 argued for the need to deny public social services, publicly funded health care, and public education to people who are suspected of being illegal immigrants. Within a more recent context, the Patriot Act of 2001 is a powerful manifestation of an anti-immigrant climate.

7. See hooks 1990 for the postmodernist critique of identity, particularly her point that "it's easy to give up identity when you have one" (28).

4. Claustrophobic Exile

1. *Two Men and a Wardrobe* won several prestigious international awards in the experimental films category in San Francisco (1958); in Vancouver, Canada (1960); and in Amsterdam, Holland (1960). Polanski made these films while a student in the directing department at the Polish National Film School in Łódź.

2. Stachówna 1994, 41. All translations in this chapter from the Polish are my own.

3. See, e.g., Lawrence Weschler, "Artist in Exile," *New Yorker,* December 5,

1994. Weschler quotes the Polish critic Maria Kornatowska, who argues that "all Polanski's films—including *Knife in the Water*—have been about the war and, in particular, about the simultaneous combination of claustrophobia and agoraphobia that characterized the ghetto experience. In *Knife in the Water*, for instance, the water seems to be an open horizon. In reality, it encloses and entraps absolutely. And that's the quintessential Polanskian universe" (94). Following Weschler's biographical information on Polanski, I call Poland Polanski's native land. Such a formulation, however, is somewhat problematic because Polanski was born in Paris in 1933. When he was only three years old, his parents, exiles from Poland, "in a fatefully ill-judged move" (91), made a decision to go back to Cracow, Poland. Polanski survived the Holocaust and remained in Poland where he received his education and film training. He returned to France as an adult, after the release of *Knife in the Water* in 1962. In a way, Weschler's article, which calls Polanski an "artist in exile," seems very appropriate, for we are confronted with an artist who is ethnically Polish-Jewish but also has roots in France.

4. *The Tenant* is based on Roland Topor's first novel, *The Tenant* (1967). For an interesting critical reading of *The Tenant*, see Oliver 1998.

5. At the time of its release, *The Tenant* did not receive favorable reviews. The film was called "ultimately undecipherable," an "improbable story," and Polanski, the director and the main actor in the film, was labeled a "little tramp . . . born of intolerance, exile, and international vagrancy." See, e.g., John Simon, "Untenable *Tenant*," *New York Magazine*, June 28, 1976, 66–68; Mitch Tuckman, "Exiled on Main Street," *Village Voice*, July 26, 1976, 108; and Colin L. Westerbeck Jr., "Rosemary's Booby," *Commonwealth*, August 27, 1976, 563–64.

6. My thinking about desublimatory examination of abjection within art has been influenced by and is indebted to Simon Taylor's powerful essay (1993) on a rhetoric of contamination and the subversive potential of the abject.

7. Polanski, now a naturalized French citizen, has commented on the xenophobic middle-class Parisian society many times: "I had lived in Paris for a long time before I became a well-known director. I know what one feels when one is reminded ten times a day that one is not French; I know what price one pays when one is considered a second-class citizen. But, when you become famous, everything that was alien until now—your sense of dignity and your identity—suddenly become original. Beware of being an ordinary person as you are then only a painted bird." Quoted in Stachówna 1994, 65. Polanski's reference to the image of the "painted bird" undoubtedly evokes in this context Jerzy Kosinski's controversial book, *The Painted Bird* (1965). Given the text's relentless emphasis on the experiences of persecution during the Holocaust and on poignant ostracism, we are reminded of the horrific workings of the logic of ethnic purity triggered by the encounter of "difference." Trelkovsky, literally and figuratively, invokes the image of the painted bird, as he twice flies into the suicidal abyss, his body marked by heavy makeup.

8. In an interesting way, Clover comments on the problem of vision in

horror cinema: "But insofar as it [the ocular opening] introduces the narrative that necessarily turns on problems of vision—seeing too little (to the point of blindness) or seeing too much (to the point of insanity)—and insofar as its scary project is to tease, confuse, block, and threaten the spectator's own vision, the opening eye of horror also announces a concern with the way we see ourselves and others and the consequences that often attend our usual manner of perception" (1992, 166–67). Even though in *The Tenant* we are challenged by the eye that closes the narrative, the ocular horror it evokes clearly anticipates the eye of the viewer.

9. Gretchen Bisplinghoff and Virginia Wright Wexman, for example, comment on this issue: "Movies like *Repulsion*, *Rosemary's Baby*, and *The Tenant* terrify audiences because, to some extent, they force us to share the confusions of their main characters about the difference between social persecution and paranoid delusions" (1979, 8–9).

10. I am using Bordwell's discussion of the Hollywood classical model. See Bordwell and Thompson 1994, 73.

11. Among the best-known expressionist films are Robert Wiene's *The Cabinet of Dr. Caligari* (1920), F. W. Murnau's *Nosferatu* (1922) and *Faust* (1926), and Fritz Lang's *Metropolis* (1926). The entire movement had an effect on the aesthetic look of film noir and contemporary horror films.

12. Jameson 1991, 14. Jameson points out that the human figure in Munch's painting is characterized by a "lack of ears," making the cry "the absent scream" (14).

13. Mary Ann Doane, for example, argues that in a genre she calls "the paranoid woman's film" often "the house becomes the analogue of the human body" (1987, 288). In a curious way, we see this phenomenon in *The Tenant*, for the film depicts Trelkovsky's apartment as a dangerous space that "lives" and "breathes."

14. Here is Polanski's other comment (see note 7) on being foreign in France: "In Paris they always point out you are foreign. If you park your car in a wrong place, what counts is not the fact that your car is on a sidewalk, but that you speak with an accent." Quoted in Stachówna 1994, 65.

15. F. W. Murnau's *Nosferatu* is a compelling example of how such a projection works. The horrifying vampire is a foreigner, coded as homosexual and Jewish, and his figure is associated with plague and death that threaten not just individual characters but, in fact, the entire community.

16. Stachówna makes a similar argument, suggesting that the cultural element of mummification evokes "the mergence between the living and the dead" (1994, 154).

17. Hart 1994, ix. The hierarchical ideology Hart refers to is "the machine of heterosexual patriarchy."

18. Bisplinghoff and Wexman argue that the feeling of persecution in *The Tenant* is an imaginary one: "In *Rosemary's Baby*, the persecution is discovered to be genuine, while in *Repulsion* and *The Tenant* it is only imagined. But, in each

case, the effect depends on the audience sharing the fears and uncertainties of the hero or heroine through surrealistic devices such as dreams and hallucinations" (1979, 9). I have already argued that the line between hallucination and reality is explicitly delicate in the film, but the narrative does not allow us to relegate Trelkovsky's anguish and sensation of being cast as a stranger solely to the realm of illusion.

19. Jardine 1982, 59–60. Jardine calls this space coded as feminine "gynesis," "the putting into discourse of 'woman.'"

20. Another interesting link between Tarkovsky and Polanski that should be noted here is the fact that both come from the second world and both share an experience of exile. Tarkovsky was born in the Soviet Union and became one of the most celebrated young Russian filmmakers who contributed to the emergence of Russian New Cinema after Stalin's death in 1953. His most famous films are *Ivan's Childhood* (1962), *Andrei Rublev* (1965), *Solaris* (1972), *The Mirror* (1975), *Stalker* (1979), *Nostalghia,* and *The Sacrifice* (1986). The last two films were made already in exile, while most of his earlier films were treated as reactionary and nonconformist by the Soviet communist authorities. *Andrei Rublev,* which was perceived as "an allegory of art crushed by social oppression," was denied a release. The reception of *Nostalghia* in the USSR reveals perhaps the most bitter and ironic twist to Tarkovsky's artistic position: he believed that *Nostalghia* was a tribute to Russian sensibilities, but the film was attacked and renounced by the Soviet government. See Bordwell and Thompson, 538.

21. For example, communist governments in Eastern Europe relegated many censored films to "life on the shelf," not allowing them to be publicly screened or to be released outside the national borders. The fear of contamination that I discuss here should be understood as a fear generated by the crossing of normative ideologies, not just as an anxiety caused by stepping over physical national borders.

22. Among the most interesting examples that comment on the Eastern and Central European experiences of exile are Jerzy Skolimowski's *Moonlighting* (1982), the already mentioned Andrei Tarkovsky's *Nostalghia,* Paul Mazursky's *Moscow on the Hudson* (1984), Taylor Hackford's *White Nights* (1985), Barry Levinson's *Avalon* (1990), and James Gray's *Little Odessa* (1994).

23. This is how Bordwell expresses complexities embedded in the tradition of art cinema: "The narration knows that life is more complex than art can ever be, and—a new twist of the realistic screw—the only way to respect this complexity is to leave causes dangling and questions unanswered" (1985, 210).

24. Ella Shohat and Robert Stam, for example, call the second world "now non-existent" (1994, 26). If, as Shohat and Stam claim, we treat the existence of the second world based solely on its link with communism, we have to agree. But such a formulation simplifies a very complex issue and overlooks the political situation and the actual existence of many Eastern and Central European communities. "Communism" is a tricky term because once-socialist Poland, for

example, did not officially perceive itself as communist when it was a Soviet-bloc country. Even though state socialism per se officially came to an end with the fall of the Berlin Wall in 1989, the space once called the second world is not entirely free from its legacy. In a similar way, postcolonial places are not free from the agonizing inheritance of colonialism simply because they have already been proclaimed officially free and independent. Thus, ex-Soviet-bloc countries, which even now slowly enter the economic realm of transnational capital, still linger and quiver between what they once were and what they are not yet.

5. ANATOMIES OF ABJECTION

1. The country's new name, however, was questioned by Greece, which refused to acknowledge the republic until it changed its name, claiming that "Macedonia" was historically a Greek term and that its use implies a territorial claim to the Greek region of Macedonia. Greece also objected to the imagery of Alexander the Great's sixteen-ray Star of Vergina on the Macedonian flag, further intensifying the tension between the two countries. In February 1994 Greece imposed an economic blockade that was in effect until September 1995, when the two countries agreed to establish diplomatic relations. The Former Yugoslav Republic of Macedonia (FYROM) agreed to remove the controversial Star of Vergina from its flag; Greece consented to lift its embargo.

The most intense internal ethnic tensions between Macedonian Slavs and the country's large Albanian minority developed before the country was admitted to the United Nations during an extensive period when it was not recognized by the international community. In 1993 the United Nations delegated peace-keeping troops to prevent the war in Bosnia from spreading to Albania. In 1998, however, three years after fighting ended in the rest of the old Yugoslav federation, the battles in Kosovo began. Ninety percent of the FYROM's Albanians reside on the borders with Albania and the Serbian province of Kosovo, which has long been regarded as the most volatile region in the former Yugoslavia (two wars in the Balkan Peninsula, in 1912 and in 1913, had been fought over Kosovo). In March 1999 NATO began air attacks against the Federal Republic of Yugoslavia after its refusal to accept an international peace plan for Kosovo. After Serbian police and Yugoslav army intensified assaults on ethnic Albanians in Kosovo, many were forced to flee to Montenegro, Albania, and the FYROM. See Mojzes 1994; Zarkovic 2000; and Schwartz 1993.

2. See, e.g., Ian Fisher, "Albanians' Many Children Unnerve Macedonia's Slavs," *New York Times,* August 11, 2001, at http://www.nytimes.com/2001/08/11/international/europe/11MACE.html. This interesting article describes how the birthrate in Macedonia is hotly debated: "On both sides of the ethnic line, birthrates are acknowledged as perhaps the fundamental fact of politics here." The issue, as Fisher describes it, is that the Albanians are supposedly having more babies than the Slavs; some believe that this situation is dictated by the fact that the ethnic Albanians have a more conservative culture in which women rarely

work outside of the home and are encouraged to have large families. The rapidly changing demographics, in turn, causes an anxiety that the Slavic majority could eventually become a minority in the FYROM and that the structures of power could change in favor of the Albanians. The article argues that the issue of birthrates lingered in the background of peace negotiations, ending a six-month rebellion by ethnic Albanian guerrillas demanding greater political rights: "Demographics may also, ultimately, lay down the logic for the biggest nightmare for many Macedonian Slavs: territorial division along ethnic lines, as has happened in Bosnia and Kosovo. That, they argue, is exactly what Albanian leaders are planning for the long run."

3. Critics and reviewers did not always appreciate this point. See, e.g., Teresa Esser, "Surreal Images and Situations Carry *Before the Rain*," *Tech*, March 10, 1995. Esser calls the film confusing, difficult, bungled; perceives Macedonia as "technologically backward"; and suggests that the film will "make you appreciate the relative peace and tranquility of life in the United States" (6). Esser's position is precisely the attitude the film critiques: envisioning violence as happening somewhere else and perpetuating the oppressive dichotomy between the "tranquil" West and barbaric, violent non-Western places. Similarly, Iordanova reproduces the binaristic logic of the rational West/irrational Balkan community when she writes about Aleksandar that "having come from the civilized and rational west, he encounters a world consumed by ugly and violent intolerance" (1996, 886).

4. *Rethinking History: The Journal of Theory and Practice* 4, no. 2 (July 2000). *Before the Rain* was a coproduction (England, France, and Macedonia). It won international awards at the 1994 Venice International Film Festival and the 1994 São Paulo International Film Festival; it was also nominated for an Academy Award for best foreign-language film in 1995.

5. Andrew Horton, review of *Before the Rain*, *Cineaste* 21 (1995): 44.

6. In his interview with Horton, Manchevski acknowledges that Aleksandar Petrovic is the spiritual father of his film. Indeed, *Before the Rain* draws structurally and conceptually on Petrovic's 1965 Yugoslav war film, *Three,* which, told as a triptych, frames the protagonist's three different perspectives on World War II (Horton 1995, 45).

7. Naficy's *Accented Cinema* features analyses of exilic filmmaking globally and covers a wide variety of contemporary diasporic cinema created by directors from different geopolitical locations: Ghasem Ebrahimian, Ann Hui, Emir Kusturica, Mira Nair, Gregory Nava, and Trinh Minh-ha (2001, 8).

8. Naficy argues that the difference between recent transnational filmmakers and European directors who moved to the United States in the 1920s and 1940s is that most of the earlier immigrants were absorbed by the Hollywood studio system, while the transnationals of the last two decades frequently produced their work via independent filmmaking channels (1996, 121–22).

9. See, e.g., Lucy R. Lippard's discussion on the social and historical

awkwardness that underlies the terminology used to refer to intercultural art and artists who frequently live between cultures. Ethnicity is one of the notions Lippard scrutinizes, noting that the word "ethnic" is "ambiguous in its application to any group of people anywhere (though it is, significantly, rarely applied to WASPs) who maintain a certain habitual, religious, or intellectual bond to their originary cultures" (1990, 17).

10. Iordanova makes a useful point about the transnationality of *Before the Rain*, arguing that it is precisely its cosmopolitan status that enabled the production and then the wide distribution of the film: "Had the director depended solely on domestic finance and subsidies, I doubt that such a film would be made in Macedonia, or in any other of the Balkan countries.... Unlike other Balkan films that rarely make it beyond the festival circuit, the film was widely distributed in the West in 35 mm and on video" (2000, 147).

11. Manchevski 2000, 129–30. See also Andrew Horton, "Oscar-Nominated 'Rain' to Screen at Tulane," *New Orleans Times-Picayune*, February 22, 1995. In this interview, Manchevski explains his resistance to creating a film that could be perceived as a realistic documentary: "I didn't want the film to comment on any event or events happening right now. You see, I don't know enough about the war. I haven't lived there for years. I wanted rather for my story to be pulled out of those events in its style, music, and in its content, too.... What is important is that I do not mean my film to be taken as a documentary of actual events" (E5).

12. For example, Slavoj Žižek sees *Before the Rain* as portraying "the Balkans as the timeless space on which the West projects its phantasmatic content," while Iordanova believes that, at least on some level, the film reiterates that "the Balkans are different; that it is all about the 'Other'; that nothing can be done; that there is no way to solve the problems that are destroying this 'Other' from within." Slavoj Žižek, "Underground, or Ethnic Cleansing as a Continuation of Poetry by Other Means," *InterCommunication* 18, at http://www.ntticc.or.jp/pub/ic_mag/ic018/intercity/zizek_e.html; and Iordanova 1996, 887.

13. I thank Áine O'Healy for pointing out that, perhaps despite its multicultural intentions, the film largely privileges the Macedonian Christian community, and the visual and aural qualities of the setting in the first part of the narrative serve to romanticize the timeless qualities of the Christian nation.

14. The identity of the stranger/killer is quite troublesome. Manchevski mentions that the nationality of the anonymous man is of no importance because the point is to show the universality of violence: "It doesn't matter what nationality the killer is. It's not explained on purpose. We don't subtitle his dialogue because I was trying to say that we are not immune to what is going on elsewhere in the world. You cannot switch channels. It doesn't work that way. By not doing anything or not doing enough, you're an accomplice" (Stone 1997, 823). But, of course, the nationality of the killer matters in this context. Even though the man's words are not subtitled, it is obvious that he speaks Serbian.

15. It is significant that, although fictional drama, the film shows us photographs of the faces and bodies of real victims of the ethnic war. The credits reveal the various photographers of each of the pictures: Ranko Cukovic's "Emaciated Man—Bosnian Refugee," Luc Delahave's "Child with 1 on Forehead," Jon Jones's "Man with Gas Mask," Patrick Chauvel's "Woman in Graveyard," Marco Armenta's "Two Children Dead in the Morgue," and W. Betsch's "Punk Soldier with Swastika Armband." Like the documentary footage in *Welcome to Sarajevo*, which blurs the line between fiction and documentary, these photographs, too, erase the clear line between narrative fiction and reality.

16. Another compelling film about an exile's return is Theo Angelopoulos's *Ulysses' Gaze* (1995), a poetically moody narrative about an American man's journey through the landscape of "his" Balkans. Through its visual motifs of fog, clouds, and misty mise-en-scène, which underline the exile's hallucinatory return, the film draws on the legacy of Andrei Tarkovsky's *Nostalghia* and reminds us that the native-turned-foreigner occupies an unstable, murky position within one's kin.

17. The difficult social position of women from the former Yugoslavia and their double oppression is also foregrounded in Gregor Nicholas's *Broken English* (1996), which is about refugees/immigrants from Bosnia who settle in New Zealand.

18. The issue of "taking sides," as Iordanova points out, holds special significance in the post-Yugoslav moment, as imposed ethnic identification (expected to be performed along the lines of a fixed-identity politics) propelled nationalist phobias: "With the break-up of Yugoslavia, the compulsory taking of sides was one of the most difficult experiences for its former citizens. No matter how unwillingly, everybody in Yugoslavia had to undergo an imposed reidentification— from the inclusive concept of 'Yugoslav,' cultivated for decades but now abandoned overnight, people had to switch to a restrictive concept of belonging and confine themselves to a clear-cut ethnic identity" (2000, 148).

19. Erik Tängerstad makes an interesting point about this moment, drawing on Manchevski's admission that he played the role of a prisoner: "Writing himself into the script in this manner, Manchevski has more than made an ironic remark on 'the death of the author.' Depicting himself as the executed and not the executioner, Manchevski suggests that he, like his imagined character Aleks, cannot find a neutral position from which to objectively describe 'reality'" (Tängerstad 2000, 178–79).

20. Žižek 1994, 2. The ethical issue of the ownership of war images from Bosnia is also compellingly represented in *Beautiful People*.

21. See, e.g., Mary Dickson, "The Faces of Violence," *Private Eye Weekly*, July 29, 1997, at http://www.slweekly.com/ae/cinema/cinema_rain.html; and Roger Ebert, review of *Before the Rain, Chicago Sun-Times*, March 10, 1995, at http://www.suntimes.com/ebert/ebert_reviews/1995/03/969362.html.

22. My thinking about the violence of vomit is indebted to Julia Kristeva's

work on abjection. Discussing the "shattering violence of a convulsion," Kristeva suggests a seeming paradox: "I expel *myself*, I spit *myself* out, I abject *myself* within the same motion through which 'I' claim to establish *myself*. . . . During that course in which 'I' become, I give birth to myself amid the violence of sobs, of vomit" (1982, 3). The "I" establishes its selfhood through self-abjection; the act of vomiting is simultaneously an act of "becoming" an "I."

Bibliography

Abu-Jaber, Diana. 1993. *Arabian Jazz*. New York: Harcourt Brace.
Aciman, André, ed. 1999a. "Permanent Transients." In *Letters of Transit: Reflections on Exile, Identity, Language, and Loss*. New York: New Press.
———. 1999b. "Shadow Cities." In *Letters of Transit: Reflections on Exile, Identity, Language, and Loss*. New York: New Press.
Ahmad, Aijaz. 1987. "Jameson's Rhetoric of Otherness and the 'National Allegory.'" *Social Text* 17: 3–25.
Alvarez, Julia. 1984. *Homecoming: New and Collected Poems*. New York: Plume.
———. 1992. *How the García Girls Lost Their Accents*. New York: Penguin Books.
———. 1994. *In the Time of the Butterflies*. New York: Plume.
———. 1995. *The Other Side/El Otro Lado*. New York: Plume.
———. 1997. *Yo!* Chapel Hill, N.C.: Algonquin Books.
———. 1998a. "A Clean Windshield." In *Passion and Craft: Conversations with Notable Writers*, ed. Bonnie Lyons and Bill Oliver. Urbana and Chicago: University of Illinois Press.
———. 1998b. *Something to Declare*. New York: Plume.
———. 2000. *In the Name of Salomé*. New York: Plume.
Anzaldúa, Gloria. 1987. *Borderlands/La Frontera: The New Mestiza*. San Francisco: Aunt Lute Books.
Auster, Lawrence. 1990. *The Path to National Suicide: An Essay on Immigration and Multiculturalism*. Monterey, Calif.: American Immigration Control Foundation.

Bammer, Angelika, ed. 1994. Introduction to *Displacements: Cultural Identities in Question*. Bloomington: Indiana University Press.

Barrerra, Mario. 1992. "Story Structure in Latino Feature Films." In *Chicanos and Film: Essays on Chicano Representation and Resistance*, ed. Chon A. Noriega, 245–68. New York: Garland.

Bartkowski, Frances. 1995. "Careless Baptism: Eva Hoffman's *Lost in Translation*." In *Travelers, Immigrants, Inmates: Essays in Estrangement*, 109–17. Minneapolis: University of Minnesota Press.

Basch, Linda, Nina Glick Schiller, and Cristina Szanton Blanc. 1994. *Nations Unbound: Transnational Projects, Postcolonial Predicaments, and Deterritorialized Nation-States*. Amsterdam: Gordon and Breach.

Bauman, Zygmunt. 1990. "Modernity and Ambivalence." In *Global Culture: Nationalism, Globalization, and Modernity*, ed. Mike Featherstone. London: Sage.

———. 1997. "The Making and Unmaking of Strangers." In *Debating Cultural Hybridity: Multi-Cultural Identities and the Politics of Anti-Racism*, ed. Pnina Werbner and Tariq Modood. London: Zed Books.

———. 1998a. "Assimilation into Exile: The Jew as a Polish Writer." In *Exile and Creativity: Signposts, Travelers, Outsiders, Backward Glances*, ed. Susan Rubin Suleiman. Durham, N.C.: Duke University Press.

———. 1998b. *Globalization: The Human Consequences*. New York: Columbia University Press.

Behdad, Ali. 1993. "Traveling to Teach: Postcolonial Critics in the American Academy." In *Race, Identity, and Representation in Education*, ed. Cameron McCarthy and Warren Crichlow, 40–49. New York: Routledge.

———. 2000. "Global Disjunctures, Diasporic Differences, and the New World (Dis-)Order." In *A Companion to Postcolonial Studies*, ed. Henry Schwartz and Sangeeta Ray, 396–409. Malden, Mass.: Blackwell.

Behdad, Ali, and Laura Elisa Pérez. 1995. "Reflections and Confessions on the 'Minority' and Immigrant I.D. Tour." *Paragraph* 18: 64–74.

Benamou, Catherine. 1988. "El Norte." *Areito* 10: 52–55.

Bhabha, Homi K. 1994. *The Location of Culture*. New York: Routledge.

———. 1996. "Unpacking my Library . . . Again." In *The Postcolonial Question: Common Skies, Divided Horizons*, ed. Iain Chambers and Lidia Curti. New York: Routledge.

Bisplinghoff, Gretchen, and Virginia Wright Wexman. 1979. *Roman Polanski: A Guide to References and Resources*. Boston: G. H. Hall.

Bordwell, David. 1985. *Narration in the Fiction Film*. Madison: University of Wisconsin Press.

Bordwell, David, and Kristin Thompson. 1994. *Film History: An Introduction*. New York: McGraw-Hill.

Brimelow, Peter. 1995. *Alien Nation: Common Sense about America's Immigration Disaster*. New York: Random.

Bromley, Roger. 2000. *Narratives for a New Belonging: Diasporic Cultural Fictions.* Edinburgh: Edinburgh University Press.
Brownstone, David M., Irene M. Franck, and Douglass L. Brownstone. 1979. *Island of Hope, Island of Tears.* New York: Wade.
Buchanan, Patrick. 2002. *The Death of the West: How Dying Populations and Immigrant Invasions Imperil Our Country and Civilization.* New York: Thomas Dunne Books.
Burgoyne, Robert. 2000. "Ethnic Nationalism and Globalization." *Rethinking History: The Journal of Theory and Practice* 4: 157–65.
Carb, Alison B. 1988. "An Interview with Bharati Mukherjee." *Massachusetts Review* (Winter): 645–54.
Chang, Robert S. 1997. "A Meditation on Borders." In *Immigrants Out! The New Nativism and the Anti-Immigrant Impulse in the United States,* ed. Juan F. Perea, 244–53. New York: New York University Press.
Chavez, Leo R. 1992. "Border Reality." In *Between Two Worlds: The People of the Border.* Photographs by Don Bartletti. Oakland, Calif.: Oakland Museum.
———. 1997. "Immigration Reform and Nativism: The Nationalist Response to the Transnational Challenge." In *Immigrants Out! The New Nativism and the Anti-Immigrant Impulse in the United States,* ed. Juan F. Perea. New York: New York University Press.
Chicago Cultural Studies Group. 1994. "Critical Multiculturalism." In *Multiculturalism: A Critical Reader,* ed. David Theo Goldberg, 114–39. Malden, Mass.: Blackwell.
Clément, Catherine. 1988. *Opera, or The Undoing of Women.* Trans. Betsy Wing. Minneapolis: University of Minnesota Press.
Cleveland, Fredrick A. 1927. *American Citizenship as Distinguished from Alien Status.* New York: Ronald Press.
Clover, Carol J. 1992. *Men, Women, and Chain Saws: Gender in the Modern Horror Film.* Princeton, N.J.: Princeton University Press.
Cox, Karen Castellucci. 2001. "A Particular Blessing: Storytelling as Healing in the Novels of Julia Alvarez." In *Healing Cultures: Art and Religion as Curative Practices in the Caribbean and Its Diaspora,* ed. Margarite Fernández Olmos and Lizabeth Paravisini-Gebert. New York: Palgrave.
Davies, Carole Boyce. 1998. "Migratory Subjectivities." In *Literary Theory: An Anthology,* ed. Julie Rivkin and Michael Ryan. Malden, Mass.: Blackwell.
Davis, Jude, and Carol R. Smith. 1997. "Conclusion: Aliens from *Star Wars* to *Independence Day.*" In *Gender, Ethnicity, and Sexuality in Contemporary American Film.* Chicago: Fitzroy Dearborn Publishers.
de Lauretis, Teresa. 1987. *Technologies of Gender: Essays on Theory, Film, and Fiction.* Bloomington: Indiana University Press.
Derrida, Jacques. 1981. *Dissemination,* trans. Barbara Johnson. Chicago: University of Chicago Press.
DeSalvo, Louise. 2003. "Color: White/Complexion: Dark." In *Are Italians*

White? How Race Is Made in America, ed. Jennifer Gugliemo, and Salvatore Salerno. New York: Routledge.

Divakaruni, Chitra Banerjee. 1995. *Arranged Marriage*. New York: Doubleday.

Doane, Mary Ann. 1987. "The Woman's Film: Possession and Address." In *Home Is Where the Heart Is: Studies in Melodrama and the Woman's Film*, ed. Christine Gledhill. London: British Film Institute.

Dorfman, Ariel. 1998. *Heading South, Looking North: A Bilingual Journey*. New York: Penguin Books.

Douglas, Mary. 1966. *Purity and Danger*. New York: Praeger.

duBois, Page. 1991. *Torture and Truth*. New York: Routledge.

Feagin, Joe R. 1997. "Old Poison in New Bottles: The Deep Roots of Modern Nativism." In *Immigrants Out! The New Nativism and the Anti-Immigrant Impulse in the United States*, ed. Juan F. Perea, 13–43. New York: New York University Press.

Fjellestad, Danuta Zadworna. 1995. "'The Insertion of the Self into the Space of Borderless Possibility': Eva Hoffman's Exiled Body." *Melus* 20 (Summer): 133–47.

Fregoso, Linda Rosa. 1993. "From Il(l)egal to Legal Subject: Border Construction and Re-construction." In *The Bronze Screen: Chicana and Chicano Film Culture*, 65–92. Minneapolis: University of Minnesota Press.

———. 1999. "Recycling Colonialist Fantasies on the Texas Borderlands." In *Home, Exile, Homeland: Film, Media, and the Politics of Place*, ed. Hamid Naficy. New York: Routledge.

Fuentes, Victor. 1992. "Chicano Cinema: A Dialectic between Voices and Images of the Autonomous Discourse Versus Those of the Dominant." In *Chicanos and Film: Essays on Chicano Representation and Resistance*, ed. Chon A. Noriega, 233–43. New York: Garland.

Goldberg, David Theo, ed. 1994. "Introduction: Multicultural Conditions." In *Multiculturalism: A Critical Reader*, 1–41. Malden, Mass.: Blackwell.

Gómez-Peña, Guillermo. 1988. "Documented/Undocumented." In *The Graywolf Annual Five: Multicultural Legacy*, ed. Rick Simonson and Scott Walker. Saint Paul, Minn.: Graywolf Press.

———. 1989. "The Multicultural Paradigm: An Open Letter to the National Arts Community." *High Performance* 12 (Fall): 17–27.

———. 1995. "Bilingualism, Biculturalism, and Borders." In *English Is Broken Here: Notes on Cultural Fusion in the Americas*, Coco Fusco. New York: New Press.

Gomez-Vega, Ibis. 1997. "Metaphors of Entrapment: Caribbean Women Writers Face the Wreckage of History." *Journal of Political and Military Sociology* 25 (Winter): 231–47.

Grewal, Inderpal, and Caren Kaplan, eds. 1994. "Introduction: Transnational Feminist Practices and Questions of Postmodernity." In *Scattered*

Hegemonies: Postmodernity and Transnational Feminist Practices, 1–33. Minneapolis: University of Minnesota Press.

———. 1999. "Transnational Feminist Cultural Studies: Beyond the Marxism/ Poststructuralism/Feminism Divides." In *Between Woman and Nation: Nationalism, Transnational Feminism, and the State*, ed. Caren Kaplan, Norma Alarcón, and Minoo Moallem, 349–63. Durham, N.C.: Duke University Press.

Guarnizo, Luis Eduardo, and Michael Peter Smith, eds. 1998. "The Locations of Transnationalism." In *Transnationalism from Below*, 3–34. New Brunswick, N.J.: Transaction.

Guglielmo, Jennifer, and Salvatore Salerno, eds. 2003. *Are Italians White? How Race Is Made in America*. New York: Routledge.

Hall, Stuart. 1992. "European Cinema on the Verge of a Nervous Breakdown." In *Screening Europe: Image and Identity in Contemporary European Cinema*, ed. Duncan Petrie. London: British Film Institute.

———. 1996. "When Was 'the Post-Colonial'? Thinking at the Limit." In *The Postcolonial Question: Common Skies, Divided Horizons*, ed. Iain Chambers and Lidia Curti. New York: Routledge.

Haney-López, Ian F. 1996. *White by Law: The Legal Construction of Race*. New York: New York University Press.

Hart, Lynda. 1994. *Fatal Women: Lesbian Sexuality and the Mark of Aggression*. Princeton, N.J.: Princeton University Press.

Hirsch, Marianne. 1994. "Pictures of Displaced Girlhood." In *Displacements: Cultural Identities in Question*, ed. Angelika Bammer, 71–89. Bloomington: Indiana University Press.

Hoffman, Eva. 1989. *Lost in Translation: A Life in a New Language*. New York: Penguin Books.

———. 1999. "The New Nomads." In *Letters of Transit: Reflections on Exile, Identity, Language, and Loss*, ed. André Aciman. New York: New Press.

Hondagneu-Sotelo, Pierrette. 2001. *Doméstica: Immigrant Workers Cleaning and Caring in the Shadows of Affluence*. Berkeley: University of California Press.

hooks, bell. 1990. *Yearning: Race, Gender, and Cultural Politics*. Boston, Mass.: South End Press.

Horton, Andrew. 1995. "Cinema across the Oceans: An Interview with Milcho Manchevski." *Cineaste* 21: 45.

Ignatiev, Noel. 1995. *How the Irish Became White*. New York: Routledge.

Iordanova, Dina. 1996. "Conceptualizing the Balkans in Film." *Slavic Review* 55 (Winter): 882–90.

———. 2000. "*Before the Rain* in a Balkan Context." *Rethinking History: The Journal of Theory and Practice* 4: 147–57.

———. 2001. *Cinema of Flames: Balkan Film, Culture, and the Media*. London: British Film Institute.

Jacobson, David, ed. 1998. "Introduction: An American Journey." In *The Immigration Reader: America in a Multidisciplinary Perspective*. Malden, Mass.: Blackwell.
Jacobson, Matthew Frye. 1998. *Whiteness of a Different Color: European Immigrants and the Alchemy of Race*. Cambridge, Mass.: Harvard University Press.
Jameson, Fredric. 1991. *Postmodernism, or The Cultural Logic of Late Capitalism*. Durham, N.C.: Duke University Press.
Jardine, Alice. 1982. "Gynesis." *Diacritics* 12: 54–65.
Kaplan, Caren. 1987. "Deterritorialization: The Rewriting of Home and Exile in Western Feminist Discourse." *Cultural Critique* 6 (Spring): 187–98.
Kesić, Vesna. 2002. "Muslim Women, Croatian Women, Serbian Women, Albanian Women . . ." In *Balkan as Metaphor: Between Globalization and Fragmentation*, ed. Dušan I. Bjelić and Obrad Savić. Cambridge: MIT Press.
Kristeva, Julia. 1982. *Powers of Horror: An Essay on Abjection*, translated by Leon S. Roudiez. New York: Columbia University Press.
———. 1986. "The System and the Speaking Subject." In *The Kristeva Reader*, ed. Toril Moi. New York: Columbia University Press.
———. 1991. *Strangers to Ourselves*, trans. Leon S. Roudiez. New York: Columbia University Press.
———. 1993. *Nations without Nationalism*, trans. Leon R. Roudiez. New York: Columbia University Press.
Kuhn, Annette. 1992. "Border Crossing." *Sight and Sound* 2 (July): 13.
Lippard, Lucy R. 1990. *Mixed Blessings: New Art in a Multicultural America*. New York: Pantheon Books.
List, Chris. 1989. "*El Norte*: Ideology and Immigration." *Jump Cut* 34: 27–31.
———. 1996. *Chicano Images: Refiguring Ethnicity in Mainstream Film*. New York: Garland.
Lowe, Lisa. 1996. *Immigrant Acts: On Asian American Cultural Politics*. Durham, N.C.: Duke University Press.
Manchevski, Milcho. 2000. "Rainmaking and Personal Truth." *Rethinking History: The Journal of Theory and Practice* 4: 129–34.
Miłosz, Czesław. 1988. "On Exile." In *Exiles: Photographs by Joseph Koudelka*. New York: Aperture Foundation.
Mitchell, David. 1999. "The Accent of 'Loss': Cultural Crossings as Context in Julia Alvarez's *How the García Girls Lost Their Accents*." In *Beyond the Binary: Reconstructing Cultural Identity in a Multicultural Context*, ed. Timothy B. Powell. New Brunswick, N.J.: Rutgers University Press.
Mohanty, Chandra Talpade. 1995. "Under Western Eyes: Feminist Scholarship and Colonial Discourses." In *Post-Colonial Studies Reader*, ed. Bill Ashcroft et al. New York: Routledge.
———. 1998. "Crafting Feminist Genealogies: On the Geography and Politics

of Home, Nation, and Community." In *Talking Visions: Multicultural Feminism in a Transnational Age,* ed. Ella Shohat. Cambridge: MIT Press.

Mojzes, Paul. 1994. "Travels in the Balkans: Tensions and Aspirations in Macedonia." *Christian Century,* May 11, 499.

Mukherjee, Bharati. 1988. "The Management of Grief." *The Middleman and Other Stories.* New York: Grove Press.

Naficy, Hamid. 1996. "Phobic Spaces and Liminal Panics: Independent Transnational Film Genre." In *Global/Local: Cultural Production and the Transnational Imaginary,* ed. Rob Wilson and Wimal Dissanayake. Durham, N.C.: Duke University Press.

———. 2001. *Accented Cinema: Exilic and Diasporic Filmmaking.* Princeton, N.J.: Princeton University Press.

Oliver, Kelly. 1998. "Abjection in Fassbinder's *Despair* and Polanski's *The Tenant.*" In *Subjectivity without Subjects: From Abject Fathers to Desiring Mothers,* 43–51. New York: Rowman and Littlefield.

Ong, Aihwa. 1999. *Flexible Citizenship: The Cultural Logics of Transnationality.* Durham, N.C.: Duke University Press.

Palumbo-Liu, David, ed. 1995. Introduction to *The Ethnic Canon: Histories, Institutions, and Interventions.* Minneapolis: University of Minnesota Press.

Payant, B. Katherine, and Toby Rose, eds. 1999. *The Immigrant Experience in North American Literature: Carving Out a Niche.* Westport, Conn.: Greenwood Press.

Reeves, Pamela. 2000. *Ellis Island: Gateway to the American Dream.* New York: Crescent Books.

Roberts, Dorothy E. 1997. "Who May Give Birth to Citizens? Reproduction, Eugenics, and Immigration." In *Immigrants Out! The New Nativism and the Anti-Immigrant Impulse in the United States,* ed. Juan F. Perea, 205–19. New York: New York University Press.

Robertson, George, et al., eds. 1994. "As the World Turns: Introduction." In *Travellers' Tales: Narratives of Home and Displacement.* New York: Routledge.

Rosario-Sievert, Heather. 1997. "Conversation with Julia Alvarez." *Review: Latin American Literature and Arts* 54 (Spring): 31–37.

Rosenstone, Robert, A. 2000a. Editorial. *Rethinking History: The Journal of Theory and Practice* 4: 123–25.

———. 2000b. "A History of What Has Not Yet Happened." *Rethinking History: The Journal of Theory and Practice* 4: 183–93.

Rubenstein, Roberta. 2001. "Inverted Narrative as the Path/Past Home: *How the García Girls Lost Their Accents,* Julia Alvarez." In *Home Matters: Longing and Belonging, Nostalgia and Mourning in Women's Fiction.* New York: Palgrave.

Rushdie, Salman. 1991. "Imaginary Homelands." In *Imaginary Homelands: Essays and Criticism, 1981–1991.* London: Granta Books.

Rutherford, Jonathan, ed. 1990. "The Third Space: Interview with Homi Bhabha." In *Identity: Community, Culture, Difference,* 207–21. London: Lawrence and Wishart.

Saadawi, Nawal El. 1997. "Why Keep Asking Me about My Identity?" In *The Nawal El Saadawi Reader.* New York: Zed Books.

Said, Edward. 1979. *Orientalism.* New York: Random.

———. 1984. "The Mind of Winter: Reflection on Life in Exile." *Harper's,* September, 49–55.

Sapiro, Virginia. 1984. "Women, Citizenship, Nationality: Immigration and Naturalization Policies in the United States." *Politics and Society* 13: 1–26.

Sawchuk, Kim. 1992. "Unleashing the Demons of History: An Interview with Coco Fusco and Guillermo Gómez-Peña." *Parachute* 67: 22–29.

Schiller, Nina Glick. 1999a. "Transmigrants and Nation-States: Something Old and Something New in the U.S. Immigrant Experience." In *Handbook of International Migration: The U.S. Experience,* ed. Charles Hirshman, Josh DeWind, and Philip Kasinitz, 94–119. New York: Russell Sage.

———. 1999b. "Who Are These Guys? A Transnational Reading of the U.S. Immigrant Experience." In *Identities on the Move: Transnational Processes in North America and the Caribbean Basin,* ed. Liliana R. Goldin, 15–44. Austin: University of Texas Press.

Schiller, Nina Glick, and Georges Fouron. 2001. "'I Am Not a Problem without a Solution': Poverty and Transnational Migration." In *The New Poverty Studies: The Ethnography of Power, Politics, and Impoverished People in the United States,* ed. Judith Goode and Jeff Maskovsky. New York: New York University Press.

Schwartz, Jonathan. 1993. "Macedonia: A Country in Quotation Marks." *Anthroplogy of East Europe Review* 11 (Autumn), at http://condor.depaul.edu/~rrotenbe/aeer/aerr11_1/schwartz.html.

Seyhan, Azade. 2001. *Writing Outside the Nation.* Princeton, N.J.: Princeton University Press.

Sharpe, Jenny. 2000. "Is the United States Postcolonial? Transnationalism, Immigration, and Race." In *Postcolonial America,* ed. C. Richard King, 103–21. Chicago: University of Illinois Press.

Shaviro, Steven. 1993. *The Cinematic Body.* Minneapolis: University of Minnesota Press.

Shohat, Ella. 1991. "Ethnicities-in-Relation: Toward a Multicultural Reading of American Cinema." In *Unspeakable Images: Ethnicity and the American Cinema,* ed. Lester D. Friedman. Chicago: University of Illinois Press.

———. 1992. "Notes on the 'Post-Colonial.'" *Social Text* 10: 99–113.

———. ed. 1998. Introduction to *Talking Visions: Multicultural Feminism in a Transnational Age,* 1–62. Cambridge: MIT Press.

Shohat, Ella, and Robert Stam. 1994. *Unthinking Eurocentrism: Multiculturalism and the Media*. New York: Routledge.
———. 1996. "From the Imperial Family to the Transnational Imaginary: Media Spectatorship in the Age of Globalization." In *Global/Local: Cultural Production and the Transnational Imaginary*, ed. Rob Wilson and Wimal Dissanayake, 145–70. Durham, N.C.: Duke University Press.
———, eds. 2003. *Multiculturalism, Postcoloniality, and Transnational Media*. New Brunswick: Rutgers University Press.
Singh, Amritjit, and Peter Schmidt, eds. 2000. "On the Borders between U.S. Studies and Postcolonial Theory." In *Postcolonial Theory and the United States: Race, Ethnicity, and Literature*, 3–69. Jackson: University Press of Mississippi.
Sklar, Robert. 1993. *Film: An International History of the Medium*. New York: Prentice Hall.
Smith, Marian L. 1998. "'Any woman who is now or may hereafter be married': Women and Naturalziation, ca. 1802–1940." *Prologue* 30: 146–53.
Spivak, Gayatri Chakravorty. 1997. "Diasporas Old and New: Women in the Transnational World." In *Class Issues: Pedagogy, Cultural Studies, and the Public Sphere*, ed. Amitara Kumar. New York: New York University Press.
———. 2002. "Resident Alien." In *Relocating Postcolonialism*, ed. David Theo Goldberg and Ato Quayson. Malden, Mass.: Blackwell.
Stachówna, Grażyna. 1994. *Roman Polanski i Jego Filmy* [Roman Polanski and His Films]. Warsaw: Wydawnictwo Naukowe PWN.
Stam, Robert. 1991. "Eurocentrism, Afrocentrism, Polycentrism: Theories of Third Cinema." *Quarterly Review of Film and Video* 13: 217–37.
Stone, Judy. 1997. *Eye on the World: Conversations with International Filmmakers*. Los Angeles: Silman-James Press.
Tängerstad, Eric. 2000. "*Before the Rain*—After the War?" *Rethinking History: The Journal of Theory and Practice* 4: 175–83.
Taylor, Simon. 1993. "The Phobic Object: Abjection in Contemporary Art." In *Abject Art: Repulsion and Desire in American Art*, 59–83. New York: Whitney Museum of American Art.
Todorova, Maria. 1994. "The Balkans: From Discovery to Invention." *Slavic Review* 53 (Summer): 453.
Tölölyan, Khachig. 1996. "Rethinking Diaspora(s): Stateless Power in the Transnational Moment." *Diaspora* 5: 3–36.
Topor, Roland. 1967. *The Tenant*. Trans. Francis K. Price. New York: Bantam.
Trinh T. Minh-ha. 1987. "Introduction." *Discourse* 8: 3–9.
———. 1994. "Other Than Myself/My Other Self." In *Travellers' Tales: Narratives of Home and Displacement*, ed. George Robertson et al. New York: Routledge.
———. 2001. "Not You/Like You: Postcolonial Women and the Interlocking Questions of Identity and Difference." In *The Longman Anthology of Women's Literature*, ed. Mary K. DeShazer. New York: Longman.

U.S. Public Laws. 1790. 1st Cong. Naturalization Act. *A Bill to Establish an Uniform Rule of Naturalization, and to Enable Aliens to Hold Lands under Certain Restrictions.* New York.

Vázquez, David. 2003. "I Can't Be without My People: Julia Alvarez and the Postmodern Personal Narrative." *Latino Studies* 1: 383–402.

Wallace, Michele. 1994. "The Search for the 'Good Enough' Mammy: Multiculturalism, Popular Culture, and Psychoanalysis." In *Multiculturalism: A Critical Reader,* ed. David Theo Goldberg, 259–68. Malden, Mass.: Blackwell.

West, Dennis. 1995. "Filming the Chicano Family Saga: An Interview with Gregory Nava." *Cineaste* 21: 26.

Zaborowska, Magdalena J. 1995. *How We Found America: Reading Gender through East European Immigrant Narratives.* Chapel Hill: University of North Carolina Press.

Žarković, Dragoljub. 2000. "A Serbian Journalist Answers Critics." *Nieman Reports* 54 (Summer): 79+.

Žižek, Slavoj. 1994. *Metastases of Enjoyment: Six Essays on Woman and Causality.* London: Verso.

———. 1997. "Multiculturalism, or The Cultural Logic of Multinational Capital." *New Left Review* 225: 28–51.

Film and Video

Before the Rain. 1994. Dir. Milcho Manchevski. PolyGram Film Productions.

Calling the Ghosts. 1996. Dir. Mandy Jacobson and Karmen Jeliničić. New York: Bowery Productions, Women Make Movies.

Ellis Island. 1997. History Channel Greystone Production. A & E Home Video, New York Video Group.

El Norte. 1983. Dir. Gregory Nava. Independent Productions.

Journey to America. 1989. Prod. Charles Guggenheim. PBS Video.

Men in Black. 1997. Dir. Barry Sonnenfeld. Columbia TriStar Home Video.

My Family, Mi Familia. 1995. Dir. Gregory Nava. New Line Cinema.

Nostalghia. 1983. Dir. Andrei Tarkovsky. Opera Film Produzione/Sovin Film.

Performing the Border. 1999. Dir. Ursula Biemann. Women Make Movies.

Surname Viet Given Name Nam. 1989. Written and dir. Trinh Minh-ha. New York: Women Make Movies.

The Tenant. 1976. Dir. Roman Polanski. Paramount Pictures Film. Based on Roland Topor's *The Tenant.*

A World of Art: Works in Progress: Guillermo Gómez-Peña, The Temple of Confessions. 1997. S. Burlington, Vt.: Annenberg/CPB Project.

Index

abjected body, 105, 107
abjection: abject as a third category, 105; abjected aliens, 35; abjected position, 152; the abyss of, 36, 42; act of, 107; and ambiguity, 125; in *Before the Rain* 131; cinematic narrative of, 105; and claustrophobia, 49; and dirt, 46; in *El Norte*, 28; of female, 116–17, 119; of foreignness, 114; and gender difference, 115; identification with 147; and immigrants, 153; and in-betweenness, 48; and Indianness, 54; in *Men in Black*, 5; and ontological otherness, 126; performance of, 154; and phobia of otherness, 122; power of, 154; and quivering ontologies, 27; racialized realm of, 44; and scream, 106; sublimation of, 143; in *The Tenant*, 29, 102–3; and transnationality, xiv; and valorized national identity, 14; and vomit, 145. *See also* contamination, difference, logic of dirt, pollution, race, scum

Abu-Jaber, Diana, 59, 73
accented body, 28, 57, 61, 63
accented cinema, 132
accented identity, 60, 61, 63; discomfort of, 65; and speech, 64, 67
accentless body, 60
accentless identity: and speech, 63
Aciman, André, 22, 61
Adorno, Theodor W., 98
Ahmad, Aijaz, 158n7
alien: and antialien discourse, 10–11; and antialien websites, 9–10; categories of, xiii; contamination, 35, 37, 39; and cosmopolitanism, 24, 149; discursive affects of, xvi; dual meaning of, xiii; and Ellis Island, 38; in *El Norte*, 28, 36, 40–43, 46, 49, 53–54; etymology of, xvi; and exclusion from citizenship, 14–16; and foreigner's ontological status, 114; in *How the García Girls Lost*

Their Accents, 28, 60, 63, 73; "I," 88; and INS testing process, xii; legal rendition of, xvi; in *Lost in Translation*, 81; in *Men in Black*, 3–9; and mobility, 150; and ontological otherness, 126; and Patriot Act, 12; and *pharmakon*, 27; and pollution, 46; and postmodernity, 26; resident, 87–88, 149; and science-fiction, xvii–3; and 1790 Naturalization Act, 14; and spectatorship, 3; and strangerhood, 17; in *The Tenant*, 29, 107; and transnationality, xiv–xv, 3, 20–21, 34; and U.S. immigration restrictions, 13; and women, 14, 25; and women of color, 39, 49. *See also* alienhood, cosmopolitanism, difference, foreigner, immigration, race, whiteness

alien body, 27, 153, 155

alienhood: and academia, 20; and contemporary immigration, 37; and cosmopolitanism, 24; definition of, xiii–xiv; and discursive violence, xvi; and Ellis Island, 38–39; in *El Norte*, 41–43, 49, 53, 55; and feminist theory, 26; and foreignness, 33; genealogy of, xiii; in *How the García Girls Lost Their Accents*, 60; illegal category of, 7; in *Lost in Translation*, 29, 79; in *Men in Black*, 5–9; and mobility, 34; and origin quotas, 16; parameters of, 11; and *pharmakon*, 27; and postmodernity, 30; and post-9/11, 12; resident, 87; rhetoric of, 9; and transnationality, 21; and U.S. immigration restrictions, 13. *See also* alien, cosmopolitanism, difference, foreigner, immigration, race, transnationality, whiteness

Alien Nation (Brimelow), 10

Alvarez, Julia, xiv, 28, 59, 60–65, 74–75

American Citizenship as Distinguished from Alien Status (Cleveland), 15

American immigrant literature, 59

American nativism, 13, 37

Americanness: authentic, 60; homogenization of, 18; hyphenated, 73; legitimate, 13, 73; privileged, 59; pure and true, 16, 34

American transnational literature, 59–60; and exilic narratives, 72

anthropoemic strategies, 17–18, 74

anthropophagic strategies, 17–18, 74

antialien actions, 10–12

antialien fears, 154

antialien rhetoric, 10–11

anti-immigration: and abuse, 66; and alienhood, xi; and aliens, 27; and discourse, 11; and national origin quotas, 39; and post-9/11, 12; and rage, 94; rhetoric of, 18; sentiments, xii, 10; and U.S. immigration history, 37; and violence, 41

Anzaldúa, Gloria, 40, 41

Arabian Jazz (Abu-Jaber), 73

Arranged Marriage (Divakaruni), 72

assimilation: and abjection of aliens, 27; and aliens, xvi–xvii; and anthropophagic strategies, 17; coercive, 63, 64, 73, 74; complete, 64; in *El Norte*, 49, 54; and immigrant rage, 93; and immigrants, 89–90; in *How the García Girls Lost Their Accents*, 28; in *Lost in Translation*, 28, 78–83; in *The Tenant*, 114

Auster, Lawrence, 10, 27

Balkanism, 130, 133

Balkans, 21, 25, 29, 129–31, 133–34, 138

Bammer, Angelika, 30

Barańczak, Stanisław, 123

Bartkowski, Frances, 168n2

Bartletti, Don, 41
Basch, Linda, 59
Bauman, Zygmunt, xv, 9, 17–18, 33, 71–75, 150, 152
Beautiful People (Dizdar), 131
Before the Rain (Manchevski), 29–30, 129–34, 136, 143, 145
Behdad, Ali, 22, 61
Berlin Wall, xv, 21, 129, 150, 152
Bhabha, Homi, K., xiv, 23
Biemann, Ursula, 161n26
bifocal identity, 86
binary logic: and alien, 9; and the Balkan conflict, 131; and hierarchy of alien/native, 73; of native vs. other, 75; and transnational feminism, 25–26
Bisplinghoff, Gretchen, 170n9, 170n18
border crossing, xi, xiv; and abjection, 35; and becoming transnational, 34; in *Before the Rain,* 132; and bridging cultures, 35–36; cinematic, 40; 41, 43, 48, 49, 54; and Ellis Island, 37–39; in *El Norte,* 28–29; and exile 22; in *How the García Girls Lost Their Accents,* 58, 60–61; and legal rendition of aliens, xvi; in *Men in Black,* 4; in *The Tenant,* 125; and transnationalism, 21, 24–25. *See also* alien, cosmopolitanism, immigration, liminality, transnationality
border identity, 21, 25, 153
Borderlands/La Frontera (Anzaldúa), 41
Bordwell, David, 105
Brimelow, Peter, 10, 37
Bromley, Roger, 21, 24
Buchanan, Patrick, 11
Burgoyne, Robert, 145

Calling the Ghosts (Jacobson, Jelinčič), 129, 161n28
Chang, Robert S., 15

Chavez, Leo R., 34, 37, 39
cinematic body, 126
Cinematic Body, The (Shaviro), 101
citizenship: and definition of alien, xvi; flexible, 24–25; history of, 14–16; and naturalization, 88; and Operation Restoration, 12; and 1790 Naturalization Act, 14; and U.S.-born children, 13; and whiteness, 14; women's, 14. *See also* alien, exile, race, racial logic of citizenry, whiteness
Claustrophobia: and homogenous community in *Before the Rain,* 131; and spatiality in *El Norte,* 28, 33, 36; 42, 47–49; in *The Tenant,* 29, 102–3; and space, 113, 121. *See also* liminality
clean body, 5
cleanliness: and homogeneity, 67; and immigrant contamination, 92; and logic of dirt, 65; and logic of purity, 39; in *Men in Black,* 7. *See also* ethnic cleansing, logic of purity
Clément, Catherine, 101–2, 106, 123
Cleveland, Frederick A., 15
Clover, Carol J., 103
contamination: in *El Norte,* 35, 37, 39–41, 49; immigrant, 94; in "The Last Immigrant," 154; in *Lost in Translation,* 91–92; in *Men in Black,* 5; in *The Tenant:* 125; textual, 93. *See also* abjection, antialien rhetoric, anti-immigration, logic of dirt, pollution, scum
cosmic citizenry, 58. *See also* Passport to the Universe
cosmic subjectivity, 58
cosmopolitanism: etymology of, 24; and exile, 139; and hypercosmopolitan identity, 58; and identity, 149–50; in *Men in Black,* 5; and quivering ontologies, 75; and

resident alien, 149; versus alien, 24. See also alien, transnationality
Cox, Karen Castellucci, 166n13

Danticat, Edwidge, 59
Davies, Carole Boyce, 165n6
Davis, Jude, 158n1
Death and the Maiden (Polanski), 102–3
Death of the West, The (Buchanan), 11
de Lauretis, Teresa, 116, 117
Department of Homeland Security, 12
Derrida, Jacques, 27, 71
DeSalvo, Louise, 16
difference: and abjection, 115; and academia, 18–20; and accented speech, 66; and alienness, 11; apartheid type of, 9; and art, 143; and conservative multiculturalism, 64–65; consumption of, 74, 153; epistemic, 126; ethnic 108, 113–14; and foreignness, 121; and gender, 115, 141; in "The Last Immigrant," 153–54; in *Lost in Translation,* 81, 91, 98; in *Men in Black,* 3–9; and mobility, 152; and quivering ontologies, 27; sexual, 119, 122; slogans of, 31; and strangerhood, 17, 75; and "third space," 23; as usable and palatable, 20; and xenophobia and xenophilia, 60. See also abjection, diversity, hybridity, multiculturalism, pedagogy, race, whiteness
dirty body, 4, 65
discursive violence, xvi, 25, 66, 75
Divakaruni, Chitra Banerjee, 59, 72
diversity: and academia, 19–20, 30–31; and anxiety over aliens, 10; and conservative multiculturalism, 65; and discursive multiculturalism, 75; ethnic, 18; management of, 60; and narration, 62; and rhetoric of purity, 41. See also difference, for-

eigner, hybridity, multiculturalism, pedagogy, race
Dizdar, Jasmin, 131
Doane, Mary Ann, 170n13
Dorfman, Ariel, 59, 73
Douglas, Mary, 159n3
duBois, Page, 146

Eastern Europe, 16, 38–39, 78, 94, 97, 150–52
Ellis Island, 17, 36–40
Ellis Island, 38
Ellis Island Immigration Museum, 16, 17, 37
El Norte (Nava), 28, 30, 33, 35–36, 39, 41–43, 45, 48–49, 53–54
Emmerich, Roland, 3
Enhanced Border Security and Visa Reform Act of 2002, 159n10
ethnic authenticity, 136
ethnic cleansing, 21, 29, 129, 131, 136, 140, 146
ethnic violence, xvi, 130–31, 133–34, 138, 142, 144
Eurocentric logic, xv, 15, 58
Eurocentrist racism with a distance, 19
exile: and accent, 63–65; and alien, xiii; in *Before the Rain,* 29–30, 137; cinematic expression of, 125–26; cinematic narratives of, 102, 124; contrapuntal exilic consciousness, 45; dialectics of, 139; and etymology, 83; exiled position, 84, 125; exiled subjecthood, 89; exilic consciousness, 22–23; exilic elsewhere in *El Norte,* 33, 44; exilic experiences, 3; exilic identity, 46, 72; exilic journeying, 34; exilic longing, 140; exilic ontology, 70; exilic position, 22, 48, 49; exilic quivering, 61; exilic status, 131; exilic subjectivity, 28, 61, 75, 88; and foreign body, 147; and for-

eigner, 103, 106, 108, 114, 122; in *How the García Girls Lost Their Accents*, 59–62; internal, 98; and liminality, 68–69; in *Lost in Translation*, 78–81, 90–93, 96–97; and naturalization, 88; in *Nostalghia*, 123–24; and ontological ejection, 83; as performative condition, 27; pleasures of, 45; and postmodernity, 20–21, 26; as sexy, 22; and shuttling transnationals, 70–72; in *The Tenant*, 29, 102; and "third space," 23–24; and transnational cinema, 132; and transnational positionality, xiv; and transnational strangers, 73; and trespassing, 60; and uprooted refugees, 35. See also alien, foreigner, globalization, logic of exile, logic of impossibility, immigration, quivering ontologies, transnationality
exiled body, 88
exiled "I", 30, 83, 95, 99
exilic elsewhere, 33–34, 40, 44, 54
Exit into History (Hoffman), 79
Expressionism, 108, 110; expressionist cinema, 111
"extreme aesthetic behavior," 153

Feagin, Joe R., 41
first world, xiv, xv, 26; and "America," 93; and "international" identity, 153; and origin quotas, 16; and torture, 146; and U.S.–Mexican border, 35
Fjellestad, Danuta Zadworna, xv
Ford, Henry, 18
foreign body, 4, 89, 94, 105–7, 114, 126–27
foreigner: and alienhood, xiii–xvi, 9; and alien ontological status, 114; and antialien rhetoric 11; and anti-immigrant violence, 41; in *Before the Rain*, 131, 140; and claustrophobia, 103; and difference, 115; and Ellis Island, 38; in *El Norte*, 36; etymology of, 33; and exile, 126; and exile, 27; feminized, 120–21; figure of 110; foreigner's foreignness, 75, 127; and garbage, 112–13; in *How the García Girls Lost Their Accents*, 60, 66–67, 69, 73; identification with, 109; and the logic of impossibility, 123; in *Lost in Translation*, and otherness, 79, 81–82, 87–88, 91–92, 94; in *Men in Black*, 4–9; and noise, 122; in *Nostalghia*, 124; romanticized notion of, 95; and scream, 104, 107, 111; and stranger, 102, 105–6; in *The Tenant*, 29, 101; and U.S. immigration history, 15–16. See also abjection, alienhood, difference, exile, hybridity, otherness, race, xenophilia, xenophobia
foreignness: and contamination, 92; and difference, 75, 115; and discriminatory logic of exile, 124; and Eurocentric logic, 15; as exotic-erotic, 95; fear of, 114; and heterogeneity, 114; and immigrant rage, 94; and new epistemological model, 114; and spectatorship, 109, 127
Fouron, Georges, 58, 59
Fregoso, Linda Rosa, 40, 42
Fusco, Coco, 154
Fuss, Diana, 119

Garcia, Cristina, 59
Geok-lin Lim, Shirley, 26, 27
globalization: xiv–xv; and mobility, 150; and transnationality, 21; and transnational subjecthood, 34. See also alien, cosmopolitanism, postmodernity, transnationality

Gómez-Peña, Guillermo, 53, 149, 153, 154
Gomez-Vega, Ibis, 167n22
Grewal, Inderpal, xiv, 25, 26, 60
Guarnizo, Luis Eduardo, 23

Hall, Stuart, 24, 129
Haney-López, Ian F., 14, 16
Hart, Lynda, 5, 119
Heading South, Looking North (Dorfman), 73
heterophilia, 75
Hirsch, Marianne, 168n2
Hoffman, Eva, xiv, 21–22, 24, 28–30, 59, 72, 77, 79, 99
Homecoming (Alvarez), 61
Hondagneu-Sotelo, Pierrette, 10, 25, 39
Horton, Andrew, 132, 136
hooks, bell, 168n7
How the García Girls Lost Their Accents (Alvarez), 28, 30, 60–63, 65, 68, 71, 73–75
hybridity: in *Before the Rain,* 139–40; in *El Norte,* 42; and in-betweenness, 73; in *Lost in Translation,* 80, 83, 94–95, 98; and position, 62, 140; and selfhood, 69, 71; and stranger, 63, 72; and "third space," 22– 25; and transnationality, 21; and U.S. immigration history, 17
hybridization, 22–23, 34, 42

ideology of purity, 130
Ignatiev, Noel, 160n15
illegal alien, xiii; and conservative websites, 9–10; in *El Norte,* 41–42, 53; and Eurocentric logic, 15; in *Men in Black,* 4; and Patriot Act, 13; and post-9/11, 12; and transnational identity, 34
illegal alienhood, 39, 53
IllegalAliens.US, 9–10
illegal elsewhere of exile, 54

Immigrant Experience in North American Literature, The (Payant and Rose), 164n2
immigrant rage, 93–94, 97
immigration: and abjected foreigner, 124; and acceptable identity, 54; and alienhood xii–xiii; and alienhood, 37; and antialien discourse, 10–11; and binational immigrants, 70–72; and border crossings, 48; and contamination, 92; and difference in *The Tenant,* 111; and dispensable bodies, 50; and displacement, 90; and Ellis Island, 16–17, 36–40; in *El Norte,* and entering the U.S., 35; and fear of immigrants, 113; and female body, 49; in *How the García Girls Lost Their Accents*; and immigrant bodies, xvii; and immigrant meaning, 98; and Ku Klux Klan, 38; and Light Up the Border, 41; in *Lost in Translation,* 77–79, 84; and migrations, 58; and narratives of assimilation, 79–82; and national origin quotas, 16; and otherness, 114; and rage, 93–94, 97; and resident alien, 87; and rhetoric of purity, 40; and 1790 Naturalization Act, 14; and transnational aliens, 39; and transnational identity, 58; and transnational positionality, 25; and transnationalism, 59; and U.S. restrictions, 13–16; and whiteness, 14–16, 38–39; and women's citizenship, 14. *See also* alienhood, antialien rhetoric, assimilation, citizenship, Ellis Island, race, transnationality, whiteness
Immigration Act of 1924, 16
Immigration Naturalization Service (INS), xi, xii, xiii, 3– 4, 7, 36
in-betweenness: and American litera-

ture, 59; and border crossings, 48; and epistemological advantage, 23; exilic, 62, 73; and location, 126; and selfhood, 149; and shuttling transnationals, 71; and stranger, 140. *See also* border crossing, liminality
in-between space, 48, 72, 78–80, 86, 95–96
Independence Day (Emmerich), 3
indiscreet body, 5
international students, 19–20
In the Name of Salomé (Alvarez), 61, 63
In the Time of the Butterflies (Alvarez), 61
Iordanova, Dina, 129–30
Island of Hope, Island of Tears (Brownstone, Franck, Brownstone), 37

Jacobson, Mandy, 161n28
Jacobson, Matthew Frye, 14, 16
Jameson, Fredrick, 111
Jardine, Alice, 123, 126
Jelinčič, Karmen, 161n28
Journey to America, 39
Kaplan, Caren, xiv, 25, 26, 36, 60
Kesić, Vesna, 162n28
Kincaid, Jamaica, 59
Knife in the Water (Polanski), 101

Kraut, Alan, 38
Kristeva, Julia, 33, 35, 54, 75, 97, 102, 105, 107, 110, 114, 127, 145, 149, 150, 153
Kuhn, Annette, 9
Ku Klux Klan, 38
Kundera, Milan, 79

Last Immigrant, The (Gómez-Peña), 153–55
Latin America, xv, 11, 35, 36, 42, 152, 153
Latina/o literature, 61, 73–74

Lee, Chang-Rae, 59
lesbian: becoming, 120; and exclusion, 121; as a haunting secret, 119, in *The Tenant*, 102, 104, 107, 114–16
Light Up the Border, 41
liminality: in *Before the Rain*, 129, 131, 140, 144; in *El Norte*, 46–47, 49; and exile, 22; 27–29; in *How the García Girls Lost Their Accents*, 61, 68–69, 71; liminal identities, 59; liminal space, 153
Lippard, Lucy R., 173n9
List, Chris, 163n8
Lodge, Cabot Henry, 38
logic of difference, 101, 154. *See also* exile, difference, foreignness, whiteness
logic of dirt, 5, 65. *See also* abjection, contamination, pollution, scum
logic of ethnic cleansing, 130
logic of ethnic violence, 130, 142
logic of exile, 124
logic of impossibility, in *Before the Rain*, 29; in *El Norte*, 44; in *The Tenant*, 123
logic of exilic impossibility, 30
logic of national identity, 71, 133
logic of origins, 139. *See also* citizenship, exile, national origin quotas, race
logic of purity, 7, 38; and alienhood, 29; in *Before the Rain*, 131; in *El Norte*, 42; ethnic, 13, 132, 134, 136; in *How the García Girls Lost Their Accents*, 61; racial 11, 41; in *The Tenant*, 105. *See also* cleanliness
logic of racial hatred, 145
logic of white Anglo culture, 54
Lost in Translation (Hoffman), 28, 30, 72, 77–78, 79, 88, 94–97
Lowe, Lisa, 15

Manchevski, Milcho, xiv, 29–30, 130–34, 136, 144, 146

McCullough, David, 39
Men in Black (Sonnenfeld), xi, 3, 5, 7, 9
Men in Black II (Sonnenfeld), 7
Mexicans: in *Men in Black,* 4–5
Mexican-Americans: and border, 43; in *El Norte,* 39–40
Miłosz, Czesław, 79
Mitchell, David, 62, 68
Mohanty, Chandra Talpade, xi, xiv, 146
Mukherjee, Bharati, 27, 68
multiculturalism: and academia, 18–20; and antialien actions, 10; anti-racist multicultural feminism, xiv; and consciousness, 75; conservative, 64–65; and consumption of difference, 60; and cosmopolitanism, 149; discursive, 75; and exile, 22; and feminism, 20; and feminist discourses, xv; and foreigner, 92; and homogenization of Americanness, 18; homogenizing, 73–74; and identity, 72; and literature, 74; multicultural euphoria, 61; polycentric, xiv; radical, xiv; rhetoric of, 9; and transnational feminist practices, 26; and whiteness, 13; "with a human face," 19. *See also* difference, diversity, pedagogy
Munch, Edvard, 110, 111
My Family, Mi Familia (Nava), 35–36, 40

Nabokov, Vladimir, 79
Naficy, Hamid, 24, 30, 39, 49, 132–33
narrative illogic: in *Before the Rain,* 134
national origin quotas, 16, 39
national purity, 41, 130, 131
nativistic racism: and Asian immigrants, 15
naturalization: aliens excluded from, 15; and humiliation, xii; and resident alien, 87; and whiteness, 16; and women's citizenship, 14. *See also* alien, citizenship, immigration
Nava, Gregory, xiv, 28, 35–36, 39–43, 54
New Europe, 152
New Latin American Cinema, 36
1921 First Quota Act, 16
1965 Immigration and Nationality Act Amendments, 16
No Man's Land (Tanovic), 131
nondocumented alien, 49
Nostalghia (Tarkovsky), 123–24

Ong, Aihwa, 21, 24–25
Opera, or The Undoing of Women (Clément), 101, 106
operatic death, 102, 105–6, 120
Operation Restoration, 11
otherness: and alien, 24; in *Before the Rain,* 30, 131, 133, 144–45; consumption of 19; in *El Norte,* 35; and exile, 31; and foreignness, 114, 122–26; in *How the García Girls Lost Their Accents,* 65–66, 73–75; in "The Last Immigrant," 154; in *Lost in Translation,* 79, 91; in *Men in Black,* 3; phobia of, 122; in *The Tenant,* 107; space of, 123; and stranger, 124; and strangerhood 17. *See also* alien, difference, exile, foreigner, logic of difference, phobia
Other Side, The/El Otro Lado (Alvarez), 61

Palumbo-Liu, David, 74
Passport to the Universe, 56–59
Path to National Suicide, The (Auster), 10
Patinkin, Mandy, 38
Patriot Act, 12–13
Payant, Katherine B., 164n2
pedagogy: and authentic authority, 149; and multiculturalism and

feminism, 20. *See also* alien, difference, diversity, multiculturalism
Pérez, Laura Elisa, 61
Pérez, Loida Martiza, 59
Performing the Border (Biemann), 161n26
pharmakon, 27, 71
phobia: and citizenship, 9; cultural, 113; and nationalism, 102, 131; of otherness, 122; phobic model of community, 102, 114, 127; social, 113, 122. *See also* difference, foreigner, otherness
Polanski, Roman, xiv, 29, 101–4, 111, 123–24, 126
pollution: and antialien rhetoric, 11; racialized idea of, 5. *See also* logic of dirt; scum
postmodernity, 20; and anthropophagic/anthropoemic strategies, 74; in *Before the Rain*, 132; and feminist theory, 26; in *Lost in Translation*, 78, 95, 97; postmodern stranger, 18, 75; and shuttling transnationals, 71; and theory and exile, 22
Pratt, Mary Louise, 13

quivering body, 154
quivering ontologies, 27, 75, 134, 139–41
quivering of being, 97, 114
quivering subjectivity, 72, 131

race: and abjection, 44; and academia and diversity, 19; and American transnational literature, 59–60; and dark skin and dirt, 46; and definition of alienhood, xiii; and Ellis Island, 39; and etymology of alien, xvi; and exclusions from U.S. citizenship, 15; and exilic cinema in *El Norte*, 35; and hatred, 145; and hierarchy, 54; as ideological construct, 16; and Light Up the Border, 41; and Mexican–U.S. border, 40; "nativistic racism," 15; and Operation Restoration, 11–12; and post-9/11, 12–13; scum and dirt in *Men in Black*, 5; and 1790 Naturalization Act, 14; and structures of oppression, 53; and superiority, 65; and superiority, 7; and transnational cinema, 133; and transnational feminist practices, 26; and transnational mothers, 25; and transnationality, 24; and violence in *Before the Rain*, 131; and whiteness, 15–16; and wounds, 53. *See also* alienhood, citizenship, difference, diversity, multiculturalism, transnationality
racial logic of citizenry, 15
racial violence, xvi, 29, 131
racist logic: in *El Norte*, 53
Reeves, Pamela, 37
religious violence, 29, 131
Repulsion (Polanski), 102–3
resident alien, xiii, 87–88, 149
rhetoric of fear, 53
rhetoric of hate, 136
rhetoric of purity, 40
Roberts, Dorothy E., 13, 16
Robertson, George, 21
Roosevelt, Theodore, 16, 18
Rose, Toby, 164n2
Rosemary's Baby (Polanski), 102
Rosenstone, Robert A., 134, 146
Rubenstein, Roberta, 166n15
Rushdie, Salman, 140

Saadawi, Nawal El, 165n8
Said, Edward, 9, 20, 45–46, 71, 73
Santiago, Esmeralda, 59
Sapiro, Virginia, 14
Schiller, Nina Glick, 58–59
Scream, The (Munch), 110–11

screaming body, 105, 107–8, 111, 116
Screening Europe (Petrie), 129
scum: in *Before the Rain*, 136; in *Men in Black*, 4–5
second world, xiv, xv, 21, 26, 150–52; in *Before the Rain*, 132; in *Lost in Translation*, 28–29, 96; in *The Tenant*, 102, 125–26
Secret, The (Hoffman), 79
1790 Naturalization Act, 14
Seyhan, Azade, 24
Sharpe, Jenny, 160n21, 167n17, 168n26
Shaviro, Steven, 101, 126
Shohat, Ella, xv, 11, 15, 23
Shtetl (Hoffman), 79
Sifuentes, Robert, 153
Sklar, Robert, 125
Smith, Carol R., 158n1
Smith, Marian L., 14
Smith, Michael Peter, 23
Something to Declare (Alvarez), 61
Sonnenfeld, Barry, 3, 7
space-off: in *The Tenant*, 116–17
Spivak, Gayatri Chakravorty, 21
Stachówna, Grażyna, 168n2
Stam, Robert, xv
stranger: and alienhood, xii–xvi, 9; and "alien nation," 11; and anthropophagic/anthropoemic strategies, 17; in *Before the Rain*, 131, 138, 140; and coercive assimilation, 17; and displacement, 90; and exile, 21; in *How the García Girls Lost Their Accents*, 28, 59, 60, 63, 71–72, 75; ontology of, 74, 75; and *pharmakon*, 27; postmodern, 18; resident alien in *Lost in Translation*, 87; in *The Tenant*, 102, 105, 114, 123, 125; and translation, 90; transnational, 73. *See also* alien, assimilation, foreigner, transnationality
strangerhood, 17, 64, 72, 75

students of color: as exotic specimens, 20
Szanton Blanc, Cristina, 59

Tänge rstad, Erik, 175n19
Tanovic, Danis, 131
Tarkovsky, Andrei, 123–24
Taylor, Simon, 169n6
Teethful Smile (Polanski), 101
Tenant, The (Polanski), 29–30, 101–7, 110–11, 113, 117, 124–26
"third space," 23–25
third world, xiv, xv, 10, 11, 21, 26; in *Before the Rain*, 132; in *El Norte*, 35, 40; in *Lost in Translation*, 96; in *The Tenant* 126
Thomas, Anna, 35
Todorova, Maria, 129–30
Tölölyan, Khachig, 157n1
Tragedy of Macbeth (Polanski), 102
translation: act of, 78; bodily, 96; body in, 98; dialectical space of, 98; in *El Norte*, 34, 50; etymology of, 78; in *How the García Lost Their Accents*, 68; lived, 79; in *Lost in Translation*, 28, 77, 78, 84, 88–91; and translating border, 99
transmigrants, 59
transnational cinema of exile, 28
transnational cultural studies, 58
transnational crossings, 58, 61, 70–71, 134, 138
transnational exilic cinema, 24, 29, 35–36, 49; and U.S. immigration history, 39; 132–33
transnational exilic narratives, 72, 77, 96
transnational exilic subjectivity, 30
transnational exilic texts, 26
transnational feminist practices, xiv
transnational feminist studies, xv
transnational feminist cultural studies, 25–26
transnationality: and alienhood, 21–22;

and aliens, xv, 20, 27–28; becoming transnational in *El Norte,* 33–35; in *Before the Rain,* 132–33; and capitalism, 58; and cinema, 24, 36, 39, 49; and crossings, 61, 70–71, 134, 138; definition of, 59; and exilic identities, 33; and feminist theory, 26; and flexible citizenship, 24–25; and global economy, 146; in *How the García Girls Lost Their Accents*; and identity, xiv, 58, 60–61, 71; and INS evaluation, xii; and literature, 24; and location, 75; and logic of impossibility, 44; in *Lost in Translation,* 77, 96; and meaning of, xiv; and migrations, 20, 58; and mothers, 25; and narrative illogic, 144; and national affiliation, 150; and Passport to the Universe, 58; and position, 5, 24–25, 34, 41, 60; and resident alienhood, 149; and shuttling transnationals, 71; and subjecthood, 34, 59; in *The Tenant,* 125–26; and "third space," 23–25; and use of alien women, 25. *See also* alien, border crossing, cosmopolitan, exile, globalization, immigration
Travellers' Tales (Robertson), 20
trespassing transnational, 28, 60
Trinh, T. Minh-ha, 9, 20, 23, 33–34, 61
Two Men and a Wardrobe (Polanski), 101

unclean body, 7
uncleanliness: and dark skin and dirt, 46. *See also* abjection, contamination, logic of dirt, pollution, race, scum
undocumented alien, 10; and citizenship, 13
Unthinking Eurocentrism (Shohat and Stam), 167n20

Wallace, Michele, 167n17
Welcome to Sarajevo (Winterbottom), 131
Wexman, Virginia Wright, 170n9, 170n18
When Angels Fall (Polanski), 101
whiteness: and alien, 7, 9; and antialien rhetoric, 11; and Ellis Island, 38; "ethnic core" of, 10; historical infatuation with, 13; masculine, 14; racial, 16; and racial logic of citizenry, 15; and racial superiority, 65; as a selective category, 16; and 1790 Naturalization Act, 14; and stereotyping of blackness/whiteness, 53. *See also* alienhood, citizenship, difference, race
Winterbottom, Michael, 131
A World of Art (Gómez-Peña), 153

Vázquez, David, 61
Vdare.com, 9
violence of vomit, 134, 144

xenophilia: and difference, 60; xenophilic representation, 130
xenophobia: and difference, 60; and foreignness, 114; and the Holocaust, 103; and immigrants-as-vultures, 94; and legitimate Americanness, 73; and nationalism, 132; and racism, 69; xenophobic community, 106; xenophobic representation, 130; xenophobic sentiments, 37

Yans, Virginia, 39
Yo! (Alvarez), 61–62

Zaborowska, Magdalena J., 158n6, 168n2
Žižek, Slavoj, 19, 129–30, 143
Zolberg, Aristide R., 16–18, 38

KATARZYNA MARCINIAK is associate professor of English at Ohio University, where she teaches feminist theory and transnational literature and cinema. She is also an affiliated scholar at the Center for Feminist Research at the University of Southern California. She is the editor of *Postmodernism*, a volume in the textbook series Symposia: Readings in Philosophy, and she has published in *Camera Obscura, Cinema Journal, differences,* and in the AFI Film Reader, *East European Cinemas*.

www.ingramcontent.com/pod-product-compliance
Lightning Source LLC
Chambersburg PA
CBHW071841230426
43671CB00012B/2027